(Re)Presentations of the Female Body in the works of Canadian Women Writers

for

Sidhivinayak and Saraswati

(Re)Presentations of
the Female Body
in the works of
Canadian Women Writers

KAMALA GOPALAN

Prestige

an international publishing house

Published by
Prestige Books
3/28, East Patel Nagar
New Delhi 110 008
Ph. 9818755529
email: prestigebooks@gmail.com
website: asiabookclub.com
ISBN: 978-81-906183-5-9

Printed at Chaman Offset Press, New Delhi 110 002

Contents

Acknowledgments

At the very outset I have to thank my guide Dr. Coomi Vevaina my friend and philosopher who inspired me to work on Canadian Literature ever since she taught me at the Certificate course offered by SNDT University in 1995. Her enthusiasm, drive and motivation saw me through some of the most difficult times through the last six years that it has taken for this project. Her spiritual strength and positive reinforcement spurred me on to complete the work.

I am grateful to the teaching faculty at the Canadian Studies centre at the SNDT University, particularly Dr. Shirin Kudchedkar who encouraged and helped me generously with a large number of books and journals from her personal collection generously and with her words of wisdom. Dr. Krishna Sarbadhikary helped me with books from her personal collection as well and I am extremely grateful to her for the rare books she gave me. My thanks to Dr. Om P. Juneja for his concern and help during my visit to the MS University of Baroda's Canadian Studies centre which I visited to gather research materials.

The renowned Canadian poet Penn Kemp helped me with her insights and her books not just during her visits to India but also through frequent e-mails. Dr. Susan Swan responded quickly to my e-mail requests and shared information and insights with me and I am grateful to both of them for the interest they showed in my work. I am extremely grateful to Dr. Mary Conde at Queen Mary and Westfield College, University of London for her help during my four week stay at her college and her sustained interest in my work and the numerous books by Canadian writers she continues to send me generously. The library staff at the Queen Mary and Westfield College as also the Humanities Library and Rare Books' Collection Library at State University of New York at Buffalo, United States were most helpful in my attempts to gather material for my research.

I am grateful to the faculty at the Department of English, University of Mumbai, particularly Dr. Nilufer Bharucha for making it possible for me to participate in the Academic Links Programme which the University of Mumbai has with Queen Mary and Westfield College. This enabled me to enrich my thesis by meeting scholars like Dr. Sue Billingham, Dr. Lynette Hunter and Dr. Coral Ann Howells and discuss my work with them. I would like to thank the non-teaching staff at the Department of English, University of Mumbai for their help, particularly, Mrs. Bharati Chitre for her near-perfect typing of the dissertation. I am grateful to Dr. Gopalakrishnan, Principal of S.I.W.S College of Commerce and Science for readily granting me leave and encouraging me to complete this dissertation as also Ms. Daya Sridhar for her timely help in giving the final touches to this work.

This work would not have been possible without the sacrifices of my family, particularly my husband T. Gopalan who was my moral support and companion in seeing the fruition of the work and my son Anand, for his creative and lively discussions with me on critical theory and for supplying the first two lines of the thesis to help me overcome the proverbial writer's block at the beginning of my work. His help during my stay at Buffalo can just be termed invaluable. I am eternally grateful to my mother Gomathi Krishnan for her support of all my academic endeavours and my friend Usha for holding the fort at crucial times.

KAMALA GOPALAN

Chapter One

Introduction: Theories of "Writing the Body"

I read writing the body, I read the body,
I write the body, I write writing the body.

1.1 (Re)presentation

Before entering and exploring the entire corpus of theories constituting this school of feminism, it is essential to both clarify and problematize certain concepts that the book proposes to grapple with. The first is that of 'representation.' The dictionary assigns at least three meanings to the verb form 'represent'—"(i) Bring clearly before the mind, especially by description or imagination. (ii) Display to the eye, make visible (esp.) exhibit by means of painting, sculpture, etc.; reproduce in action or show, play, perform, act the part of. (iii) Symbolize, serve as embodiment of etc." Even a cursory understanding of the meanings of the word brings into focus the performative aspect as being the most prominent in the act of representation. Judith Butler, very ably, in the very first page of her first chapter, in *Gender Trouble* titled "Subjects of Sex / Gender / Desire" problematizes the notion of representation which always presumes something already there to be re/presented with the words:

> The domains of political and linguistics "representation" set out in advance the criterion by which subjects are formed, with the result that representation is extended only to what can be acknowledged as a subject. In other words, the qualifications for being a subject must first be met before representation can be extended. (1-2)

This calls into question the possibilities of representing identities whose subjecthood would have to be established first. At this point it is useful to recall Foucault's observation that "juridical systems of power produce the subjects they subsequently come to represent" (qtd. Butler 2).

Structures of power operate to form, define and reproduce subjects. Judith Butler extends Foucault's idea to problematize the category of "women" and points out that this category, "the subject of feminism, is produced and restrained by the very structures through which emancipation is sought" (2).

1.2 The Female Subject

The ongoing debate on the notion of subjectivity has also brought into forefront the plethora of 'feminisms' that have come into being—many of them simply by virtue of questioning the homogenizing tendency of "mainstream white feminism." The term 'woman' becomes a site of contest and dissatisfaction. As Butler points out: "since gender intersects with racial, class, ethnic, sexual, and regional modalities of discursively constituted identities . . . it becomes impossible to separate out 'gender' from the political and cultural intersections in which it is invariably produced and maintained" (3). Black feminists and writers of colour have been crying themselves hoarse trying to draw attention to the oppression generated by the hegemonizing notion of a universal female subject. In their writings, this observation is often accompanied by hurt and humiliated accounts of either tokenism or sheer callousness meted out to them even in academia.

When Simone de Beauvoir, in *The Second Sex* asserts that, one is not born but rather becomes a woman, she set into motion a radical re-visioning of the concepts of sex and gender, often used interchangeably till then. It also seriously challenges the Freudian dictum: Anatomy is destiny. While some neo-Freudians and theorists have reworked the tenet, others such as Jacques Lacan and Juliet Mitchell have worked within the Freudian paradigm without questioning its basic tenets. Their theories, in part have also been attempts to resurrect Freud. The idea of gender, being a socio-cultural construct and product of socialization processes rather than a given, has provided impetus to Gender Studies for over three decades. The results of these have often provided interesting breakthroughs and far-reaching implications for the idea of the subject. As Judith Butler states:

> When the constructed status of gender is theorized as radically independent of sex, gender itself becomes a free floating artifice, with the consequence that man and masculine might just as easily signify a female body as a male one, and woman and feminine a male body as easily as a female one. (6)

French feminists like Julia Kristeva and Hélène Cixous have endorsed this view amply. In fact, Kristeva insists on bisexuality in all humans when she refers to the androgynous aspects of the male and the female in all our psyches. In this debate, very little has been said of the body and its materiality. As Butler puts it, "the body is figured as a mere instrument or medium for which a set of cultural meanings are only externally related. But 'the body' is itself a construction, as are the myriad 'bodies' that constitute the domain of gendered subjects" (8). When "the body" is brought back to centre stage, it manages to challenge all artificial binaries of Western thought—nature-culture, body-mind, reason-intuition etc.

The idea of 'subjectivity' needs to be scrutinized from various angles. It is vital for this dissertation to trace the development of some of the theories governing the practice of "writing the body." Many of these theories have emerged as off-shoots of psychoanalysis and most of them have appropriated key concepts from Lacan's re-reading of Freud such as "the Mirror Stage" and the ego-I formation. Almost all of them are violent reactions to the psychoanalytic paradigm and even parody it.

1.3 Lacan, the Law-giver

As with Freud, feminists have had a love-hate relationship with Lacan. Psychoanalytic theories dissolve in great part binaries such as reason and passion that dominated earlier concepts of subjectivity and in this sense, have had a liberating value. However, Freud's cultural norm of subjectivity remains focused on the male. (Female sexuality does not develop as in male children but is explained with reference to masculine sexuality in terms of absence or lack). Differentiation is a crucial step in the development of ego-self identity in the Freudian schema. A quick review of these ideas will enable understanding of how Lacan uses Freudian concepts as points of departure. The two main ideas that have been reworked by Lacan are the Freudian concept of the ego and his theory of sexuality.

In "Beyond the Pleasure Principle," Freud records his observation of the compulsive—repetition game played by his grandson—that of throwing away and retrieving his cotton reels. Earlier he states how the newborn child experiences himself as an absolute subject, undifferentiated from his world. This is prior to any relationship being established. To preserve this sense of wholeness and universal unity, he seeks to be attached to a crucial object—the mother's breast. This attachment brings along with it the danger of its loss or absence. This situation is replayed as it were in the game of loss and retrieval. Juliet Mitchell, in her examination of the Freudian idea of the emergence of ego-self identity states:

> Thus the distinguishing act is accomplished and mastered and the object is first realized as an object in its absence. So, too, is the child first perceived by itself in its own distinctness in strict emulation of this presence and absence of the object (the mirror game). In a footnote, Freud confirms his interpretation that the game represents recognition of the mother's comings and goings—and from this recognition of the baby's own existence. (Mitchell 383)

Mitchell later adds:

> The baby, whose unified world is broken apart by the comings and goings of the mother on whom its body depends for survival, in his turn represents the terrors of this loss first with a toy, then with itself. The self is, then, perceived as the self first as an object (the cotton reel) and as an identification (with the mother, in whose absence the baby had done exactly what she had done to him in his perception—the baby leaves himself and then finds himself in a mirror). We can see from this game that the child constitutes the other as object, constitutes himself as the other in the eyes of another for himself. (383-84)

Absence, desire for the absent and reappearance of the desired object are thus crucial in the process of differentiation, which is itself central to the child's perception of its self as being different from the object of its desire—the mother's breast and thereby the mother herself.[1] Mitchell puts it precisely thus: "The subject is constituted as the opposition between presence and absence, its foundation is dependent upon the discovery of difference." (386)

Freud had two models based on two different views of the ego. Elizabeth Grosz terms these as the realist and the narcissistic views. She traces the realist view to a posthumously published draft of an essay, "The Project for a Scientific Psychology." Grosz terms this a proto-psychoanalytic text. He is to have drawn on this model for psychological terminology in *The Interpretation of Dreams* (1900). He is said to have returned to it in "The Ego and the Id" (1923) and Grosz points out that he affirms this in *An Outline of Psychoanalysis* (1938) at the very end of his life.

The narcissistic view is developed in "The Three Essays on the Theory of Sexuality" (1905) which was written during his middle period of writing. He elaborates on this view further in "On Narcissism: An Introduction" (1914) but abandoned it for a while and returned to the model in the last paper published in his life time, "The Splitting of the Ego in the Process of Defence" (1938). The realist view of the ego perceives it as a 'reality principle,' a kind of filter which strives to control the thrusting energies of the Id and makes it compromise to the demands of reality which impinges on the organism. Freud compares the ego to the rider of a horse who has to harness the energies of the horse (which represents the Id). It has to constantly play a balancing game as Elizabeth Grosz puts it:

> As a rational mediator, it strives to protect the organism from threats and danger from the social; and at the same time, it strives to procure maximum satisfaction and pleasure for the wishes of the Id that it also serves, while ensuring the smooth reproduction of social norms and values. (25)

The ego, in this case is a rational mediator between the uncontrolled energies of the Id and the harsh rigours of socio-cultural reality. The narcissistic ego is seen as a storehouse of libido. The ego is able to view itself as a libidinal object.[2] Grosz describes the narcissistic ego as "entirely fluid, mobile, amorphous series of identifications, internalizations of images/perceptions invested with libidinal cathexes" (28).

The infant invests libido on its self and on external objects. This is different from autoeroticism. Since it invests libidinal energy on external objects, its form is variable. The three main points stated by Grosz when summarizing Freud's narcissistic view of the ego are crucial to an understanding of Lacan's theory of the Mirror Phase:

> far from being a self-contained or potentially autonomous entity, the ego is paradoxically intersubjective; it depends on the subject's relation with the other;
> instead of being dominated by the demands of reality and a logic of expediency and compromise, the ego is governed by fantasy, and modes of identification, and introjection, which make it amenable to the desire of the other;
> rather than defending the Id against the demands of reality, the ego defends against a part of itself. The subject that takes itself as its own object is fundamentally split, as a subject and an object. (31)

It is this view of the ego that Lacan uses for developing his idea of the Mirror Phase and the development of the ego from the pre-Oedipal to the Oedipal stage and ties it in with acquisition of language and establishes his notions of the Symbolic Order and the Semiotic. Lacanian psychoanalysis (and much postmodernist fiction) views human agency, determination and identity as simply the illusory effects of the individual's discursive positioning within a necessarily patriarchal culture which he terms the Law of the Father. Lacan returns to Freud's work on narcissism emphasizing that the ego cannot be centred on itself, self-determining and integrated because the ego is formed in alienation, in an identification with an 'other' which produces only an illusion of wholeness. Lacan's theory focuses on the Mirror Stage. This concept is central to the notion of the construction of an alienated subjectivity. The first point of departure from Freud that Lacan establishes is his reworking of the idea of the ego. His view of the ego subverts the Cartesian cogito in that anything but reason is involved in the process of achieving the ego-self identity. Using Freud's narcissistic model Lacan goes beyond it to seek the genesis of this ego in the 'Mirror Stage' of the child's development (from five months to eighteen months). Grosz points out: "Lacan hovers between seeing the mirror stage as purely internal, biologically regulated process; and as a linguistically structured, socially regulated relation." (32)

Essentially in this stage, the child first achieves recognition of the distinction between the (m)other/mirror-image (self as other). Along with this is also the recognition of lack or absence—an absence of gratification of needs. There is an emergence of self-reliance. The child experiences the first psycho-sexual drives and there would be auto-eroticism with the child substituting parts of its own body for gratification in the absence of the mother. When the child sees its image in the mirror, there is a tension between the illusion of solidity, unity/wholeness of the image seen with the fragmentation or 'anatomical incompleteness' experienced by it. It has not yet achieved motor coordination and Lacan refers to it as 'hommelette.' Lacan based these observations on cross-species studies. The creative leap that he makes is by disengaging the biological base on which the Freudian framework rests by bringing it into the socio-cultural sphere. In other species, instincts play a vital role and the maturation process, language and law regulate the human being's existence. Absence or lack is the crucial part of the mirror stage. Elizabeth Grosz sums up these ideas very coherently thus:

> The child can only give up this hermetically sealed circuit of need and satisfaction by accepting that the (m)other is not within its control, being a separate object. The 'fullness,' the completeness that the child experiences through the maternal supplementation of its needs is interrupted by lack. The child is no longer in that happy state of satisfaction, protected by and merged with the (m)other. From this time on lack, gap, splitting will be its mode of being. It will attempt to fill its (impossible, unfillable) lack. Its recognition of lack signals an ontological rift with nature or the Real. This gap will propel it into seeking an identificatory image of its own stability and permanence (the imaginary), and eventually language (the symbolic) by which it hopes to fill the lack. The child loses the 'pure plenitude' of the Real and is now constituted within the imaginary (i.e. the order of images, representations, doubles, and others) in its specular identifications. (35)

1.4 **Lacan and "Writing the Body":**

Lacan's notion of 'imaginary anatomy' is of critical interest to theorists of 'writing the body.' There is a tension set up by the discrepancy between the specular image of unity/solidity and the fragmentation and unease actually experienced. While studying the phenomena of the phantom limb and hysteria, Lacan observes for instance, that often pain cannot be located in the real anatomy of the body, it inhabits the space occupied by the imaginary body. He writes: "It all happens as if the body-image had an autonomous existence of its own, and by autonomous I mean here independent of objective structure." (Lacan 1953: 13)
With reference to this, Grosz also adds:

> in many dreams there is evidence of the pre-oedipal body-image, particularly in dreams about the dissolution of bodily unity and control. The body is often divided or fragilized along the lines of pre-oedipal significance, with organs appearing in odd places and unusual arrangements. (45)

All this points to the conclusion that the body-image is governed by socio-cultural expectations. The self is a 'construct' dominated by images of others. The identity of the self emerges in "otherness" or essentially alienation. The imaginary anatomy does not necessarily coincide with bodily-felt experiences. This imaginary is the internalization of cultural expectations of the corporeal schema.

Judith Butler explores this idea fully and incorporates the notion of "discursive positioning of bodies" in her scholarly work *Bodies That Matter*. There is a third entity that emerges to mediate the dual imaginary relation and that is the Father; Lacan again refers to the dead or the symbolic father whose laws and prohibitions are played out through the real father. He takes on the role of the castrator and the Name-of-the Father. It is on account of his intervention that the Oedipal drama is played out symbolically, in that the child who aspired to become the object of the mother's desire, the phallus is confronted with the phallus in the figure of the father. He signifies all the social mores and restrictions and thus incest is prevented. This notion also seems to be drawn from concepts set out by Freud in *Totem and Taboo*.[3] The success of this stage signals the child's entry into the Symbolic Order where the Phallus is the Signifier of all signifiers. The Mirror Stage leaves the child with a split ego—the child remains bound to the other and cannot participate in social exchange with others. The playing out of the Oedipal situation is essential in Lacanian theory as well for the child's ascension into the Symbolic Order and to emerge as a socially functional and sexually differentiated individual. How does Lacan differ from Freud in his theory of sexuality?

Elizabeth Grosz observes that "The Three Essays" represent Freud's most clearly elaborated developmental account of infantile sexuality (54). In his account, the individual undergoes infantile psycho-sexual stages like the oral, the anal and the genital with their respective erotogenic zones successfully to emerge as a sexually adequate (heterosexual) adult. Freud is very close to biological determinism in his theory.[4] His theory treats sexual drives as a given and relies on instincts and the species' survival impulses. Lacan looks to language and linguistic processes for his analysis of sexual drives. Grosz observes in her study of Lacan:

> Where Freud develops an etiological model of sexual maturation from the child's first psychosexual impulses to adult forms of genital sexuality, Lacan rarely uses a developmental model, analyzing sexuality instead as it is manifested in the transferential relation between analysand and analyst—in, that is, the data of the analysand's speech. His object is sexuality in so far as sexuality is the 'reality of the unconscious.' Lacan's account of sexuality draws subtle distinctions between need, demand and desire. These three are expressions that correspond to the orders of human existence that Lacan defines as the Real, the Imaginary, and the Symbolic. (59)

1.5 Need, Demand and Desire and the Girl-Child's Position in the Symbolic Order

Needs are part of nature and are more or less universal and basic to survival. They look for sources of satisfaction critical to the being's survival. Grosz points out:

> Need, as purely natural or instinctual, is short-lived; it is rapidly overlaid by a structure of meaning and significance that envelops it in imaginary and symbolic relations, transforming it into demand and desire. When the child recognizes the absence of the mother, biological or instinctual need becomes converted into social, imaginary and linguistic functions. (60)

This occurs in the Mirror Stage. Demand is the articulation of need. It needs language. Language is derived and learned from the mother and therefore demand is dependent on the other. It is insatiable. It converts a quasi-biological need to a linguistic-social occurrence. Lacan, in explanation of the transition from need to demand and thereby into language states:

> it is in the oldest demand that the primary identification is produced, that which is brought about by the mother's omnipotence, that is to say, the identification that not only suspends the satisfaction of needs from the signifying apparatus, but also that which fragments them, filters them, models them upon the defiles of the structure of the signifier. Needs become subordinated to the same conventional conditions as those of the signifier in its double register: the synchronic register of opposition between irreducible elements, and the diachronic register of substitution and combination, through which language, even if it does not fulfill all functions structures everything concerning relations between human beings. (qtd. Grosz 61-62)

He uses Saussurean ideas to bring out the distinctions between needs and demands. Demands are thus insatiable—one leading to another, addressed to the omnipotent, phallic mother, in essence nostalgically desiring that unity even if it means annihilation of the self.

The third term central to Lacan's theory is desire. Grosz records that Lacan owes this concept to Hegel, particularly from *The Phenomenology of Spirit* where Hegel posits desire as a lack and absence (64). The indebtedness of French feminists' subversion of the notion of desire as lack, is quite evident as well. Lacan sees desire as a gap separating need from demand. Like demand, desire also is oriented toward the Other. Unlike demand, it is beyond conscious articulation. It becomes repressed as unconscious material. Lacan clarifies thus:

> desire is situated in dependence on demand—which, by being articulated in signifiers, leaves a metonymic reminder that runs under it, an element that is not indeterminate which is the condition of both, absolute and inapprehensible, an element necessarily lacking, unsatisfied, impossible misconstrued, an element that is called desire. (qtd. Grosz 65)

Since demand is the child's first access to the social order, it is subject to familial pressures whereas as Grosz suggests:

> Desire is concerned only with its own processes, pleasures, and internal logic, a logic of the signifier. While such a logic can support social laws and values, it is also able to subvert or betray them, based as it is on expelled, socially inappropriate, repressed wishes. (65)

This last idea is seized on and appropriated by the French feminists, particularly Kristeva. In her interpretation of Lacan's concept of desire, Grosz states:

> Desire opens the subject to a broader world of signification or infinite semiosis: a world in which it has access to systems of meaning unregulated by any individual or group, and unrestricted in the range of its possible messages. Desire thus institutes a new relation to and in language. (66)

In these ideas are contained the germs of theories of writing the body. The repressed, unconscious material (pre-Oedipal) becomes a rich repertoire for the writers to draw on since it contains all that is left unarticulated. For the child's ascension into the Symbolic Order the figure of the Father is necessary. Lacan seems to be referring to the father invoked by Freud in *Totem and Taboo*, in that the power of the dead father of prehistory is more potent than that of a real father. What is significant to the feminists in the Lacanian analysis is that the acquisition of language and the achievement of sexual differentiation are within the patriarchal order, where the Phallus is the most potent signifier. In both the Freudian and Lacanian frameworks, the girl's Oedipus complex is simply the discovery that she and her mother are 'castrated.' This inadequacy makes her turn to her father to focus her libidinal drives. But this only strengthens her inadequacies. The mother is the most powerful agent of the Law of the Father since she carries the law within her. She evokes the authority of he who is absent. For the child, the giving up of the loved object is rewarded by the position of a speaking subject in culture. For the girl it is impossible to become a speaking subject without entering the Symbolic Order since language and law are the properties of this order.

At this point, it is however, necessary to point out a significant difference in the Freudian and Lacanian explanation of sexual maturation. Lacan does not see women as castrated in an anatomical sense. He merely sees them perceived by the child as powerless in relation to the father. This is a demotion from her position as an omnipotent, Phallic mother. The denigration occurs only when the child, on entering the Symbolic Order, perceives the power vested in the Phallus as a signifier and the mother as being subservient to it in the social order. The girl's position in the Symbolic is necessarily marginal since she cannot become a speaking subject without entering the Symbolic Order. She necessarily has to abandon her original love object but cannot help identifying with the other in terms of her lack and the powerlessness associated with it. She remains in alienation.

1.6 Lacan's Theory of Language Acquisition

Freud's ideas of condensation and displacement as important procedures of the unconscious, are essential to the understanding of Lacan's theory of language. According to Lacan, the unconscious is structured like a language. What aspects of the unconscious is he referring to? Condensation and displacement are the two techniques of disguise used by the unconscious. As Elizabeth Grosz explains:

> With condensation, a compression of two or more ideas occurs, so that a composite figure, image or name, drawing on and leaving out features of both, is formed. In this way, a single image in a dream is able to represent many different wishes or thoughts through compression of common features and elimination of (relevant) differences. In the case of displacement, the significant, unconscious wish is able to transfer its intensity or meaning to an indifferent term, allowing the latter to act as its delegate, thus disguising it. The insignificant idea is able to represent the more significant one without the repressed features of the significant idea breaking the barriers of censorship. (87)

Lacan draws on the ideas of condensation and displacement while appropriating some ideas of linguistics developed by Ferdinand de Saussure to explain the functioning of the unconscious. The assumption on which his theory rests is that the unconscious is structured like a language. It then becomes necessary to use linguistics and semiotics. The contents of the unconscious are taken to be signifiers. He essentially remains within the Freudian paradigm, merely elaborating its key concepts like the unconscious and relying on the psychoanalytic techniques such as free association, based on the analysand's speech. He uses Saussure's notions of the signifier and the signified but assigns more importance to the signifier over the signified and gives the formula S/s, which is read as: the signifier over the signified, "over corresponding to the bar separating the two stages." (qtd. Grosz 94)

He also uses Saussure's notion that if any signifier refers to any given signified, it does so through a whole chain of signifiers. No single signifier is attached to a single signified as there is a sliding over the chain of signifieds. There is therefore, no essential core of meaning one can eventually arrive at. Each term can be understood only in relation to another or in difference.

All terms can be understood only in relation to language as a whole. Grosz aptly sums up the Lacanian position thus:

> Lacan's conception of the primacy of the signifier in representation correlates with his subversion of the primacy of the subject in his account of the mirror phase. He problematizes the common presumption of consciousness or intentionality regulating discourses. For him, language does not represent the subject's preexisting intentions of ideas; the subject no longer constitutes language or functions as its master, but conversely, is constituted as a subject by language. (97)

This point has proved to be of utmost relevance to feminists who critique language as being a creation of patriarchy which cannot be useful to women writers, who wish to write themselves into existence. According to them, women writers either have to adopt a male orientation, having internalized the language of patriarchy, or need to use subversive techniques. The notion of subjectivity that emerges is also noteworthy, since it is clear that it is language that constitutes the subject. Again, it particularly problematizes the subjectivity of women, since it is necessarily patriarchal language that determines that subject. A woman cannot become 'a speaking subject' unless she enters the Symbolic Order and imbibes the language of patriarchy. This move necessarily entails the child's acknowledgement of maternal castration. Lacan further draws on the work of Roman Jakobson to explain the Freudian ideas of condensation and displacement. Jakobson's two central ideas are 'selection' and 'combination.' Jakobson is here elaborating Saussure's concepts of the syntagmatic (combinatory) and paradigmatic (selective) relations (Grosz 98). Jakobson identifies selection or similarity as metaphoric and combination or contiguity as metonymic. Lacan in turn uses these terms to elaborate ultimately on the idea of the paternal metaphor and metonymy to explain desire.[5] To quote Lacan:

> The creative spark of metaphor does not spring from the presentation of two images, that is, of two signifiers equally actualized. It flashes between two signifiers one of which has taken the place of

> the other in the signifying chain, the occulted signifier remaining present through its (metonymic) connection with the rest of the chain. (157)

Lacan identifies metaphor with the Freudian notion of condensation with the substitution of one term for another. In metonymy, the relation between what is repressed and what substitutes for it is based on contiguity. Grosz links his notion of metonymy to desire thus:

> In this movement from one term to its substitute, Lacan will recognize the movement of desire. Desire too is based on a chain of substitution whereby the first (lost object of desire generates a potentially infinite chain of only partially satisfactory) substitutes. (100)

Metonymy is identified with the Freudian notion of displacement. There is again a sliding of the signifier over the signified. This can be related to the child's initiation into language in the form of demand. Language substitutes for the lack of the desired object, lack of identity etc. There is a 'lack' at the level of language itself in that there is no fixed relation between the signifier and the signified i.e. the meaning of each sign.

Going back to the idea of the paternal metaphor, it is crucial to the very attainment of subjecthood for the child. Lacan uses his general formula of signifying substitution:

S S → S (1 / S) - to explain a psychotic who has failed to register or

S^1 X

to represent the paternal metaphor and is unable to position himself in the formula suggested above.

The symbols used can be substituted by the following terms:

Name-of-the-father Desire of the mother→ Name of the father O

Desire of the mother Signified to the subject Phallus

Castration is crucial to the child's position in the symbolic. The subject O is always positioned in relation to the phallus. Therefore, the signifier crucial to the child's sense of 'I' is the phallus. The zero is described by Lacan as an 'hommelette,' a 'little' man more closely resembling a scrambled egg than an identity (104).

Thus the paternal metaphor is a powerful one, encompassing within it not just male institutions of power but the entire social structure that dictates social mores and constitutes law and language. It is that from which an individual, be it a man or woman, derives his/her identity.

1.7 Critiquing Lacan

Much of Lacan's critique can be done from within his model. The most obvious one is that both Freud and Lacan have Eurocentric models. They establish patriarchy as the 'norm' of social order and other ways as being deviant. Both have built their theories around sexual taboos that have prevailed in western society. Both deny women positive identities and desire since women are essentially defined by absence or lack.

Besides this, the model does not sustain its internal logic. When one considers Lacan's notion of desire, it is essentially based on the idea of repression. In the first volume of *The*

History of Sexuality, Foucault criticizes the idea of desire as propounded by Lacan on the grounds that it presumes an original desire that has ontological integrity and a priori status with respect to the repressive law. Butler sums up Foucault's position in the following words:

> This law, according to Foucault, subsequently silence or transmutes that desire into a secondary and inevitably dissatisfying form or expression (displacement). Foucault argues that the desire which is as both original and repressed is the effect of the subjugating law itself. In consequence, the law produces the conceit of the repressed desire in order to rationalize its own self-amplifying strategies, and, rather than exercise a repressive function, the juridical law, here as elsewhere, ought to be reconceived as a discursive practice which is productive or generative—discursive in that it produces the linguistic fiction of repressed desire in order to maintain its own position as a teleological instrument. (65)

In other words, desire is desire due to the law that gives it context. This critique is of course part of Foucault's attempt to historicize the very idea of sexuality and that it is situated within power matrices and is constructed within specific historical practices, both discursive and institutional.

1.8 Writing is a Necessity

The Freud-Lacan model draws a lot of flak from Hélène Cixous, particularly in her path-breaking essay, "The Laugh of the Medusa." She ascribes the host of negative stereotyping that women have been subjected to the Freudian notion of 'castration' and Lacan's notion of 'lack.' These notions have contributed in large part to women's repressed sexuality and their reduced position in the Symbolic Order in which they are no longer speaking subjects and consequently are unable to write themselves into being. Referring to the psychoanalytic account of femininity she writes:

> Here we encounter the inevitable man-with-rock, standing erect in his old Freudian realm, in the way that, to take the figure back to the point where linguistics is conceptualizing it "anew," Lacan preserves it in the sanctuary of the phallus (ϕ) "sheltered" from *castration's lack*! Their "symbolic" exists, it holds power—we, the sowers of disorder, know it only too well. But we are in no way obliged to deposit our lives in the banks of lack, to consider the constitution of the subject in terms of drama mangling restaged, to reinstate again and again the religion of the father. Because we don't want that. We don't fawn around the supreme hole. We have no womanly reason to pledge allegiance to the negative. The feminine (as the poets suspected) affirms: ". . . And yes," says Molly, carrying *Ulysses* off beyond any book and toward new writing: "I said yes, I will. Yes." (341)

Cixous particularly objects to woman being compared to the dark continent which is unexplorable with all the concomitant stereotypes. She stresses that women are neither dark nor unexplorable and women's sexuality cannot be homogenized or classified. It is infinitely rich just as her Imaginary is. Throughout the essay she waxes eloquent about the need for women to write the body but also states that writing in the feminine cannot be codified. She expresses this idea in these words:

> It is impossible to *define* a feminine practice of writing, and this is an impossibility that will remain, for this practice can never be theorized, enclosed, coded—which doesn't mean that it doesn't exist. But it will always surpass the discourse that regulates the phallocentric system; it does and will take the place in areas other than those subordinated to philosophico-theoretical domination. It will be conceived of only by subjects who are breakers of automatisms, by peripheral figures that no authority can ever subjugate. (340)

She is, however, very emphatic about woman's need to write. Regarding language, she feels that it has always been a male domain and hence there is a need to appropriate it and improvise from within:

> If woman has always functioned "within" the discourse of man, a signifier that has always referred back to the opposite signifier which annihilates its specific energy and diminishes or stifles its very different sounds, it is time for her to dislocate this "within," to explode it, turn it around, and seize it; to make it hers, containing it, taking it in her own mouth, biting that tongue with her own teeth to invent for herself a language to get inside of. And you'll see with what ease she will spring forth from that "within"—the "within" where once she so drowsily couched—to overthrow at the lips she will cover the foam. (343)

In an essay titled "Sorties," Cixous outlines the various dichotomies that have dominated thought since times immemorial through various agencies of patriarchy of which ironically, man is also a victim. She seems to take a slightly softer stand towards the masculine in this piece as she writes:

> Phallocentrism is. History has never produced, recorded anything but that. Which does not mean that this form is inevitable or natural. Phallocentrism is the enemy. Of everyone. Men stand to lose by it, differently but as seriously as women. And it is time to transform. To invent the other history. (96)

In the "Laugh of the Medusa," she seems to be advocating androgyny in the construction of gender identity. This is of course, very close to the Kristevan position. However, she is at pains to divorce herself from all Freudian connotations inherent in the term 'bisexuality' as is seen in the following words:

> Bisexuality: that is, each one's location in self (*réperage en soi)* of the presence—of both sexes, non-exclusion either of the difference or of one sex, and from this "self-permission," multiplication of the effects of the inscription of desire, over all parts of my body and the other body. (341)

Clarifying the respective positions of the three major French feminist thinkers, Coomi Vevaina writes in an article entitled, "Black Woman, 'Righter' and the Anguish of English":

> Unlike Irigaray, Cixous and Kristeva refuse to differentiate between masculine writing (literatur) and feminine writing (l'écriture feminine) on the basis of the writer's gender. Both refuse to collapse language into biology for they rightly believe that men are able to write in the feminine mode and women in the masculine mode, depending on whether their thinking is rooted in the Symbolic order or the semiotic order. In other words, the feminine as a position in discourse is not the exclusive preserve of women. (269)

Cixous gives the writing of Jean Genet as an illustration of a male writer writing in the feminine. Irigaray however, would differ and suggest that this is neither possible nor desirable. Cixous however, does concede that even when a woman is theorizing, she is never linear and draws her story into history. Cixous, in her own essay forges a new style of writing theory—that which is not clinical but one in which emotion percolates to the deepest layers. She is, in this essay, however, more concerned that women write breaking centuries of silence due to the censorship imposed on their bodies:

> Women must write through their bodies, they must invent the impregnable language that will wreck partitions, classes, and rhetoric, regulations and codes, they must submerge, cut through, get beyond the ultimate reserve-discourse, including the one that laughs at the very idea of pronouncing the word "silence," the one that, aiming for the impossible, stops short before the word "impossible" and writes it as "the end." (342)

Thus although Cixous, Irigaray, and Kristeva start from the same premise, they do reach slightly different conclusions on writing the body and women's need to evolve a new language.

1.9 Luce Irigaray and "Writing the Body"

Although Luce Irigaray's critical thinking seems close to that of Julia Kristeva, a careful consideration of their concerns will reveal vast differences in their positions and their methodology. According to Grosz in her book *Sexual Subversions*:

> Her project is both to undo the phallocentric constriction of women as men's other and to create a means by which women's specificity may figure in discourse in autonomous terms. Her challenge revolves around two central themes: that of the cultural debt to maternity, the creation of a means of representing the mother's relations to the child beyond the orbit of the symbolic father's authority; and that of adequately representing and constructing an autonomously conceived female sexuality, corporeality and morphology. Each requires more than a reorganization and equalization of socialization and child-rearing practices (as feminists like Chodorow, Dinnerstein et al proclaim); they imply a profound and difficult reorganization of the forms and means of representation—a reorganization of language itself. (109)

Thus Irigaray's concerns lead her to the area of language as one of the representational systems. She is likewise, concerned with deconstructing all systems of phallocentric discourses, including psychoanalysis itself. The female subject is deduced by Freud from the male model. According to Irigaray, this is based on sameness or identity with the male subject. Irigaray aims at the defining of woman's subjectivity autonomously. She focuses on this aspect in *The Speculum of the Other Woman* in the following words:

> Freud discovers—in a blind reversal of repressions—certain variously disguised cards that are kept preserved or stored away and that lie beneath the hierarchy of values of the game, of all the games, the desire for the same, for the self-identical, the self (as) same, and again of the similar, the alter-ego, and, to put it in a nutshell, the desire for the auto . . . the homo . . . the male, dominates representational economy. 'Sexual difference' is a deviation from the problematics of sameness, it is,

> now and forever, determined within the project, the projection, the sphere of representation, of the same. The 'differentiation' into two sexes derives from a priori assumption of the same, since the little man that the girl is, must become a man minus certain attributes whose paradigm is morphological—attributes capable of determining, of assuring, the reproduction—specularization of the same. A man minus the possibility of (re)presenting oneself as a man = a normal woman. (26-27)

Thus a woman cannot be an autonomous subject due to the very process of acquisition of selfhood in the Freudian paradigm. She is defined by her lack and this further valorizes man's phallic position. Irigaray, therefore, aims at representing woman in other than phallocentric terms. This is an ambitious project requiring a lot of rigour methodologically and the project is bound to have far reaching implications for:

> To reconceive of woman and feminity in terms independent of men and masculinity requires a major reorganization of sexual, linguistic and socio-symbolic systems, and indeed of desire itself. More specifically, it requires reconceiving the female body as a positivity rather than lack. (*SS* 110)

In a facile manner, Irigaray's critics have often dismissed her position as expressive of biological essentialism. It is vital to understand her emphasis on the morphology rather than anatomy of the body. She refers to the body conceived and lived through socio-linguistic construction and emphasizes the social and psychical dimensions of the body. She recognizes that sexuality is the production of images of representation and other signifying practices. Power and language construct reality in as much as they reflect reality. She relies on psychoanalysis both as a tool of deconstruction as well as the main target of her criticism.

Irigaray's view of feminine sexuality is that it is polymorphous, in that it is not located in any specific organ but dispersed all over the body and the dominant image she uses is of fluidity and multiplicity as opposed to rigidity and singularity. She puns on the word 'lips' and insists that 'jouissance' is indescribable and polymorphous.

Likewise, she feels that patriarchal discourses exhibit solidity and stability with their obsession with logos. To describe jouissance, she harks back to the pre-Oedipal stage of the multiple zones of pleasure but wishes to extend it to adult sexuality. The image of the two lips also is illustrative of autoeroticism and self-containment of the female body.

According to her man has paid the price for his identification with the phallus by his alienation from his own corporeality. Irigaray says:

> In the system of production that we know, including sexual production, men have distanced themselves from their bodies. They have used their sex, their language, their technique, in order to go further and further in the construction of a world which is more and more distant from their relation to the corporeal. But they are corporeal. It is necessary therefore for them to reassure themselves that someone (a woman) is indeed the guardian of their body for them (qtd. Grosz *SS* 83-84).

By exploring the mother-daughter relations Irigaray shows deep concern in order that she may be able to zero in on more positive models. She also desires to establish a genealogy for women—connections she believes have been effaced and need to be established and reasserted. She believes this area to be shrouded in mystery and mystique inasmuch as a dark continent would be and feels that though an exploration of this terrain would prove threatening to the social order, it is a debt that culture owes to the maternal.

She envisages a complete reversal of the mother-daughter relation which would require the daughter's abandonment of her attachment to the phallic mother and the commencement of her relation to her mother on woman-to-woman basis.[7] This project entails an even more ambitious effort for:

> To be able to trace a female genealogy of descent entails new kinds of language, new systems of nomenclature, new relations of social and economic exchange—in other words, a complete reorganization of the social order. (123)

This would necessitate a restructuring of not only the mother-daughter relation but language and desire itself. These would be steps necessary for representing mother and daughter as self-referential subjects.

Elizabeth Grosz in her perceptive study on Irigaray points out that, contrary to popular understanding of her work, she does not seek to establish a new language for women but to utilize the existing language system to subvert knowledges and dominant modes of representations and question their claims to universal truths.

These ideas are central to the present thesis since many of the writers being studied attempt precisely what Irigaray suggests through their works. Some others, while theorizing about their fiction, even suggest that they are inventing a new language, stripped of its vestiges of patriarchy. Most of the writers being studied are as concerned with 'metalanguage' as is Irigaray. The Québecoise theorists and writers of both Anglophone and Francophone Canada certainly owe a great debt to French feminist theories. These larger concerns take Irigaray into the area of Derridean deconstruction and the notion of difference.

This notion even underlies her core idea—that which states that a woman's relation to the dominant social order is structured the same way as the unconscious to the conscious. There is always a threat of spilling out, rupturing out of the confines causing disruption.

The image of the speculum offers an alternative to Lacan's flat mirror in which she sees an alienated being reflected. As Alice in Wonderland did, the woman writer should walk through the mirror and see the wonderland beyond.

The first step towards this endeavour is for women to master patriarchal Agreement discourses, knowledge and social practices so that they can use their tools and techniques to subvert them from within. They should be able to challenge and reject all binaries postulated by patriarchy's dominant discourses and be able: "To speak with meanings that resonate, that are tactile and corporeal as well as conceptual, that reverberate in their plurality and polyvocity" (*SS* 132). In this way, life and languages could be regarded in a holistic manner.

1.10 Kristeva's Theory of Language and Subjectivity

The point of departure that Julia Kristeva makes from the Lacanian framework, although she is essentially rooted in the paradigm, is as Butler puts it:

> Lacan claims that we can never tell the story of our origins precisely because language bars the speaking subject from the repressed libidinal origins of its speech; however, the foundational moment in which the paternal law institutes the subject seems to function as a metahistory which we not only can but ought to tell, even though the founding moments of the subject, the institution of the law, is as equally prior to the speaking subject as the unconscious itself. (67)

Kristeva assigns a very crucial and creative role for maternity, whereas the phase of the infant-mother intimacy of the pre-Oedipal stage is practically glossed over by Lacan. She builds her theory from Lacan's Mirror Stage which signals a clear distinction between the Semiotic and the Symbolic Order and considers the positive attributes of the girl child being for a longer period in a symbiotic relation with the mother. She uses the Greek notion of "chora" as being the material of the unconscious, accessible to the woman writer, Kristeva, herself of course looks at avant garde works by male writers to study the ruptures that the Semiotic makes into the Symbolic. Since she is firmly positioned in the Lacanian paradigm, she considers only male writers, since they are fully instituted in the Symbolic Order being able to do this.

Kristeva's definition of the semiotic is grounded in psychoanalysis. The maternal space is of great significance since the primal drives repressed by the Symbolic originate there. Judith Butler clarifies this idea thus: "'the maternal body' designates a relation of continuity rather than a discrete subject or object of desire; indeed, it designates that jouissance which precedes desire and the subject/object dichotomy that desire presupposes." (82) Applying this to the realm of language she extends the interpretation in the following way:

> If the Symbolic and the semiotic are understood as two modalities of language, and if the semiotic is understood to the generally repressed by the Symbolic, then language for Kristeva is understood as a system in which the Symbolic remains hegemonic except when the semiotic disrupts its signifying process through elision, repetition, mere sound, and the multiplication of meaning through indefinitely signifying images and metaphors. In its Symbolic mode, language rests upon a severance of the relation of maternal dependency, whereby it becomes abstract (abstracted from the materiality of language) and univocal; this is most apparent in quantitative or purely formal reasoning. In its semiotic mode, language is engaged in a poetic recovery of the maternal body, that diffuse materiality that resists all discrete and univocal signification. (82-83)

For her, poetic language implies a return to the maternal space. She, in keeping with Freud and Lacan, maintains that the incest taboo is necessary for the formation of the subject. She also seems to accept the assumption that culture is equivalent to the Symbolic but as Butler points out:

> Her strategic task, then is neither to replace the Symbolic with the semiotic nor to establish the semiotic as a rival cultural possibility, but rather to validate those experiences within the Symbolic that permit a manifestation of the borders which divide the Symbolic from the semiotic. (85)

However, maternity is a space which women as such cannot inhabit. It cannot be spoken especially by mothers. At the same time she valorizes maternity and poetry as privileged practices within the Symbolic Order. Regarding the inability of women to articulate the semiotic, she writes in the *Tale of Love*:

> It is not possible to say of a woman that she *is* (without running the risk of abolishing her difference), would it perhaps be different concerning the *mother*, since that is the only function of the 'other sex' to which we can definitely attribute existence. And yet, here too, we are caught in a paradox. First we live in a civilization where the *consecrated* (religions or secular) representation of femininity is absorbed by motherhood. If, however, one looks at it more closely, this motherhood is the *fantasy* that is nurtured by the adult, man or woman of a lost territory. (qtd. Grosz 162)

Elizabeth Grosz, in her discussion of the Kristevan position, observes that Kristeva's position remains surprisingly close to Lacan's conception of an unknowable feminine 'jouissance.' This explains her interest in the study of avant-garde texts because it dwells on the unspeakable and unarticulated. This is however, only within the reach of the male author. For Kristeva, the maternal space is equally significant for both the male and the female in the individuation process. However, only the male writer is able to access the material which is the repressed feminine because as Grosz puts it in summarizing the Kristevan view:

> It is only from a position within the Symbolic that it can be ruptured or transgressed. It is only those who actually occupy the position of speaking / representing subject who can undermine or subvert the limits of representation. (164)

This would obviously exclude women who would not be in a position to transgress the limits of such an order. In *Women's Time,* Kristeva discusses the third generation of women or rather a third attitude emerging, while tracing briefly the history of the women's movement. She advocates this third attitude where she feels the very dichotomy of the sexes would become irrelevant:

> The very dichotomy man/woman as an opposition between two rival entities may be understood as belonging to metaphysics. What can 'identity,' even 'sexual identity,' mean in a new theoretical and scientific space where the very notion of identity is challenged. (397)

She clarifies that she is not advocating the notion of a hypothetical bisexuality by would be a "de-dramatization of the 'fight to the death' between the rival groups and thus between the sexes" (398). This would not be a result of some reconciliation, according to her. This view is based on her original tenets regarding the division between the semiotic and the Symbolic and a belief that this founding division would be interiorized by every person—male or female. She states:

> This process could be summarized as an interiorization of the founding separation of the socio-Symbolic contract, as an introduction of its cutting edge into the very interior of every identity whether subjective, sexual, ideological, or so forth. (398)

She further mentions the multiplicity of every person's identifications, suggesting the fluidity of identity. This seems almost reminiscent of the polyvocity of the child in Freud's pre-Oedipal stage.

Critics like Judith Butler see Kristeva's attempt at subverting the Oedipal Stage of the Freudian model as futile since she firstly remains attached and dependent on the notion of the Symbolic Order. Secondly she denies the female subject a speaking position. Butler questions the viability of the construct of the primary relationship to the maternal body and whether it is a knowable experience according to the linguistic theories of Kristeva and Lacan. Another relevant point of criticism that Butler levels at Kristeva is that "the prediscursive maternal body is itself a production of a given historical discourse, an effect of culture rather than its secret and primary cause" (*GT* 80-81).

Butler objects to the fact that the maternal space with its repressed material and subversive potential is posited and then withdrawn by Kristeva and thereby she denies the semiotic an emancipatory ideal. Also according to Butler, Kristeva does not essentially challenge "the structuralist assumption that the prohibitive paternal law is foundational to culture itself. Hence, the subversion of paternally sanctioned culture cannot come from another version of culture, but only from within the repressed interior of culture itself, from the heterogeneity of drives that constitutes culture's concealed formulation" (86).

Thus Kristeva does not question the premises of the Freud-Lacan model. Her views on homosexuality are also problematic since she views it as psychosis or culturally unintelligible practice. Since poetic language is a return to the maternal body, it would be for women, both displaced maternal dependency and displaced homosexuality.

Butler very vehemently expresses her critique of the Kristevan injustice to the lesbian and women's maternal experience:

> Kristeva describes both the maternal body and lesbian experience from a position of sanctioned heterosexuality that fails to acknowledge its own fear of losing that sanction. Her reification of the paternal law not only repudiates female sexuality, but denies the varied meanings and possibilities of motherhood as a cultural practice. But *cultural* subversion is not really Kristeva's concern, for subversion, when it appears, emerges from beneath the surface of culture only inevitably to return there. (87-88)

Finally as Judith Butler observes, what is construed as maternal instinct itself may be a cultural construct put in naturalistic vocabulary (91). This criticism has been amply demonstrated by theorists such as Adrienne Rich, Nancy Chodorow and others. It has to be acknowledged however, that the Kristevan notion of "chora" has generated a lot of interest in the subtle nuances of the mother-daughter relationship on the part of writers as well as theorists. Writers of the 'body-writing school' have also explored this aspect of a woman's life fully trying to wrench it free of the masculinist bias that the Freud-Lacan models have in their understanding of it or rather their indifference to it altogether.

At this point, it is logical to turn to Luce Irigaray's subversion of the psychoanalytic models using psychoanalysis itself strategically and finally to her views on women's writing.

1.11 Canadian Theorists

Canadians theorists build on the ideas of French feminist thinkers in terms of exploring language and women's relationship to language. Linda Hutcheon points out that the critique of totalizing systems and so-called 'universal truths,' which is to be found in poststructuralist literary theory is enacted in literature by women writers through the study of sexual differences.

She finds this happening particularly through the devices of intertextuality. Intertextuality, according to her, has several narrative functions and in her article 'Shape Shifters: Canadian Women Novelists and the Challenge to Tradition' says:

> It implicitly contests the Romantic notion of uniqueness or originality and single meaning. And it does so in much the same way as does post structuralist theory today. It can, at times, also be seen as a kind of parodic play that implies ironic differences at the very heart of similarity. (226)

Hutcheon assigns a very important role to the use of parody by women writers. She examines parody briefly in an essay on Marian Engel's ironic parody of the picaresque in her novel *Lunatic Villas*. Hutcheon makes an interesting point about how the male wilderness novel has been domesticated by Canadian women novelists in the form they have invented namely, the cabin or cottage novel and cites examples from Margaret Atwood's *Surfacing,* Margaret Laurence's *The Diviners*, Marian Engels' *Bear* and Audrey Thomas' *Intertidal Life*. These writers use parody for social and cultural critique and through the works of novelists like Alice Munro, Margaret Laurence and Margaret Atwood, Hutcheon points out that we can gauge what it is to be female and grow up in repressive small-town in Canada. In order to do this, the traditional bildungsroman undergoes a lot of change the subject being women. Hutcheon calls the writers 'shape shifters' as they have innovated not only thematically but formally as well.

It would be useful at this juncture to examine how women writers deal with the wilderness theme. This is related to the nature-culture divide as also to its corollary notion, that of what Frye calls 'the garrison mentality.' It would be necessary to problematise the idea of wilderness since that has always traditionally been male space. When talking about the garrison, Frye says:

> Small and isolated communities surrounded with a physical or psychological "frontier," separated from one another and from their American and British cultural sources: Communities that provide all that their members have in the way of distinctively human values, and that they are compelled to feel a great respect for the law and order that holds them together, yet confronted with a huge, unthinking, menacing and formidable physical-setting. Such communities are bound to develop what we may provisionally call a garrison mentality. (342)

The garrison mentality is traditionally accompanied by a loathing of wilderness due to its danger and solitude. The nature-culture dichotomy has also been used to disenfranchise women and others who are seen as close to nature. Heather Murray in her article, "Women in the Wilderness," while examining this problematic writes:

> Wilderness in Canada is where you make it, or where you imagine it to be. It is not a place, but a category, defined as much by absences and contrast as by positives and characteristics. (75)

The wilderness may often be a pseudo-wilderness as in Atwood's *Surfacing* or in Ethel Wilson's *Swamp Angel*. In *Surfacing* there is also real wilderness underwater, which is accessible. Since writers like Atwood and Laurence problematize the nature-culture dichotomy in their works, there is a problematization of their female characters' relation to the garrison as well. This will be examined more closely in later chapters. Such an examination will also bring to light their handling of the female body and its experiences within the framework of the patriarchal social order.

1.12 Influences of "Writing in the Feminine"

It is well documented that the ideas held dear by the English-Canadians of a feminist erotics are indebted to those of the continental French theorists: Hélène Cixous, Luce Irigaray and Julia Kristeva, as well as to Quebecoise writers like Nicole Brossard and Madeleine Gagnon. As mentioned earlier, these theorists in turn derive much from the work of Jacques Lacan though they problematize some of his views. The central focus is on his notion of 'the Mirror Stage' in which the female subject cannot gain access to the Symbolic Order and is relegated to the margin, she is displaced and silenced. These tenets of Lacan's theory which they draw on make them turn their attention to language in general and woman's writing in particular.

Donna Bennett, in her article, "Naming the Way Home" asserts that female sensuality would then demand a female erotic and an aesthetics of a different kind. She writes:

> Female writing . . . could eliminate boundaries between such categories as form and content, or signified and signifier, without destroying the categories themselves. In other words, feminine writing would not be restricted by pre-existing concepts such as 'genres' and 'conventions,' but would be able to absorb these concepts and transform, redefine or replace them. (242)

France Théoret has most eloquently addressed herself to the need for describing 'writing in the feminine.' This is also rooted in the dramatic reversal in the position of the speaking subject. The 'I' is no longer an object and can look at itself and others differently.

According to Théoret, women's writing is characterized by the tension between the two opposing tendencies of formalism and feminist consciousness. The speaking subject in formalism is devoid of background and merely exists in the text. Formalism's absorption with language has been of interest to feminists but they are also aware that language is not neutral. As Théoret brings to focus this issue in her article "Writing in the Feminine":

> Language in the feminine has situated its problematic in the area of enunciation. The speaking subject becomes at times the central figure in writing, as does its social and individual inscription. (363)

Women writers have been also led into examining and questioning the genres. They write purposefully mixing genres like fiction, autobiography and the diary. In defiance of the sterile and clinical postulates of male theoretical formulations, they write theory—fiction. Théoret aptly describes it as:

> Propos[ing] both advances in the area of fiction, i.e. of life linked to a certain sensibility, and theoretical advances which give abstract form to what can be generalized from subjectivity. Such writing, because of its undoubted connection with the frequently repeated assertion that private life is political, conserves, includes both thought and emotion. 'Thought in emotion, emotion in thought.' (363)

There is a blurring of the boundary between theory and fiction deliberately in rejection of the linearity and solidity offered by traditional theory. Thought and the consciousness that gives rise to it remain related. Writers like Louky Bersianik and Yolande Villemaire are engaged in stripping language bare of its sexist biases and reworking it. Théoret points out that writing in the feminine is also a writing of memory. It takes into account how the feminine subject is constituted in history. 'Writing the body' does not merely focus on the body experiences of women but brings into question larger issues of language and subjectivity. Of course it stands to question which language and whose subjectivity is under discussion. One cannot ignore discourses of power operating within this framework. The very notion of 'jouissance' needs to be problematized since the charges of biological essentialism and prescriptive tendencies have to be answered.

1.13 Contestations by Women of Colour

In the present thesis, there is an attempt to examine the entire notion of women's body experiences from the perspective of 'the other' or 'the coloured body' and study texts by women of colour to understand their larger concerns as well as their experiences of the body which are quite different from those of white women. The fact of their being in a triple bind of race, gender and colour radically changes what bells hooks calls, 'looking relations.' Their works need to be studied not only in terms of what is expressed but also for its silences. Women writers of colour view the body and subjectivity differently as Coomi Vevaina writes, "Contrary to Lacan's theory of selfhood, the female narrators of Dionne Brand, Claire Harris, Lillian Allen, Marlene Nourbese Philip and Afua Cooper locate the missing part of themselves not in the word of the father but in the being and the word of their foremothers and mothers (Naming . . . 215).

Again, the pitfall of trying to homogenize the experiences of all women of colour has to be avoided since each ethnic group has to be treated differently. Feminism needs to be contextualized. Given this fact, is it still possible to theorize keeping in mind their differences?

Firstly, women of colour resent the homogenizing tendencies of white, liberal mainstream feminists and do not accept its separatist tendencies. Writers like Alice Walker prefer to refer to themselves as 'womanist' rather than 'feminist.' Walker's view is that the struggles of Third World women as feminists are a part of their community's struggles against racism, and economic exploitation. Her view is that mainstream (liberal, gender-specific) feminism has been too narrow to include these broader concerns. A purely gender-specific view of oppression would not amply explain black women's struggle. The era of slavery had constantly juxtaposed images of black and white women.

Discussing this aspect Cheryl Johnson-Odin in her article "Common Themes, Different Contexts, Third World Women and Feminism" writes:

> Black women were cast as non-women, as "unfeminine," as a necessary precondition for exploiting both their productive and reproductive labour to the fullest. But the definition of "feminity" foisted upon white women was that of totally dependent beings. Consequently, for every "Aunt Jemima"

> who was maligned as a non-woman, there was a "Miss Ann" imprisoned by the definition of her femınity. (318-19)

Thus they were subjected to different stereotypes of the feminine. Their experience of the "male gaze" and sexuality are undoubtedly vastly different. Johnson-Odin, in the same article also points out how in addition to broadening the parameters of feminism, working with a common agenda is also difficult. She cites the issue of female circumcision as an example to illustrate this difficulty. Many African women have taken up the battle against female circumcision by resenting the sensationalizing of the campaign by First World feminists (322). There is a real concern therefore among Third World feminists that their issues should not get submerged in the mainstream theory and that they should not get ghettoized as a sub-culture of feminism.

Writers like Audre Lorde have pointed out that even radical feminists with their emphasis on difference, have absences in their writing where women of colour are concerned. She discusses this in a poignant "Open Letter to Mary Daly." She finds that even a sensitive, radical writer like Daly, in her book *Gyn/Ecology* uses solely goddess-images that are white, Western European, Judeo-Christian thereby omitting Black goddesses. She writes protestingly: "What you excluded from *Gyn/Ecology* dismissed my heritage and the heritage of all other non-European women, and denied the real connections that exist between all of us." (95)

She feels that even an important, ground-breaking work like *Gyn/Ecology* uses a patriarchal western-European frame of reference. She further points out that in erasing or neglecting even the traditions of history of non-white women, such theorists only devalue their own words and that this serves the forces of racism and separation between women. She puts it very forcefully in these words: "When patriarchy dismisses us, it encourages our murderers. When radical lesbian feminist theory dismisses us, it encourages, its own demise." (98)

Lorde perceptively points out that although the oppression of women is a reality across all boundaries of race and colour, it is not identical within those boundaries. A critique such as this is a constant reminder to women of colour that it is easy to be swept off by the rhetoric of the so-called Radical feminist theories but it is necessary to critically examine who is being included and excluded and who is being addressed. In her piece titled "The Master's Tools Will Never Dismantle the Master's House," Audre Lorde goes a step further in considering the creative role of difference from the perspective of completely marginalized groups like the poor, lesbian, Black women. This is a further criticism levelled at the Radical feminists who, according to her, advocate the mere tolerance of difference between women. Lorde terms this attempt as the grossest reformism and writes: "For difference must be not merely tolerated, but seen as a fund of necessary polarities between which our creativity can spark like a dialectic." (99)

Due to this creative role assigned to difference, the connectedness and interdependency between women becomes unthreatening. Patriarchy always views this as suspect. Speaking for the triply marginalized women, she writes of the impossibility of functioning within patriarchal society while liberal and some radical feminists advocate subverting from within. Her position, on a superficial reading, seems close to Radical feminism, in its celebration of difference but, on a closer examination it is clear that it is a necessary and strategic stand taken outside the centre. Moreover, it is a stand that divorces itself very vehemently from white, Radical feminism as well. It also clarifies that the experiences of the triply marginalized women of colour are very different from those of white women and is also positioned quite differently vis-à-vis the dominant social order. In a similar vein Gloria Anzaldua foregrounds the marginalized position of a coloured woman writer. Writing is a luxury but is necessary for her survival. Often she is alienated from high literary circles and is always justifying how she came to write. She says that a lesbian of colour is not only invisible but does not exist. Lesbians of colour, being trained in the mainstream educational system, come to writing, having imbibed dominant, high brow theories of art. Anzaldua says:

> They convince us that we must cultivate art for art's sake. Bow down to the sacred bull, form. Put frames and metaframes around writing. Achieve distance in order to win the coveted title "literary writer" or "professional writer." Above all do not be simple, direct, nor immediate. (167)

She is quite bitter about the privileging of these tenets of "high" culture and its art forms. In the same article she warns the Third World woman academic of the danger of "selling out one's own ideologies" (167) and about the temptation of uncritically absorbing the current 'feeling-fads' and 'theory fads.' She also warns of the cooption inherent in this and the danger of white feminist establishment's appropriation of their cause. She lashes out at the tokenism meted out to the woman writer of colour who writes for survival against all odds, including poverty. Anzaldua quotes Luisah Teish who, when speaking to a group of predominantly white feminist writers, hoped to draw their attention to the Third World women's experience:

> If you are not caught in the maze that (we) are in, it's very difficult to explain to you the hours in the day we do not have. And the hours that we do not have are the hours that are translated into survival skills and money. And when one of those hours is taken away it means an hour not that we don't have to lie back and stare at the ceiling or an hour that we don't have to talk to a friend. For me it's a loaf of bread. (qtd. Anzaldua 167)

These words movingly describe the hand to mouth existence of these women for whom writing is a luxury but nevertheless, a necessity and a mission. Describing her own need to write Anzaldua says:

> Why am I compelled to write? Because the writing saves me from this complacency I fear. Because I have no choice. Because I must keep the spirit of my revolt and myself alive. Because the world I create in the writing compensates for what the real world does not give me. By writing I put order in the world, give it a handle so I can grasp it. I write because life does not appease my appetites and hunger. I write to record what others erase when I speak, to rewrite the stories others have miswritten about me, about you. (169)

The woman writer of colour thus has different problems to deal with where her identity and subjecthood are concerned. She has to confront not just marginalization and alienation as a woman but also by virtue of her race. Anzaldua advises the woman writer of colour that it is essential to bring lived experience into one's writing and that no topic is trivial. One should not try to be universal and humanitarian at the cost of the particular, the feminine and the specific historical moment. She believes that writing empowers and advocates writing about all that one knows and feels, including body experiences. She says:

> Your skin must be sensitive enough for the lightest kiss and thick enough to ward off the sneers. It you are going to spit in the eye of the world, make sure your back is to the wind. Write of what most links us with life, the sensation of the body, the images seen by the eye, the expansion of the psyche in tranquillity: moments of high intensity, its movement, sounds, thoughts. Even though we go hungry we are not impoverished of experiences. (172)

She seems to be advocating writing the body not for its own sake but to bring the realities of life into writing and to establish connection with one's own self. Again, at the surface level, there is a seeming similarity that she would share with white women writers, who are writing in the feminine but in the experiences of the body itself there are bound to be vital differences linked with one's skin colour and marginal position in society. In such a context, the body has completely different significations. There is also the problem of the connection of racial and sexual oppression and women of colour would not like to splinter off from their common struggle against racial oppression in which they would like to support their men. This remains the main issue of contention between mainstream feminists and women of colour. This however does not imply that women of colour are not being exploited by their men or are not aware of it. Strategically they find it essential for them to fight unitedly against racial oppression. The discrimination meted out by black men, especially to black women involved in intellectual pursuits, is two fold. Discussing black, male attitudes towards intellectual, black women they write:

> We discovered that all of us, because we were "smart" had also been considered "ugly," i.e. "smart-ugly." "Smart-ugly" crystallized the way in which most of us had been forced to develop our intellects at great cost to our "social" lives, The sanctions in the Black and white communities against Black women thinkers is comparatively much higher than for white women, particularly ones from the educated middle and upper classes. (214)

This statement makes it clear that though they do not share the separatist lesbian stance, they feel even more of a necessity to fight biological determinism of all kinds. They are also very sensitive to accusations that black feminism divides the Black struggle.

The problems of the immigrant woman writer of colour in Canada often centre around the issue of authenticity of voice. As the Afro-Caribbean Canadian poet Claire Harris, puts it in her article "Poets in Limbo": "How to be true to the black self; to the female self; how to reflect accurately the Canadian experience?" (116)

The colonization of the Caribbean wiped out the religion, language and cultural forms of the black people. They were dehumanized even as they were enslaved. This led to tremendous alienation even as they tried to regain their lost identities and voices. The absence of roots and traditions make the task that Harris talks about even more difficult. The poet Dionne Brand in an interview expresses this succinctly:

> When you grow up black anywhere in the western world, there is uneasiness . . . an anxiety of place. It is as if there is nothing behind you. So when you hear people putting pieces into place, you recognize it as "the something" that was absent. (qtd. Harris, 117)

Much of the oral tradition which was lost in the process of colonization has to be re/membered as a part of the recuperative process. Since writers like Claire Harris, Dionne Brand and M. Nourbese Phillip are trained in the mainstream, formal educational system, they have to "detoxify" the English language to adapt it to express a black, female sensibility. The first step in their attempts to re/cover their selves, is to turn to their childhood experiences and the second step is towards claiming the black self. There is a metaphoric turning to Africa—a mythologized mother, in search of sources. This is followed by the recognition of the oppression that blacks anywhere in the world face. Claire Harris expresses this idea in the following words:

> That the diaspora has made the world 'home' is our good fortune. It has given us an insight into those we share this planet with, our intimate strangers, and our reluctant sisters. Liminality, the space between two worlds, is a place of paradox. . . . A potent space of creativity and fullness. (125)

Thus the experience of diaspora becomes a source of potency and creativity for the immigrant woman writer of colour. The Asian immigrant woman writer's experience of the diaspora is a different one altogether. She has to struggle to find an authentic voice, be true to her roots and be heard in the "new world" struggling to reach beyond stereotypical responses like indifference or Orientalism in new avatars.

Himani Bannerji discusses this problem of finding a voice in her article "The Sound Barrier: Translating Ourselves in Language and Experience." She writes about the marginalization experienced by these writers in the following words:

> Our voices are mostly absent, or if present, often out of place with the rest of the expressive enterprises. A singular disinterest about us or the societies we come from, thus who we are substantively not circumstantially, is matched equally by the perverted Orientalist interest in us (the East as a mystic state of mind to the West) and our own discomfort with finding a cultural-linguistic expression or form which will minimally do justice to our selves and formations. And this has not to do with language facility, or ability to comprehend, negotiate or navigate the murky waters of a racist-imperialist 'new world.' (30)

She also believes in the creativity that the diaspora can yield. According to her the very experience of fragmentation and dislocation can give rise to new content and forms.

These immigrant writers often do not dwell on the body in the celebratory manner of the white postmodern feminists and surely not for its own sake. It often becomes a part of the racial oppression and experience of otherization. There is a further marginalization that is experienced by virtue of it being a coloured body, not falling within the prescribed standards of "femininity" or "beauty" of the dominant, white culture.

Trinh Minh-ha is very supportive of the feminists' stand that women must write their bodies and feels that they need to rethink the body to re-appropriate femininity. The body, with its deadened parts, must be reclaimed not simply to dwell on it in a narcissistic manner but in order to perceive its integrity. Women also experience writing the world differently. In an attempt to establish the wholeness of a human being Minh-ha writes in *Woman, Native, Other*: "we do not have bodies, we are our bodies, and we are ourselves while being the world" (36).

In keeping with the French feminists' position, she also feels that by writing the body, women are breaking centuries of silence and are making audible all that was erased by phallocentric discourse. Men have always spoken for and about woman in the past and even named their bodies in proprietral ways. For centuries they have succeeded in keeping woman alienated and not in possession of their own bodies. Minh-ha writes:

> Men name "womb" to separate a part of woman from woman (to separate it from the rest that forms her: body and mind), making it possible to lay legal claim to it. By doing so, they create their own contradictions and come round to identifying with their fabrication: a specialized, infant producing, organ. Women use "womb" to reappropriate it and reunite (or redefine themselves, their bodies, their places of production.) This may simply mean beating the master at his own game. But it may also mean assertive difference on differences. (37-38)

Thus Trinh Minh-ha who is very affirmative about the need to re/claim the body, opposes the idea of androgyny and cautions that if one becomes essentialist and reduces everything to the order of sex, we get locked into a "discourse directed within the apparatuses of sexuality." (39)

Traditionally, theories have positioned binaries enhancing the body/mind dichotomy and Trinh Minh-ha points out the danger of the circumstance freezing into a dogma. She turns to the spirituality in Asia which postulates three centres in the human being which connect the being within himself as well as to the cosmos. Minh-ha further points out how theories suddenly get threatening to the established social order by questioning canons and norms validated as "natural" or "human." Theory gets oppressive when it aligns itself with existing power structures and claims to be the "voice of knowledge" (42). Summing up her views on "writing the body" she writes:

> "Writing the body" is that abstract-concrete, personal-political realm of excess not fully contained by writing's unifying structural forces. Its physicality (vocality, tactility, touch, resonance), or edging and margin, exceeds the rationalized "clarity" of communicative structures and cannot be fully explained by any analysis. It is a way of making theory in gender, of making the theory a politics of every day life, thereby re-writing the ethnic female subject as a site of differences. It is on such a site and in such a context that resistance to theory yields more than one reading. (44)

Theorizing the coloured body has the potential for calling into question established Eurocentric, logocentric and phallocentric discourses, hitherto accepted uncritically as 'natural' or 'normal.' This assigns an iconoclastic role to the body of colour. Himani Bannerji's and Dionne Brand's writings show the differences in the historical experiences and construction of the female body in the two communities. Dionne Brand, in her thorough analysis of the economics at the root of gender, race and class issues of the black immigrant women in Canada, observes that black women immigrating from the Caribbean, have come mostly as independent immigrants on work permits rather than as spouses. In her article titled "A Working Paper on Black Women in Toronto: Gender, Race and Class," she points out that black women, along with other women of colour, rank as the lowest paid workers and that, contrary to popular beliefs, many black women are heads of households and primary income earners. When they came as single women it also meant no dependents, and no sex. It also often meant doing domestic and manual work as well as being sexually available to the employers.

Dionne Brand relates the issue of sexuality to the economics of migration, employment and the politics of racism. She writes: "The construction of Black women's sexuality occurs within an historical moment where patriarchy, class and race conjoin to produce oppression that is particular to Black women (223-24). She feels that the social constructs and discrimination perpetuated and bolstered by slavery has been carried forward to the "new world." In the article she goes on to demonstrate how the quality of work assigned to the Black women has not significantly changed. This has further implications for the manner in which black, female sexuality is constructed, perpetuates and sustains their role in the economy. Brand writes:

> "White femininity" played a major role in slavery: "Miss Anne"—the southern belle, the pride and purity of the white race—could not have emerged in the absence in the image of Black carnality. Racism did and still does prevent Black women from acquiring positions which white women hold, so nursing and other jobs in the helping profession are seen as the most "decent" jobs which Black women may hold. (225)

The black woman's body has been seen as unfit to do anything but "nigger work," meaning manual work. Since the time of slavery Brand points out she has been seen as a breeder. There has been a lot of ambiguity on the white man's part vis-à-vis the issue of "breeding." On the one hand there had to be a continual supply of labour and on the other hand there was a threat perceived if "they" multiplied too quickly. Brand writes vociferously:

> During slavery, the breeding of children was the production of a commodity. It replenished the supply of enslaved labour. The free expression of sexuality was, at best, risky and usually virtually impossible. The situation of Black people in America was not unlike that of animals caught and used for labour and breeding. Any attempt at family, at kinship, within this context was an act of resistance, of open rebellion. (235)

Black women's sexuality was to be harnessed to reproduce to meet the needs for accumulation of capital. What is significant, Brand says is that this mind set continues in the work place, in legislation and in language. She observes that black women employed as domestic workers on work permit are tied to their jobs and hence reluctant to report sexual assault either to the police or immigration authorities. Brand warns that although recently, the status of black women has seemingly changed for the better, attempts at co-optation smack of tokenism and leave basic oppressive structures intact. Therefore it is easy to see why the attempt to gain control over sexuality has always been an important part of the black women's struggle and rebellion.

Quite different from this is the situation of South Asian women who mostly went along with their spouses as dependents. Himani Bannerji laments their condition as one of the facelessness and in her article "Popular Images of South Asian Women" writes, "The few images of South Asian Women that do exist are primarily non-sexual, passive, docile and feminine"

(144). Writing of images of South Asian Women that are dominant in Canadian society, she writes, "Passivity, docility, silence, illiteracy, uncleanliness, smell of curry and fertility are some of the common-sense things that the dominant culture "knows" about us. They provide the content of our racist experiences—the well-aimed spit or cry of "Fucking Paki bitch!" (147). She further explains that these also become the basis of resistance. She is critical of the category of 'visible minority' since discrimination is in-built. It implies notions of "different," "not normal," "does not belong" etc. There is a codification of discrimination in such notions and signs and she proceeds to say: "Visual images in that sense are congealed social relations, formalizing in themselves either relations of domination or those of resistance." (152)

There seems to be a vicious circle at work in that once the stereotypes about a community are afloat, the community internalizes them and lives up-to the images. In turn these images get further reinforced and crystallized. While reading some of the poems in *Shakti's Words,* for instance, one senses the nostalgia and intense longing for home felt by the women poets. They also attempt to re/create the familiar spaces and rituals in the foreign land to make living a little bearable. These ideas will be taken up in one of the later chapters in this work.

NOTES

1. For a thorough psychoanalytic approach to feminist concerns and the process of individuation in the female child, see Juliet Mitchell's *Psychoanalysis* and *Feminism.*
2. Freud's notion of the narcissistic ego is crucial to Lacan's 'Mirror-Stage,' with the self observing itself.
3. The notion of the Phallus as a Transcendental Signifier probably owes its origins to the Symbolic father in Freud's *Totem and Taboo.*
4. This has always been a point of contention for feminists who strive to prove that anatomy need not be destiny.
5. Freud's ideas of condensation and displacement are used by Lacan linguistically to explain metaphor and metonymy respectively.
6. Foucault's critique of Lacan is used by Queer theorists to contest homogenizing explanations of sexual and gender identity.
7. Women writers writing the body, focus inevitably on the mother-daughter relationship which writers like Brossard term as the first lesbian love.

Chapter Two

Discontent Caused by Male Definitions of the Female Body

In the present chapter there is an attempt to study the novels of some of the mainstream women writers such as Margaret Laurence, Adele Wiseman, Margaret Atwood and Susan Swan in the context of mainly, two factors: (1) The Body in the construction of the self/the subjectivity and (2) The Body as a signifier.

The aspects to be studied within the first factor are: alienation from the body experienced by the female protagonists, the resultant body-mind dichotomy, the process of socialization that reinforces it and the consequent self-image the protagonists have. The body needs to be considered not just in its materiality but the significations it acquires in culture and patriarchy. In order to study this factor, the mother-daughter relationship, the protagonists' relationships with their peers, man-woman relationship and the women's relationships with society at large need to be considered. The body becomes a site where other power conflicts are played out. The paradoxical position assigned to the body—that of valorizing it on the one hand and setting prescriptions for the 'ideal' female body on the other, becomes significant. The writers being studied in this chapter work from within the structures and language of patriarchal confines and yet subvert these very values by often using literary devices like parody, irony and the use of the grotesque.

The three novels by Margaret Laurence included in this study are *A Jest of God*, *The Fire Dwellers* and *The Stone Angel*. In all the three novels, the protagonists experience alienation from their bodies and this in turn affects their self-image and the very construction of their subjectivities. Discussing the problem of alienation, in both Atwood and Laurence's work, Coomi Vevaina writes:

> Alienation from other human beings, from nature, animals and the land itself is the direct outcome of the 'self-versus-other' consciousness. This static dichotomy which prevents a harmonious relationship with the environment, needs to be replaced by the 'self-and-other' consciousness. (18)

As the novels progress, it gets amply clear that the protagonists are not doomed to this alienated condition forever. Several of their characters are well on their way to self-realization. They are able to fit into the "creative non-victim" position that Margaret Atwood writes of in *Survival*. Atwood describes such a person as being able to free himself from thinking in terms of static dichotomies. He is also able to accept his own body, including its sexuality, as part of this process, accepting the versatility that it requires. Margaret Laurence strikes one as a deeply spiritual writer, who sees the move from alienation to a better state of being in slightly different terms. In most of her works there is a movement from alienation towards order and meaning; "not the making or imposing of order on chaotic fragments, but the exploration and revealing of an order that is there and is within the power of seeking men and women to apprehend" (21). In an interview with Donald Cameron, Laurence says, "Life is extraordinarily and in a way wonderfully formless, and yet the whole world, sort of examined minutely has got incredible form" (qtd. Vevaina 21). Thus her work is informed by a larger vision. The alienation and discomfort with the body experienced by her female protagonists is overcome when their vision clears and they are able to see their own positions in the cosmos or scheme of things. Often the body's liberation becomes instrumental in attaining this higher state of being. Adele Wiseman in her novel *Crackpot*, looks at the marginalization of Hoda on account of her ethnic identity, obesity, sex and poverty. Hoda overcomes her alienation both from her body and society to make space for herself and adopts a non-victim position. There is a reinscribing of the maternal body and a subversion of the Oedipal situation. Susan Swan, by means of the grotesque and parody exposes patriarchy's marginalizing of the female body of the giantess into history. The body figures as a metaphor for problematizing troubled Canadian-American relations as well. In all the texts the writers focus on the negative images of the female body circulating in society and the resultant negative self-images that govern women's lives.

2.1 Ravages of Middle Age

In *The Fire-Dwellers,* Margaret Laurence portrays the feelings of self-loathing and near panic in the protagonist Stacey caused by her aging body. Laurence also examines sexuality in the middle-aged woman in this novel. Stacey has the following thoughts while studying herself in the mirror:

> Oh Cleopatra. You old swayback. Four kids have altered me. The stretch marks look like little silver worms in parallel processions across my belly and thighs. My breasts aren't bad, and at least my ankles aren't thick. (*FD* 21)

A little later Stacey feels a physical need for her husband, perhaps any man. This seems to be more in the way of reassuring herself of her desirability rather than anything else. She seems to be objectifying her own body. The alienation from her body intensifies further and finds expression in a nightmare; where she walks through a dark and damp rain forest carrying something:

> She has to continue, bringing what she is carrying with her. The thing is bleeding from the neck stump, but that cannot be helped. The severed head spills only blood, nothing else. She has tunnelled at last through the undergrowth. Now she has a right to look. She holds it up in front of her. How is it that she can see it. What is she seeing it with? That is the question. The head she has been carrying is of course none but hers. (115)

The dream symbolizes the fear she experiences and the alienated condition she lives in. Her own objectification of her self is complete. She is quite different in her alienation from Hagar in *Stone Angel* and Rachel in *A Jest of God*. According to Coomi Vevaina:

> unlike Hagar and Rachel who exert rigid control on themselves before their partial liberation, Stacey is open, benevolent and alive. Also, unlike them, she is not terrified of the expression of passion and human need in others and is desperate to know the actual people behind their social masks. (122)

The alienation she feels is an internalization of the social prescriptions for the female body and her own mother's dicta. It informs the mother-daughter relationship as well as her relationship with her husband, Mac.

Although Stacey feels oppressed by the small town Manawaka in which she grew up, it becomes a mind set and rules her thoughts. Associated with that is her mother's domineering role in her life. Stacey has internalized her mother's values in spite of her seemingly rebellious attitude. She constantly censures herself for not being a good mother and these feelings of self-doubt affect her relations with her daughter Katie.

Social prescriptions for women's beauty result in Stacey's feelings of self-loathing of her aging body and feelings of insecurity in her relationship with her husband and her lover.

> I don't want to expose myself to him. I'm not perfect enough. He's too young. I've got on me the stretch marks of four kids, the lines of dead silver worming across my belly. Will he notice? He'd have to be blind, not to. I can't help it. I'm not twenty anymore. The padding of fat on my hips and on the inner reaches of my thighs. Goddam. I never knew it would be like this. It's different with Mac. (186)

These feelings create contradictory pulls between her maternal feelings on the one hand and the need to look young and slim on the other. She is bewildered by her own sexuality and is guilt ridden.

A woman's response to lack of sexual fulfillment in marriage has been treated subtly by Laurence in this novel. The body, as prescribed by patriarchy and its institutions is a source of discomfort and discontentment for women. In her analysis of Laurence's novels, Jill Franks writes:

> One of Margaret Laurence's strongest skills is writing convincingly about sex rendering characters' pain in response to feeling trapped within their individual consciousness at a moment when they wish to be merged with the other. All of the protagonists' sexual experiences are "strange" but perhaps that is because all of them figure the unequal power relationships that form their social contexts. (109)[1]

Contradictory demands like motherhood and the need to stay young and beautiful are made on women, resulting in their alienation from their bodies. There is complete frustration at not being able to meet role expectations and social prescriptions. Stacey admits to have envied Tess for being glamorous. This goes to show that Stacey is a victim of patriarchal ideals of beauty.

This is why she feels dowdy and fat and is in constant self-doubt. Christl Verduyn in her article titled, "Language, Body and Identity in Margaret Laurence's *The Fire-Dwellers*" suggests:

> Close examination of Laurence's *The Fire-Dwellers* . . . discloses a subtext wherein language is repeatedly shown to be an inadequate vehicle of expression for the protagonist Stacey MacAindra. At this level of disclosure, *The Fire-Dwellers* reads much more like a contemporary feminist exploration of language and "reality" than as a 'somewhat dated housewife story.' (128-29)

Verduyn sees the body experiences of the protagonist linked with limitations of conventional language and shaping her sense of self. She writes, "The physical experience of the body, always modified by the social categories through which it is known, sustains a particular view of society. There is continual exchange of meanings between the two kinds of bodily experience so that each reinforces the categories of the "other" (134). Stacey's alienation from her body results in a divided self and her "struggles with this divided self, and the separated spheres of body and brain, her struggles with language" (130).

Tess, so empty and hollow within, is constantly trying to beautify herself with cosmetics and clothing. In spite of having a beautiful body, she has a confused identity. After Tess's death by suicide, Stacey is extremely distraught and Katie is the comforter, the mother. There is a reversal of the mother-daughter relationship and Katie comes off as the stronger one, the nurturer. This is in contrast to Stacey's relationship with her mother which is at stasis.

Stacey's discontent with her body and her apprehensions about aging continue even towards the end of the novel:

> I won't be twenty-one again. I'll never have a really decent-looking pair of hips again as long as I live. I don't claim that's any tragedy. I don't even claim it's anything except ludicrous. But it's enough to make me feel relatively lousy on occasion. (*FD* 280)

Neither Stacey's relationship with Luke nor her better level of communication with Mac can alter this feeling. There is, however a realization of the presence of these attitudes within her and that perhaps could set off self-analysis and introspection as is suggested by the lines: "Give me another forty years, Lord, and I may mutate into a matriarch" (281).

Referring to Laurence's use of the ironical voice, Jill Franks writes: "Although irony may seem like a small "victory" over patriarchal expectations, it is the only resistance available to some women (like Stacey) who have decided to live with men on men's terms." (109)

Referring to the narrative structure, Laurence elaborates: "Narration, dreams, memories, inner running commentary—all had to be brief, even fragmented, to convey the jangled quality of Stacey's life." (qtd. Stovel 125)

Laurence, through Stacey's portrayal, drives home an important aspect of aging, which is, that there is rarely coordination and harmony between the mental and physical processes. As Mathew Martin observes: "The split in the narrative between Stacey's inner thoughts and outer speech often illustrate that while she may be outwardly conforming to her Oedipal role, she is sceptical about its status as the universal structure of desire." (65)[2]

This discrepancy itself could lead to the alienation a woman experiences from herself and society, poised at middle age. The mother-daughter relationship is perceived a little differently. Often it is Katie who seems worldly-wise and mature. Stacey can see her teenage viewpoint but deliberately tries to don a stereotypical matriarchal role—the manners in which she has been socialized thereby showing that she has imbibed her mother's values.

2.2 Sexual Awaking and Identity

A Jest of God can be considered as a story of Rachel's sexual awakening and her coming to terms with her body. In the constricted environment of Manawaka, she is in denial of her own needs and the image she projects is that of a prim and proper schoolmarm who is bound by duty to her mother. She admits to Nick Kazlik to having been socialized to not display emotion. She tells him that she used to envy people like him who were "Not so boxed-in" who were "more outspoken" (*JG* 88). She felt that their Ukrainian-Canadian community was more expressive and freer in communication than their Scots-Presbyterian one.

Rachel's cloistered life in Manawaka makes her almost cling to Nick for company and for her physical fulfillment as well. The socially oppressive climate of Manawaka is evident when she thinks she needs contraception but avoids going to the doctor simply so that the word does not get around. She is very apprehensive when she misses her period and is quite excited on the one hand about possibly carrying Nick's child and, on the other, is worried about the social ostracism. Fate deals with it ironically when she eventually summons up courage to go to Doctor Raven, she is told she has a tumour. He even remembers the last time she had missed her periods. Laurence portrays the suffocating social proximity and its implications particularly, for a single woman in a small town like Manawaka.

The alienation from the body is reinforced by the social establishment and relationships in the small town. Rachel is constantly in fear of her students' ridicule as well but, at the same time she feels the need for Nick. She hardly knows him as a person and yet feels the need for him and even falls in love with him and wants to bear his children. She realizes at the end that it was perhaps her own need that kept the relationship going. Being sexually uninitiated, she sought more from the relationship than he seemed ready for. The basis of the relationship seems to be initially their sexual needs rather than friendship or sharing of any emotional kind. After they achieve a physical comfort level they however, do start communicating. Rachel, however, does not take a victim position when Nick leaves abruptly without even a goodbye. She is perceptive enough to understand that there had been no real communication between them and her needs and his had been quite different. She does not even imagine that he had intentionally deceived her or trapped her:

> I don't know whether he meant to lie to me or not. As for what was happening with him and to him this summer, I couldn't say what it really was, not whether it had anything to do with me or not. (190)

Rachel does not harbour any illusions about herself or their relationship. This helps her survive and take initiatives to go on with her life. Laurence does not take a strident, feminist position vis-à-vis her heroes. Nick may merely have been instrumental in Rachel's sexual awakening.

The mother-daughter relationship in all its oppressive forms is portrayed in the novel. Rachel and her mother never openly fight but the undercurrent of animosity is omnipresent. Rachel's mother could very well be the figure of the Phallic mother with deceptively mild and polite manners. She is ever petulant and lays the guilt on Rachel who apologizes for every small thing in every conversation they have. She really keeps an iron grip on her daughter by emotionally blackmailing her and adopting a victim position. More than that, Rachel is constantly monitored by her voice running in her head with its remarks and sayings. This internalization seems to be a worse kind of oppression.

The love-hate quality inherent in every mother-daughter relationship is portrayed in a complex manner in the novel. The mother figure becomes a strong agent of patriarchy to keep and sustain a woman's alienation from her body. She is constantly chiding Rachel about her clothes or her staying out late. By constantly reminding Rachel of her weak heart, she makes unfair demands on Rachel's time and attention and this in turn serves to keep Rachel confined to the house and by her side. Each time Rachel goes out with Nick, she has to sneak into the house like a teenager and devise strategies to avoid the prying eyes of her mother.

Mathew Martin sees a subversion of the Oedipal complex and Oedipus society in *A Jest of God*, *The Fire-Dwellers* and *The Diviners*. After her relationship with Nick, Rachel overcomes her repressed sexuality and this is the beginning of her changed consciousness. She realizes that her superego is a construct and that she tends to distort reality with her own repressed fear and desires:

> From this newly acquired space Rachel inverts the Oedipal binary opposition that privileges the phallus over the womb. Rachel's supposed pregnancy is the material signifier of this change. . . . Rachel's story is a story of rehabilitation through breaking down prescribed limits and building upon the possibilities thus created. (62-63)

Like her sister Stacey in *The Fire-Dwellers* Rachel too is a victim of patriarchy.

In her study of Laurence's novels, Jill Franks writes of the covert feminist thoughts of her protagonists:

> Their feminisms lie within their own brains, and it is only through hearing their voices in the act of novel reading that we may know of their qualified liberation. This liberation is portrayed via their many-voiced internal conversations, in which it is possible to identify two particularly strong strands: one, the voice-of-conformity to societal (hence, male-dominated) standards for women's behaviour and roles; the other, the voice-of-rebellion that is ironical, cynical and often parodic of the other voice and the culture it represents. These voices can be said to assert a feminist consciousness through playful plurivocality. (100)

The covert feminist thoughts expressed by her protagonists call for experimentation however subtle in her narrative technique as well. In her analysis of the sister novels, *A Jest of God* and *The Fire-Dwellers*, Nora Foster Stovel observes:

> Laurence interweaves structural with symbolic techniques to dramatize the sisters' identity crisis, manipulating narrative method to convey the divisions between the characters' inner and outer life, subjective and objective reality. This manipulation of narrative method also structures the time sequence in a flashback technique, relating memory and desire, as the protagonists try to come to terms with the past in order to free themselves for the future. (121)

Hagar, the central female protagonist in Margaret Laurence's *The Stone Angel* seems to be the very personification of the terrible, all-powerful Mother in the Lacanian sense. She is a creation of and a spokeswoman for patriarchy and has literally been shaped and moulded by her father Jason Currie. She has never known her mother and is brought up just like the boys, taught to be proud of the Currie clan and her Scottish traditions. She turns away from human contact as if the need itself were a human failing and in fact resembles the stone angel of the title.

The novel is in the first person and as Sara Maitland puts it: "In the creation of Hagar Shipley [Laurence] has given us a character with exactly the right degree of self-knowledge to make this form work—a character who is not, by her nature either self-indulgent or easily fooled, not even by herself, but who is not so self knowing that the reader has to take her every observation as the ultimate and perfect truth." (44)

This device allows for the reader to partake of authorial irony whenever there is a gap between Hagar's observations and the reader's differing and more sensitive perceptions. Hagar sees love as a kind of weakness and remarks: "Love, I fancied, must consist of words and deeds delicate as lavender sachets, not like the things he did sprawled on the high white bedstead that rattled like a train" (*SA* 80). These notions are based on a shallow understanding of the romantic. Although she marries Bram Shipley in an act of rebellion against her father, she tries to uphold the Currie clan's values over the Shipley's more humble ones. Towards the end of her life at the age of ninety, she finally looks inward and realizes that the values of both the Curries and Shipleys are necessary for making the most of life. As Coomi Vevaina notes, "Having come to terms with her past, Hagar ceases to be the stone angel of the title and comes close to becoming a flesh-and-blood angel" (224). By then it is far too late and too much harm has been wreaked by her insensitivities on her loved ones.

In a sense her tragedy originates and culminates from her alienation from her body as well as her spirit. Calvinism does not help her. As Hugh MacLennan says: "Calvinism as understood by many of its practitioners, shifted the balance of the Christian gospel from a message of hope, love and redemption, to one of guilt, death and damnation, backwards from the Christ of the New Testament to the Old Testament God of wrath and retribution." (qtd. Vevaina 220)

The following words from the novel define Hagar's character for the reader at the very outset: "How anxious I was to be neat and orderly, imagining life had been created only to celebrate tidiness like, prissy Pippa as she passed." (*SA* 5)

She then goes on to describe other "dust-tinged" "musky" smell of things that grew untended where the Cree walked "with enigmatic faces and greasy hair" (5). Hagar's father wishes to toughen her and she hears him say that he wished she had been a boy. She is proud when he tells her that she is like him and seeks his approval. The incident when Hagar as a young girl, refuses to put on her mother's plaid shawl for her brother Dan's sake, shows her to be one who is intolerant of frailty to the point of being cruel and lacking in compassion.

Hagar is completely alienated from her husband Bram. She feels superior to him and marries him in an act of defiance. She enjoys sex with him but this she admits only to herself. In the entire novel there is only one instance when she is gentle and sympathetic, and that is when he loses his horse.

> When we went to bed that night, he started to turn to me, and I felt so gently inclined that I think I might have opened to him openly. But he changed his mind. He patted me lightly on the shoulder. (87-88)

This could have been a turning point in their relationship, had she reached out to him but Hagar, being Hagar, does not.

There is an outward denial of her body's needs and expressions and the resultant alienation from it is guided by a false sense of decorum and a Victorian guilt-ridden, false sense of superiority. This is illustrated in the following lines from the novel:

> It was not so very long after we wed, when first I felt my blood and vitals rise to meet his. He never knew. I never let him know. I never spoke aloud, and I made certain that the trembling was all inner. He had an innocence about him, I guess, or he'd have known. How could he not have known? Didn't I betray myself in rising sap, like a heedless and compelled maple after a winter? But no. He never expected any such thing, and so he never perceived it. I prided myself upon keeping my pride intact, like some maidenhead. (81)

She denies passion altogether as is evident in her reactions to a painting she sees. Hagar literally turns to stone after her son John's death when she is unable even to shed a tear.

She is unable to express her feelings even towards her grandson Steven. She feels only discomfort and embarrassment but, at the same time, feels the need to communicate. Even towards the end of the novel, she finds it difficult to tell her son Marvin that she thought him a better son than John. Hagar's tragedy lies in her distance from her own feelings and her inability to express them. This results in the failure of all her relationships with both men as well as women. This tragic flaw can be attributed partly to her upbringing and to the small-town, Scots-Presbyterian ethos. The dichotomous thinking characteristic of logocentrism results in one's losing touch with oneself—the inner core of being. The body, in this novel has several significations as Donna Pennee puts it. Referring to Hagar she says:

> In her old age, she can no longer escape the body that she has systematically repressed. But while for her this body is a source of shame, for readers it can be the source of Laurence's most sustained critique of what she called "the intertwined and simultaneous" discourses of patriarchy, empire and traditional authority. (5)

There are unique and graphic descriptions of an aged and ailing old woman's physical discomfort in the novel. It is a realm of experience which is often marginalized and even ignored, much less written about. One such illustration is contained in the following lines:

> As I brush my fingers over my own wrist, the skin seems too white after the sunburned years, and too dry, powdery as blown dust when the rains failed, flaking with dryness as an old bone will flake and chalk, left out in a sun that grinds bone and flesh and earth to dust as though in a mortar of fire with a pestle of crushing light. (54)

Donna Pennee, perceptively notes:

> Not surprisingly, then, Hagar's own incontinent body functions paradoxically in the novel, for it both registers and is a register of the repressive relations of settlement-invasion and social stratification represented in the novel. At the level of realistic detail, much of the narrative is taken up with Hagar's aged body, with its unwieldy size, its embarrassing and troublesome excesses of tears, urine, intestinal gas, and pain. (15)

In tracing the narrative strategies employed by Margaret Laurence, Brenda Beckman-Long observes that of the four Manawaka novels, *The Stone Angel* and *A Jest of God* are written in the first person but the later two, *The Fire-Dwellers* and *The Diviners* are not. In this context Beckman-Long writes:

> In this tradition of women's fiction, the inside view of first-person narration generates sympathy for the point of view of the narrator because the reader finds herself or himself located within the narrator's consciousness. Laurence borrows the confessional form to create sympathy for her protagonist through whose eyes the reader views the societal representation, as she embeds a feminist ideology to challenge a patriarchal culture. (71)

In her later two novels she shifts to third-person narration and, according to Beckman-Long, "third person narration lends authority to the text because the values and reflections expressed are not presented merely as the singular opinion of a fictional character. . . . This shift may reflect a corresponding socio-historical shift brought about by the women's movement of the late 1960s and 1970s" (72). The critic feels that the gender-specific pronoun "she" indicates the generalizing possibilities of the protagonist's experience. Elaborating on this idea Beckman-Long notes:

> Laurence's employment of an authoritative third-person narrator becomes a rhetorical strategy to convince the reader of the accuracy of the fictional representation, and the implied reader becomes Stacey's chief confessor. This strategy is particularly effective in a gendered confession. (74)[3]

2.3 The Maternal Body

Crackpot, by Adele Wiseman, is a novel about the body in all its ramifications. The materiality of the body with all its hues and odours are presented and it is a body without tangible boundaries. Hoda's body is the site on which pathos and the absurd are played out. The marginalization of this very giving body is focused on without bitterness and with great sensitivity and understatement. Hoda's birth is heralded in the tone and manner of grandeur, very similar to that adopted in the narration of events in the Bible. The novel begins thus:

> Out of Shem Berl and Golda came Rahel. Out of Malka and Benyamin came Danile. Out of Danile and Rahel came Hoda. Out of Hoda, Pipick came, Pipick born in secrecy and mystery and terror, for what did Hoda know? (*Crackpot* 9)

It is on one level a story of the first generation of Jewish immigrants in Canada and experiences of the Jewish diaspora. Hoda's parents Rahela and Danile are doubly or even triply marginalized by virtue of being Jewish and poor and Danile also being blind. Ruth Panofsky notes in her article titled "From Complicity to Subversion: The Female Subject in Adele Wiseman's Novels":

> In the figure of Hoda, *Crackpot* seeks retribution for Laiah's death and provides a revisionist reading of the earlier text which attempts to recover a place for women within Judaism and fiction. *Crackpot* is written against *The Sacrifice* as a critique where "community and social connectedness are the end of the female guest, not death." (41)

Hoda is blissfully unaware of the odds against which her parents are surviving in Canada. She is used to being an object of curiosity from early childhood due to her obesity and she revels in it and learns to capitalize much as the young giantess does in Susan Swan's novel *The Biggest Modern Woman of the World*. There are parallels between the three characters and their childhood—Joan of *Lady Oracle*, Hoda and the giantess in Swan's novel.

In all the three novels, the writers use the grotesque to convey certain tragic experiences and social realities encountered by the protagonists. Hoda encounters cruelty at school due to her obese body but defies it. She resorts to sheltering herself in fairy tales thus:

> The Prince of Wales would know who was born to become his queen.
>
> And he wasn't the only one who would know what she was really like, under the spell of fat she couldn't escape and sloppiness she couldn't control, like the Frog Princess and Beauty and the Beast and the Ugly Duckling and Cinderella too. All kinds of girls who thought they were the fairest of them all would get a surprise some day, when the young prince who was ripening in his long. chinned, pale-eyed nondescript, special kind of noble beauty would come from over the seas and not even notice them at all. (49)

There is, this naïve, illusion that Hoda harbours all her life. It is also indicative of a distorted self-image. The author adopts a tone of irony mixed with pathos. Hoda's physical ugliness and sloppiness and its irreconcilability with the fairy tale stereotypes she grew up on, set the stage for the tragedy to follow. It is as if her obesity has dulled her wits as well. The implications of her mother, Rahel's death, are beyond her comprehension and all that she can do is eat to feel secure. She associates food with her mother, since Rahel used to carry her to work and constantly feed her on tidbits. Her mother gives food substitutes for her presence. There is an alienation from her body which is like a separate entity gorging on huge amounts of food and likewise from her true feelings of grief. She is completely anaesthetized. These feelings of distance from her peer group increase with time and Hoda goes to the extent of allowing boys to touch her and eventually have sex with her, mainly in an attempt to somehow get their acceptance. She is constantly made to feel the outsider and these attitudes in turn affect her self-worth. She feels objectified and gives in to the feeling merely for acceptance as peer group approval is a strong teenage need. Her marginalized condition is due to a combination of factors such as her ethnic identity, her obesity, her sex and her poverty. However, she dreams of marriage and security like any other girl of her age would.

Her impoverished condition makes her dream even more about a future when she would be thin and beautiful like everyone else and have plenty to eat. She is compelled to live a hand to mouth existence and worry about basic necessities at an age when she ought to have been a carefree school girl. She is forced to do domestic work like her mother but even in those homes, she encounters only cruelty. The well-to-do women show no charity and are downright mean to her. She is exploited for her domestic work as well. Hoda is made to feel guilty about her appearance and Adele Wiseman sensitively captures her pathetic condition in these lines:

> Hoda didn't want to lug around such a carcass. She was used to being told in less than complimentary terms about how fat she was, and she didn't care, really she didn't. But when, interlarded with all that other stuff that all seemed so kindly meant, people said all those mean things, as if she had no feelings and she mustn't open her mouth to say anything, when she was working so hard to please them, as if it was her fault that she looked that way. (121)

These lines drive home the fact that society is cruel to fat people and associates fat with ugliness. Her body with all its social signification defines her for her teacher as well. Her teacher has these nauseous feelings at the very sight of Hoda:

> So far there had been no trouble from this one; a certain blowsy eagerness, a super-abundance of physical presence, she was one of these bodies you felt was impinging on all your senses; you might not actually be able to, but you felt as though you could even smell her at a distance. (134)

The feeling of disgust imminent in these lines harbours deep-rooted prejudices, both against Hoda's ethnicity and her body. One is too inclined to agree that women are patriarchy's most effective agents and its perpetrators. Her employment prospects are likewise marred by her body's appearance. Social ostracism of fat people is evident in the thoughts she has after she delivers her son Pipick:

> They'd see she was thinner, and they'd realize why. She slumped against the table and at the same time tried to blow out her stomach from within. But she hadn't got much thinner. And anyway, they never really looked at her that closely. She was fat, and fat was fat and people figured what's a thimbleful one way or another. (222)

The entire description of birthing is filled with pathos. Hoda's alienation from her body during the birth of her child is heart-wrenching. Being motherless, she is caught unawares and the horrors of the body and its processes astound her. There is black humour in the manner in which Wiseman describes Hoda's need to compromise herself to Yankl, the butcher, for the sake of some meat to feed herself and her father.

There is extreme pathos in the novel and the tragic climax is reached when her son Pipick comes to her as a customer for sex. It is her greatest act of love and suffering. Her body assumes maternal qualities, in its capacity to protect and heal and partly it is an amorous body with its capacity to please her son. As Ruth Panofsky puts it: "In a parodic inversion of mother-son incest, *Crackpot* turns the tale of Jocasta and Oedipus on its head. Instead of engendering tragedy and alienation as it does in the Thesbian drama, the incestuous relationship between Hoda and David facilitates the novel's comic resolution." (46)

According to Panofsky, incest becomes an act of compassion and an illustration of Hoda's selflessness.[4] The figure of Hoda assumes mythic dimensions towards the end where the story of creation is suggested and she is the Eternal, life-giving Primal Mother. Interestingly, Hoda does not degenerate and dwell in the victim position. From an exploited, young girl, she evolves into a wise, all-giving mother. The healing powers of her maternal body are evident even with her lover Lazarus who is in deep sleep, resting against her, soon after they get engaged. Hoda's body defines boundaries, in that it becomes an instrument and provider of different needs to different people, almost magical. There is eventually a magnanimity and a solidity about it that overrides the ridicule and laughter it evokes.

2.4 Alienation and Commodification of the Female Body in Consumer Society—The Split Subject

The Edible Woman by Margaret Atwood was written at the time of the baby boomers generation of women and when Betty Friedan's book *The Feminine Mystique* was published. In a perceptive analysis of the novel, Coomi Vevaina writes:

> The spiritual side of the psyche is starved by a life devoted to material prosperity. This defect is however, cunningly masked as a virtue. Consumer ethics idolizes the materially prosperous individual and regards the spiritually inclined person with disdain. To add to it, a wide variety of 'desirable' images are created for the appetite of consumers, most of whom are made to forget that happiness lies within themselves rather than in the external world. (104)

This seems to be the bane in the lives of the three main female protagonists of Atwood's three novels to be considered in this chapter—Marian in *The Edible Woman*, Joan in *Lady Oracle* and the unnamed narrator of *Surfacing.* The body becomes the site of an identity crisis struggle and of a rejuvenated identity emerging at the end of it all. All three protagonists suffer from eating disorders at different points in the novel. These disorders are themselves symptomatic of a more deep-rooted malaise in their self-images (centring on the body).

Marian seems to be a helpless bystander at the beginning who allows things to happen to her in trying to be exactly what Peter, her fiancé, wants her to be. She is alienated from the others and also from herself. Even when she and Peter make love in the tub, her mind is cut off from the rest of her, as she ironically ponders over the fact that it was she who had to tolerate the discomfort of the tub since Peter was on top of her. Betty Friedan calls the norm prescribed for white, middle-class women of her society, 'the feminine mystique.' This media propped image was, she writes, "created by women's magazines, by advertisements, television, movies, novels, columns and books by experts on marriage and family, child psychology, sexual adjustment, and by the popularizes of sociology and psychoanalysis." (qtd. Vevaina 108)

Friedan goes on to write that the image of woman that emerges from it was: "young and frivolous, almost childlike; fluffy and feminine; passive; gaily content in a world of bedroom and kitchen, sex, babies and home." (qtd. Vevaina 108) These were the baby boomers who were told that truly feminine women do not want careers, higher education and political rights.

The office virgins Lucy, Emmy and Millie are portrayed as quite dumb and constantly on the prowl. They doll up like items of confectionary to hook eligible men. Unlike these women, Clara, a wife and mother of three, is far from happy. Clara's presence explodes the myth created by feminine mystique that motherhood is the ultimate glory of a woman's life. Clara describes her unplanned babies as "barnacles encrusting a ship and limpets clinging to a rock" (*EW* 36). Clara warns Marian and Ainsley not to believe what society says about maternal instinct and says she cannot see "how anyone can love their children till they start to be human beings" (33). Joe, Clara's husband, feels that once a woman gets married, "she allows her core to get taken over by the husband. And when the kids come, she wakes up one morning and discovers she doesn't have anything left, inside, she's hollow, she doesn't know who she is any more; her core has been destroyed" (236). Marian, the day after her engagement, feels the same way and says: "my mind was at first as empty as though someone had scooped out the inside of my skull like a cantaloupe and left me only the rind to think with" (83).

Marian begins experiencing alienation and a distancing from Peter quite early in the novel. When she tries to run ahead of them in the street and behaves in an uncharacteristic manner, Peter has no clue about what is going on inside her. He behaves quite cruelly with Marian and is callous in his attitude. After their heated argument about the evening having been ruined, he humiliates her further by saying, "you're first rejecting your femininity" (80). He approves of Ainsley just to rankle Marian even more. In her study of Atwood's novel, Sonia Mycak suggests:

> This sense of fragmentation and the alienating experience of having identified a Body "somehow no longer quite her own" . . . is fundamental to the mirror-stage formation of the ego as Lacan describes it. In his account of the identificatory process whereby the infant recognizes his or her own image, the apparent unity visually introjected is in discordance with the actual bodily experience that is one of organic prematurity. (66)

The cake lady seems to function as an imaginary anatomy whereby Marian's ego takes the form of a body image introjected as a kind of psychic map.

The novel can be read also as a parody of graduate students' lives and the intellectual sterility that it contains. Duncan, Marian's graduate-student lover, says, there really seems to be no difference "between the library stack and one of those used-car graveyards" (143). Ainsley is a victim of this clinical, sterile approach as well. She chooses to have a baby simply because according to the experts,' "Every woman should have at least one baby. . . . It's even more important than sex. It fulfills your deepest femininity (40-41). It is evident as Ainsley goes on to scheme and trap Len to father her child and later Fish, that in spite of her seemingly non-conformist views, she too succumbs to the feminine mystique.

The tragedy of the characters lies in their alienated condition in consumer society. Atwood admits that the novel makes a very negative statement about society for the characters are trapped in a circle game (qtd. Vevaina, 112). Marian wants to marry Peter for all the conventional reasons. Her growing anorexia is symbolically and quiet literally indicative that she cannot "stomach" her situation anymore. The intense anorexia and the consequent nervous breakdown are essential for the rebirth of a more integrated and self-realized Marian. Her anorexia is the ultimate stage in her objectifying her own body and she puzzles over "her body's decision to reject certain foods" (179). It is as though her body has acquired a will of its own. The first and third sections of the novel are in the first person and the middle section is in the third person. The first section records the self-doubt and discontentment in Marian while the second section, in keeping with her anorexia and alienation is in the third person. In the third section, Marian comes back to consumer society but with a heightened sense of awareness after her break-up with Peter and her brief but educative interlude with Duncan. Her eating of the cake she herself bakes in the figure of a woman, is of course suggestive of the fact that she overcomes her anorexia, even as she is able to cut through the layers of the false selves that consumer, patriarchal society had camouflaged her true self in. Sharon Rose Wilson, in her analysis of Atwood's works, writes:

> Although *Surfacing's* cannibalism theme is less explicit and sustained than that of *The Edible Woman*, *Surfacing* also depicts symbolic cannibalism: imperialistic and sexist power that wastes the wasteland of narrator, land, region, and country. In addition, the novel's ritualistic eating is linked to victimization and atonement, death and rebirth. (112-13)[5]

Marian regains the lost core of her being and is able to get in touch with her self. Interestingly, she does not assume the victim position even when her relationship with Duncan falls apart. Atwood does not offer the character of Duncan as a panacea to Marian and an antidote to all her travails. He is as alienated as her in many ways. There is something intangible about him as he himself puts it:

> that I am a changeling. I got switched for a real baby when young and my parents never discovered the fraud, though I must admit they suspected something. . . . They kept telling me my ears were too big; but really I'm not human at all, I come from the underground. (141)

His character has sub-human, even animal like qualities, close to that of the trickster figure who is merely meant to help the protagonist along the path to self-realization. Duncan is completely self-absorbed and psychologically lop-sided for, when having sex, he tells Marian: "You're just another substitute for the Laundromat" (145). By saying that he felt it was happening to someone else he objectifies her as well as himself.

Atwood seems to be suggesting that men as well as women are victims of patriarchy and consumerism, since they share the alienation of their bodies and spirit. Sharon Rose Wilson, in her study of Atwood's novels, writes on her use of parody: "In *The Edible Woman* the fairy-tale intertext establishes both comic and Gothic. Not only undercutting the reliability of Marian's vision and questioning the influence of popular culture, it parodies our expectations of 'plot' in sexual relationship." (94)

Nemesis for playboy Len's exploitation of young girls comes through Ainsley. After she announces her pregnancy there is a heated exchange between them, during which Ainsley accuses Len of "uterus envy" (159)—a reversal as it were of the Freudian idea of 'penis envy.'

Alienation from the body is likewise suggested in the descriptions in the novel of Clara's pregnant body. Pregnancy is not considered a very attractive condition of the female body in patriarchy. Marian too subscribes to these views as she thinks about Clara after she delivers a baby:

> Clara was deflating toward her normal size again and she would be able to talk with her more freely: she would no longer feel as though she was addressing a swollen mass of flesh with a tiny pinhead, a shape that had made her think of a queen-ant, bulging with the burden of an entire society, a semi-person. (115)

Clara herself voices similar feelings of disgust and anxiety in the last stages of her pregnancy as she tells Marian, supposedly lightly, referring to the baby in her womb: "'Maybe it's got three heads,' and 'Maybe it isn't a baby at all but a kind of parasitic growth, like galls on trees, or elephantiasis of the navel, or a huge bunion.'" (114) These feelings of disgust perhaps may not be found in some matriarchal societies where pregnant women are even deified.

Catherine McLay points out that "the point to which Marian returns is on a higher level of reality" (qtd. Vevaina 121) but she does return to the same choices as that she had before her transformation "a career going nowhere or marriage as an exit from it" (121). The novel is not completely pessimistic about the human condition, however. Marian does take the first step in getting in touch with her self as a more integrated person.

In her third novel *Lady Oracle* Atwood overtly uses parody and satire as literary devices to subvert and thereby expose, prescriptions of love, romance and beauty imposed by the culture of patriarchy. It has even been suggested by critics that perhaps she wanted to parody the quest myth developed in *Surfacing* (Vevaina 71). During an interview with J.R. Struthers, Atwood says that Joan develops "3/4 of an inch" (qtd. Vevaina 71) for, at the end of the novel, she decides to return to Toronto to clear her friends Sam and Marlene of the charge of murdering her. Yet she continues her costume-oriented fiction-filled life style without a second thought.

From early childhood, Joan experiences alienation on account of her body. She feels objectified even as she says, while she is with Arthur: "I suppose I was like a kid's chemistry set for him: secretly he liked mixing me up, he knew, something exciting would happen" (20). The roots of these feelings can easily be traced to her childhood experiences. She resorts to a fantasized romantic life even while she is supposedly happily married to Arthur.

According to Erich Neumann, in 'The Significance of the Genetic Aspect for Analytical Psychology,' "the Self is experienced in childhood in relation to parents, initially the mother" (qtd. Vevaina 62). During this phase "the ego-self axis is most vulnerable to damage by adverse environmental influence. . . . Therefore inability to experience acceptance or rapport is felt to be identical with loss of acceptance by the Self" (qtd. Vevaina 62). Joan's mother is truly a Phallic/Terrible Mother in the Lacanian sense. Joan internalizes all the negative images that her mother creates of her and these centre on her body. The mother-daughter relationship is crucial to understanding Joan's complex character. Her identity confusion begins with her name itself. Later, when she is older she wonders if her mother had named her

> after Joan Crawford because she wanted me to be like the screen characters she played—beautiful, ambitious, ruthless, destructive to men—or because she wanted me to be successful? Joan Crawford worked hard, she had willpower, she built herself up from nothing, according to my mother. Did she give me someone else's name because she wanted me never to have a name of my own? . . . There's more than one side to Joan Crawford though. In fact there was something tragic about Joan Crawford, she had big serious eyes, an unhappy mouth and high cheekbones, unfortunate things happened to her. Perhaps that was it. Or and this is important: Joan Crawford was thin. (42)

Her mother's cruel and snide remarks about her weight reinforce her feelings of low self-esteem. Feelings of shame about her body are implanted in her. The negative self-images hinge on her mother's rejection of her body and consequently lead to self-abuse which is manifested in her eating disorder. A desperation to please and a craving for approval become recurrent behavioural patterns in all her relationships.

A moving episode in the early part of the novel is of Joan as a schoolgirl, rehearsing hard for a role as a butterfly in a school recital. Much to her disappointment, on account of her size, she is made to play a mothball by her mother and teacher. This leaves a permanent scar on her psyche. Dance is a recurrent motif in the novel. Her mother shows utter callousness in handling her daughter. From this point on, the body plays a crucial role for getting society's approval and compassion. Obesity becomes a cause for ridicule. The Brownie's refrain: "A Brownie gives in to the older folk. A Brownie does NOT give in to herself" (56), reinforces the need for approval. In an attempt to gain her mother's approval, poor Joan makes "clumsy" attempts at helping with housework. Low self-esteem persists even in her later life. Joan's excessive eating gets worse successively as her self-image worsens. She develops sado-masochistic traits for she sees overeating as a way of getting back at her mother. She says: "I ate to defy her, but I also ate from panic. Sometimes I was afraid I wasn't really there, I was an accident; I'd heard her call me an accident." (82-83)

Joan is denied pets and is forced to play with dolls, which she describes as, "those crotchless frizzy-haired plastic goddesses, with their infantile eyes and their breasts that emerged and receded gently as knees, unalarming, devoid of nipples" (84). Her mother denies her an emotional life or attachments of any kind. Her coldness alienates Joan from others as well. With reference to the mother-daughter relationship Mycak writes:

> Because of the privileged role orality and corporeality play in negotiating choric space, this struggle between mother and daughter is expressed primarily through the attempted control, on both their parts, over Joan's body. As a consequence Joan begins to assert herself by way of abjecting her own body through an immersion in anorexic dieting; and the resulting weight loss, in the context of its functioning as an attempt at detachment from the maternal, initiates her entry into the sexual arena of masculine desire. (74)[6]

She does however relate well with Aunt Lou and the two go to movies together. Despite the closeness however, she perceives her own body as an object:

> There, staring me in the face was my thigh. It was enormous, it was gross, it was like a diseased limb, the kind you see in pictures of jungle natives; it spread of forever, like a prairie photographed from a plane, the flesh not green but bluish-white with veins meandering across it like rivers. (133)

She has to come to terms with her body and rely on an external incentive (Aunt Lou's promised money) to make the change. Joan lives an emotional life through the characters in the movies. In the meantime, her self-image is shaped by how others perceive her, "To the ushers and the ticket sellers I must've appeared a huge featureless blur" (87).

Joan fantasizes that the warm and earthy Aunt Lou is her real mother for she never gets hugged or cuddled by her mother. Psychologists have pointed out that touch is an important means of communication to build a child's sense of security and self-worth, but Joan observes: "I could always recall what my mother looked like but not what she felt like" (95). She goes on to describing what Aunt Lou felt like. These experiences increase the alienation from and disgust with her own body. The only power Joan has over her mother is by tormenting her through her fatness and she glories in that. To add to it she defiantly scuttles all her mother's attempts to make her a replica of herself and triumphantly feels: "I had defeated her. I wouldn't ever let her make me over in her image, thin and beautiful" (94).

Joan feels a sense of triumph at this point seeing her mother drunk, crying and crumbling in front of her. Her self-definition is in this way a negative one. When Joan gets thinner and goes on a diet, her mother loses control over her and is devoid of any other purpose in life. It is as if she thrives on abusing her daughter. Not being able to punish her emotionally any longer, she gives in to rage and physically abuses her by plunging a knife into her. When Joan becomes thin she still feels alienated but for different reasons. The body fat had served as an insulation, a cocoon. It had been a disguise to camouflage herself as she puts it: "I also longed to be fat again. It would be an insulation, a cocoon. Also it would be a disguise. . . . Without my magic cloak of blubber and invisibility, I felt naked, pruned, as though some essential covering was missing." (157)

Joan's defence mechanism is set in motion and she develops multiple selves rather than a divided self. She continues to be haunted by her mother albeit through her visions as she realizes that the strange lady of the "Lady Oracle" poems she writes about under the influence of Automatic Writing is really her mother. Joan says:

> She never really let go of me because I had never let her go. It had been she standing behind me in the mirror, she was the one who was waiting around each turn, her voice whispered the words. She had been the lady in the boat, the death barge, the tragic lady with flowing hair and stricken eyes, the lady in the tower. She couldn't stand the view from the window, life was her curse. How could I renounce her? She needed the freedom also; she had been my reflection too long. (329-30)

Joan's search for a mother figure and a positive role model never ceases. Even after four years of marriage she admits: "I carried my mother around my neck like a rotting albatross. I dreamed about her often, my three-headed mother, menacing and cold" (213-14).

The other vision that haunts Joan is that of the Fat Lady whom she had given the face of a fat friend at high school, Theresa. This figure appears whenever she is under emotional stress and metamorphoses from a figure evoking ridicule to one getting applause. This is Joan's shadow (her repressed self) which keeps haunting her:

> She rose into the air and descended on me as I lay stretched out in the chair. For a moment she hovered around me like ectoplasm, like a gelatine shell, my ghost, my angel; then she settled and I was absorbed into her. Within my former body, I gasped for air. Disguised, concealed, white fur choking my nose and mouth. Obliterated. (321)

The negative self-image hovers around her constantly and she has difficulty integrating this image in particular, into her personality.

The multiple selves Joan develops play out the drama of the Gothic romances she writes. Joan's early childhood experience of rejection and pain makes her devour these romances and live through their characters as any emotional life is denied her. According to Lillian S. Robinson, women seek out Gothic romances "to receive confirmation, and eventually, affirmation that love really is what motivates and justifies a woman's life" (qtd. Vevaina 57) and furthermore the reader thrives on this escape fiction which offers him "a world in which excitement, mystery, danger and action occur side by side with domestic activities and social roles that women have traditionally performed. There is no conflict between these two worlds; in fact, they enhance each other" (qtd Vevaina 57). Thus fiction sustains reality. It adds to the drama in reality and this in turn is strengthened by some devices used by the writers of Gothic novels:

> Writers of popular Gothics con readers into believing that they are reading about 'real' life through elaborate descriptions of clothes, appearance and furnishings. Since the characters in these novels are cardboard stereotypes, mimesis is confined to physical resemblances between the imaginary world and its real prototype. As a writer of Costume Gothics, Joan devotes a lot of attention to the clothes of her heroines, heroes, villains and rival females for she thinks that if only she can get the clothes right, everything else will fall into place. For this purpose she does research at libraries, visits museums and frequents shops which deal in age-old articles. (Vevaina 57-58)

Problems of achieving an integrated personality affect Joan's relationships with men. Her first exposure to male sexuality is the Daffodil Man. Associated with this encounter is her mother's condemnation and anger that follow but her own experiences contradict her mother's warnings about strange men. Joan strikes relationships in adulthood with men she hardly knows and is just as quickly turned off by them. She enters these relationships with her head mystified by Gothic romances she has read and which she writes; often imagining herself as caught up in the dramatic lives of the characters. Paul, her first lover, after the first flush of their adventurous encounter is over, proves to be very patriarchal in his views on women and Joan finds traditional role expectations very uncomfortable.

Atwood parodies conventional ideas of romance and passion espoused in Gothic novels by juxtaposing the real life marriage, that of Joan and Arthur, with the Costume Gothic ideas of passion and love and deflating them even more in the process. Arthur ignores Joan's sexual needs and she turns to the Royal Porcupine to satisfy them. This relationship also is doomed to failure since she is objectified both in terms of being a celebrity and a woman.

Very like her Gothic heroines, Joan escapes when the situation gets too claustrophobic and stifling. She dons yet another identity by staging a drowning and escapes to Terremoto in Italy. By physically distancing herself from the past, however, she cannot free her psyche from the haunting figures of the past; not does it change her alienated condition. Feelings of alienation from her body persist and appear in the form of the vision of the fat lady overwhelming her to the extent of obliterating her self. Even after a dive into her inner self, she does not emerge an integrated person. Joan compares herself to a performing bear in an arena and this is evidence of her continuing feelings of low self-worth. Further she is not freed from the pattern of falling into the arms of strangers. With her head in the clouds, she continues to feed off her Gothic heroines and unwittingly hits a man at her door with a Cinzano bottle, imagining events in her life as a continuity of events in novels she conjures. From a Gothic heroine she transforms herself, perhaps temporarily into a caring nurse figure, much like the nurses in the nurse romances that Paul writes under the pseudonym, Mavis Quilp.

Alienation of women from their bodies and spirits due to the consumer society that they live in, seems to be the leitmotif running through almost all of Margaret Atwoods's novels. The unnamed narrator of *Surfacing* is as much alienated from her body and spirit as are Marian in *The Edible Woman* and Joan in *Lady Oracle*. What Atwood seems to be also reiterating is that men are not the villains that some women make them out to be. They are as much victims of patriarchy as women are and consumer society objectifies them as well. The narrator of *Surfacing* is herself guilty of objectifying the body of her lover, Joe. She fails to recognize his intense feelings and perceives him to be all body. Her description of him is as follows:

> From the side he's like the buffalo on the U.S. nickel, shaggy and blunt snouted, with small clenched eyes and the defiant but insane look of a species once dominant, now threatened with extinction. That's how he thinks of himself too: deposed, unjustly. Secretly he would like them to set up a kind of park for him, like a bird sanctuary. Beautiful Joe. (8)

She does not make an attempt to probe into his feelings even when he has nightmares. She thwarts his sexual overtures but coaxes him out into the wilderness so that her child, a demigod can be conceived amidst nature. Instead of finding out the reasons for his incommunicability, she takes comfort in it. The narrator's own insensitivity is beyond doubt a product of the consumer culture she lives in. There is ample evidence in the novel of her own alienation from her body even as she describes their love-making:

> his hands at any rate are intelligent, they move over me delicately as a blind man's reading braille, skilled, moulding me like a vase, they're learning me; they repeat patterns he's tried before, they've found out what works, and my body responds that way too, anticipates him, educated, crisp as a typewriter. It's best when you don't know them. A phrase comes to me, a joke then but mournful now, someone in a parked car after a high school dance who said with a paper bag over their head they're all the same. (73)

The description brings out the monotony and mechanical quality of their love-making. The intellect seems to be hovering above them like a superior entity, completing the compartmentalization of body and mind. The same numb attitude is evident in the graphic description of the narrator's cleaning and cooking fish as also the condition of the killed heron hung up like a lynch victim. This feeling of numbness dominates her relationship with Joe as well. When her friend Anna observes that Joe was more uncommunicative than usual, she thinks about her own lack of response: "I didn't feel awful; I realized I didn't feel much of anything, I hadn't for a long time. Perhaps I'd been like that all my life. Just as some babies are born deaf or without a sense of touch; but if that was true I wouldn't have noticed the absence." (114)

She of course has to make the inner journey to understand when it all began and that she had not always been in the alienated condition she finds herself in at the present moment. Commenting on the dualistic thinking inherent in Christianity, the Zen philosopher, Suzuki, said during a lecture in the United States: "God against man, man against God, man against nature, nature against man, nature against God, God against nature, very funny religion." (qtd. Vevaina 263)

The dichotomous thinking characteristic of Christianity reinforces the self versus other compartmentalization. The narrator, initiated by sacred totems of Amerindian religion into a process of self-discovery, comes to understand her need for wholeness and rejects compartmentalization. The novel's form, in keeping with this idea, defies classification into any particular genre. It is bildungsroman, a kunsteleroman, a detective story and a ghost story—all in one.

The alienation begins and ends with the body, and the protagonist comes a full circle. She locates the atomisation she experiences in the mind-body split which is symptomatic of and evident in the times we live in. She says:

> The trouble is all in the knob at the top of our bodies. I'm not against the body or the head either: only the neck which creates the illusion that they are separate. The language is wrong, it shouldn't have different words for them. If the head extended directly into the shoulders like a worm's or a frog's without that constriction, that lie, they wouldn't be able to look down at their bodies and move them around as if they were robots or puppets; they would have to realize that if the head is detached from the body both of them will die. (*Surfacing* 81)

When she looks at her childhood photographs and her sketches she realizes that she had been a more integrated and happy person earlier. It was later that things had gone wrong after, as she says, "I'd allowed myself to be cut in two. Woman sawn apart in a wooden crate, wearing a bathing suit, smiling a trick done with mirror . . . only with me there had been an accident and I came apart. The other half, the one locked away was the only one that could live; I was the wrong half, detached, terminal, I was nothing but a head, or no, something minor like a severed thumb, numb" (117).

Not only does she feel alienated and compartmentalized but even suffers from a low self-worth. According to R.D. Laing, insecure people "experience themselves as primarily split into a mind and a body. Usually they feel more closely identified with the mind" (qtd. Vevaina 271). These feelings of compartmentalization are related to her inability to get out of herself, reach out to others and express any form of love. She envies Anna and Joe for their ability to feel.

There is ample evidence in the novel to suggest that the narrator's estrangement is due to her past. Her father, in his pursuit of rationality, did not allow his daughter any access to the church or community. She had difficulty entering the Symbolic Order of logic and reason and the dilemma persists even in adulthood. She finds language inadequate and untrustworthy. It is due to this that she trusts the silent Joe more than other people: "I remember the hair on Joe's back, vestigial, like appendices and little toes: soon we'll evolve into total baldness. I like the hair though, and the heavy teeth, thick shoulders, unexpectedly slight hips, hands whose texture I can still feel on my skin, roughened and leathery from the clay. Everything I value about him seems to be physical, the rest is either unknown, disagreeable or ridiculous" (61)

What attracts the narrator to Joe is his earthiness and seeming closeness to nature. She, in this manner, objectifies him and ignores other aspects of his personality. She finds David especially repugnant with his Americanism and describes him as "an imposter, a pastiche, layers of political handbills, pages, from magazines, affiches, verbs and nouns glued on to him and shredding away, the original surfaces littered with fragments and tatters" (162-63).

At one point she wondered whether Hitler had been worse than the Americans and later comes to the realization that evil is not out there, camped at a distance, but within each person. She also acknowledges her affinity to David in one aspect, namely, the capacity to love. She gets more sensitized to the animal world after the heron incident and feels what people could do to animals, they could do to each other. However, she is lead to greater heights of realization only after her dive into the lake. She no longer carries around the horror of death which she had caused when aborting the foetus. The abortion caused immense guilt as is seen when she says: "Since then I'd carried that death around inside me, layering it over, a cyst, a tumour, black pearl." (155) The image of the near death of her brother caused by drowning is also laid to rest. She associates the image of the dead heron, with Christ who died to save others till she understands, while floating in the lake that death feels life:

> the swamp around me smoulders, energy of decay turning to growth, green fire. I remember the heron, by now it will be insects, frogs, fish, other herons. Thy body also changes, the creature in me, plant-animal, sends out filaments in me; I ferry it secure between death and life, I multiply. (180)

It is only after the experience of diving into the lake that she can come to terms with death and truly mourn for her loved ones.

After her first entry into the lake, symbolic of a descent into her unconscious and consequent empowerment, she feels freedom from the guilt and is rejuvenated. She feels empowered by the Indian gods after visiting their sacred place beneath the lake and this feeling helps her get in touch with her body. She wants to conceive a demigod through Joe whom she perceives as a better human on account of his half animal qualities. She promises herself that she would never teach her divine child human language (with all its falsity). She feels one with nature and her body, as is seen when she thinks of birthing: "The baby will slip out easily as an egg, a kitten, and I'll lick it off and bite the cord, the blood returning to the ground where it belongs; the moon will be full, pulling." (173)

The next time that she dives, she makes further progress in achieving integration when she can literally and symbolically discard her false coverings, clothes, the external trappings of consumer society. She says: "When every part of me is wet I take off my clothes, peeling them away from my flesh like wallpaper." (191) As also:

> The earth rotates, holding my body down to it as it holds the moon; the sun pounds in the sky, red flames and rays pulsing from it, searing away the wrong form that encases me, dry rain soaking through me, warming the blood egg I carry. (191)

In this manner, by attending to her body rhythms and acknowledging its connection to nature's rhythms, she is able to get over her alienated condition.

Simultaneously, she makes progress towards overcoming her alienation with regard to other human beings by first confronting her parents' death. She searches for them and feels betrayed by their absence. She assigns them a semi-divine status almost all her life. In the process of her search, she rediscovers her lost self, accepts their death and eventually reconciles herself to what they really were—human:

> No total salvation, resurrection, Our father, Our mother, I pray, Reach down for me, but it won't work; they dwindle, grow, become what they were, human. Something I never gave them credit for; but their totalitarian innocence was my own. (204)

This acceptance of the humanness of her parents with all their vulnerabilities, is essential for her to get back to society and get on with her life. She however, needs to see their spirits in other forms such as a jay and a wolf-shaman. The narrator's story highlights the disjointed, dismembered lives that people lead in consumer societies, devoid of magic and mystery. Consumerism even prescribes how a woman should look as the narrator ironically observes after her oneness with nature:

> They would never believe it's only a natural woman, state of nature, they think of that as a tanned body on a beach with washed hair waving like scarves; not this, face, dirt-caked and streaked, skin grimed and scabby, hair like a frayed bathmat stuck with leaves and twigs. A new kind of centrefold. (205)

There is an attempt here to subvert the glossy magazine's image of "the natural woman" for its centrefold. Atwood's ironic tone and parody of consumer society's images of "ideal" women, is a recurrent strand running through all the three novels being mentioned in this chapter.

In her discussion of irony in *Double Talking*, Linda Hutcheon writes:

> one of the postmodern additions to the critical functioning of irony would have to include an increased emphasis on its ability to subvert from within, to speak the language of the dominant order and at the same time suggest another meaning and another evaluation. This forked-tongue, even fence-sitting mode of address deconstructs one discourse, even as it constructs another. Its very doubleness can also act to contest the singleness of authority and universal value that frequently underlies it. (15-16)

The attempt to subvert from within the dominant discourse is quite evident in the works. Adele Wiseman, Margaret Atwood, Susan Swan and Margaret Laurence, do not use irony or parody as dominant modes in her writing. Laurence, nevertheless is lashing out at the strictures imposed by Manawakan society and its damaging impact on women and their relationships. However, she also holds women responsible for internalizing the values of patriarchy and their condition.

The narrator of *Surfacing* is certainly alienated from others as well. She claims that Anna is her best female friend after having known her for only two months. She remains a detached observer of Anna's travails and woes and there is no evidence of bonding between the two women. Competition and rivalry between women is actively encouraged by consumer society. Anna confides in her only when she is frustrated and disgusted with David but this closeness is momentary. The narrator, in her self-absorption cannot see the Anna-David relationship for what it truly is. Initially she envies them for their closeness but when she observes their relationship at close quarters, she understands the mutual hatred on which it is based. The more David objectifies Anna's body, the more she uses her it as a weapon. When the narrator begins to understand the dynamics of their relationship, she says:

> They knew everything about each other, I thought, that's why they're so sad; but Anna was more than sad, she was desperate her body her only weapon and she was fighting for her life, he was her life, her life was the fight: she was fighting him because if she ever surrendered the balance of power would be broken and he would go elsewhere. To continue the war. (*Surfacing* 164)

It is obvious that their relationship is sustained by hatred. This relationship serves as a foil to the narrator's relationship with Joe as in the former, there is over-communication, verbosity and excessive demonstration whereas in the latter there is almost an absence of communication except for their silent love-making episodes. There is however discontentment in both.

The narrator's relationship with her parents similarly was based on unrealistic perceptions. Since she was denied her gods, by her father's excessive obsession with rationality she created an aura of divinity around them. Even as a child she feels the need to conjure up magic and mystery:

> I pressed my fingers into my eyes, hard to make the pool of blackness ringed with violent colour. Release, red spreading back in, abrupt as pain. The secret had come clear, it had never been a secret, I'd made it one, that was easier. (111)

She has to invent and include the sacred in her life. The denial of this leads to alienation of the body and the spirit. After seeing her father's drawings, she feels he was perhaps transformed and had been granted a true vision by Amerindians' gods in their sacred places. However in order to be free of her own alienated condition she has to, first of all, get in touch with her numbed body, then nature and then attempt to reintegrate into society as a more balanced person.

Christian Bök in an article titled "Sibyls: Echoes of French Feminism in *The Diviners* and *Lady Oracle*" attempts to applications of French feminism to the works of Margaret Atwood and Margaret Laurence. In this interpretation Bök focuses on the protagonists of the two novels as writers:

> *The Diviners* and *Lady Oracle* describe writing as a cathartic process, in which the female writer renovates her life by accessing the unconscious, what Julia Kristeva might call the "semiotic" . . . the nonthetic, prelinguistic realm of experience normally suppressed by the "symbolic," the thetic, phallocentric realm of language: the *écrivaine*, as oracle or diviner, voices feminine experiences relegated by patriarchy to the margins of discourse. (80)

Drawing on Cixous' ideas, Bök establishes that the literary act of expression becomes a political gesture normally denied to woman. In the manner of French feminists who contest male defined notions of truth, Joan in *Lady Oracle* rewrites her own past life for the benefit of other people in the present. Bök explains, "eventually, these fictions become so numerous and complex that Joan must fake a suicide in order to simplify her polyvalent identity" (87)[7].

Both the writers working within the confines of traditional genres, subvert conventional notions of beauty and the female body using literary devices like parody and irony. In this context, Bök observes, with reference to Atwood:

> Both the gothic and the picaresque have traditionally reified masculine stereotypes of feminine behaviour, but the feminist satire renders these stereotypes absurd through a carnivalesque inversion of gendered conventions. Atwood uses the rules of masculine genres to satirize the rules of masculine genres. She adapts a patriarchal tradition to a feminist critique of the same patriarchal tradition. (88)

2.5 Politics of the Body and Body Politic:

Susan Swan, in the process of retelling the story of the legendary Nova Scotian giantess, Anna Swan, foregrounds several problematic areas. In a seemingly postmodernist manner, the notion of a unified subject is called to question. In her attempt to reconstruct the story of the legendary figure, she also succeeds in questioning traditional ideas regarding the authenticity of historical accounts. The critic Teresa Heffernan observes in her analysis of the novel, "Tracing the Travesty: Constructing the Female Subject in Susan Swan's *The Biggest Modern Woman of the World*":

> The concept of history as an event experienced via selective representation and interpretation in the present, supported in *The Biggest Modern Woman of the World*, challenges the notion of history as a series of tangible facts fixed in a past and fully accessible. (28)

She questions the truth claims made by history by using apparently conventional literary forms, and juxtaposing different narratives. Swan highlights the relativity of the various narratives including Anna's own journal entries. In this process, she is also able to examine the inadequacies of conventional genres available to a woman writer.

It is significant that the body becomes a site through which these issues are brought to light aside from the body itself becoming a site of contestation. In addition to foregrounding the marginalized subjectivity of Anna Swan, it is also used to examine the complex relationship that Canada has with the US. In this section, there is an attempt made to study the literary devices Swan uses to achieve the two-fold purpose of problematizing the very notions of 'self' and 'identity' and using the protagonist as a metaphor for Canada. As Marlene Goldman puts it:

> Swan's novel underscores the way in which a dominant set of nineteenth century discourses wrote the female body into existence by scientifically classifying this body among other bodies. This hierarchical classification reinforced an understanding of the female body as inferior or abnormal compared to that of the male. (65-66)

The notion of subjectivity in general and Anna Swan's in particular are examined through the corporeality of the body and its experiences. Reactions aroused by her grotesque body go to form her self-image and self-esteem beginning in early childhood. Societal expectations of her rivet around the dimensions of her body. She always arouses feelings of awe mixed with disgust and often even ridicule as she is in a triple bind being a woman, a freak and poor. This status of Anna Swan allows the writer to examine extreme conditions of objectification and commodification that the giantess experiences. She is subjected to exploitation early in life with her father making her feel special asking her to sing to the vegetable patch to make vegetables grow faster. Little does Anna realize how she would be commodified even as she thinks: "As for me, I saw my growth as a symbol of my power and energy and expected others to envy me for it. Momma might look on in dismay but she couldn't stop my dance to the stars." (*BMWW* 11)

She is exhibited in Halifax at the age of four. Looking back she understands that her body would become the source of both her livelihood and separation from her parents.

> I am sorry my size tortured my mother and pointed my destiny away from the pioneer life that my parents lived. As a child it was my greatest delight. Later it became my greatest trouble, and my struggle with the two opposing views has been the chief task of my life. (12)

It is evident from these lines that Anna retains ambivalent feelings about her body throughout her life and this in turn shapes her self-image and governs all her relationships.

Descriptions of her body and its experiences of pain and pleasure are deliberately expressed in the conventional language of patriarchy and even in Victorian terms to bring out the limitations and in-built biases inherent in such language. The writer seems to suggest that there is a silencing of the body, even the gigantic and grotesque one. In an interview with John Ayre, Susan Swan talks about her need to create a unique character like Anna:

> I suppose I'm interested in that female entity who flies up along side Superman. I may be trying to define that creature one way or another. It seems like so much of our literature and culture doesn't give women images of their beauty, their power, their intelligence in an exciting way. . . . If it doesn't have a mythic quality, it doesn't work so well for me. I find literature that just reports on life dull. I don't understand the excitement over it. (15)

There is a parodying of patriarchy's treatment of women's sexualities right through the novel. An example of this which comes immediately to one's notice is the gap between Anna's journal entry after the seduction by Ingalls and his account of the episode. He 'takes' her thinking she is asleep. She later records her feeling of pleasure in subdued Victorian terms. She writes in her diary:

> Some moments later, I was re-awakened by a pleasureful sensation in my privates and I felt the start of the downward undertow that reduces all of me to a dwarfing tremor. I opened my eyes and there was Apollo bouncing against me as if I was a vast flesh trampoline. I suppressed a smile at his mischievous face, flushed a tea-rose pink under a flying mane of yellow hair, and closed my eyes again to feign sleep. It felt so nice I wished him to continue but I thought it best not to be overt. (Victorian men are a mysterious species. They expect women to be uninterested in the physical and are easily frightened if we express enthusiasm.) (229-30)

Teresa Heffernan, noting the intertextuality the novel shares with Richardson's *Pamela* and the use of the diary points to a significant difference and writes:

> Like Pamela, Anna records her seduction in a diary at the very moment of the seduction. Sitting at her desk, Anna writes: "In the glow of the wall candle, I can see Martin's face moving closer to mine." The effect of these scenes, unlike the intended effect in Pamela, is to highlight the process of writing/recording events and underscores the inevitable gap between the act and the representation of the act. (26)

This gap is heightened when a woman wants to record her experience of sexuality as language proves to be inadequate. There has been a silencing of woman's sexuality through the centuries as is evident in the following lines from the novel:

> At fifteen, I didn't know that I was as much in charge of my sexual ecstasy as the man. I imagined it was something the male of the species did to the female and I did not connect it to the fumbling with which Momma had surprised me that night in the shanty. Had I known, I would have shown Angus how to rub me. (58)

Anna's sexuality is further suppressed by Victorian ideas of sexuality. She records Apollo's seduction of her while she pretends to sleep in her diary in the following words:

> It felt so nice I wished him to continue but I thought it best not to be overt. Victorian men are a mysterious species. They expect women to be uninterested in the physical and are easily frightened if we express enthusiasm. (229-30)

Later she is gloriously happy that she could provide pleasure to another human being. The manner in which Apollo seduces her shows the one-sided pleasure that men regard as essential to the sexual act. Anna, in keeping with the social mores of her times, quickly suppresses her bodily needs. She experiences alienation from her body on other counts as well. She feels an outcaste simply because of her size. There is a comic-tragic aspect to this feeling even as she records her loneliness at not being able to find a playmate and wonders what she could do to take her mind off her dreadful loneliness.

The objectified status of a woman's body is highlighted by the doctor's comic comparisons of her body to land and its formations: "We must respect the terrain for what it is—down to the orifices of tubular follicles on its inner cloth, the arbor vital *uterine*, the tiny—oh, very minute—oblique columns like tree branches proceeding to the light at the end of the southwest passage." (239) Earlier, when Martin inquires whether she will be able to carry a child without a hitch, the doctor's response is: "Yes, Captain. Her organ of life is in a fine creative stage." (239)

This euphemistic way of describing the uterus serves to contextualize it, in the Victorian period as well as achieve comic effect. The underlying implications lie in objectifying parts of her body as if they have an existence independent of her. Marlene Goldman, noting the significance of Swan's use of parody, writes:

> Swan's text emphasizes the individual's power to exert a measure of control over discourse through parodic appropriation. . . . This strategy goes beyond the mere repetition of official discourses because the ironic distance afforded by this type of parodic appropriation can transform imitation into 'a means of freedom' (Hutcheon, *Theory* 35). Official discourses and traditional genres can be enlisted to serve radically different causes from the ones they were originally intended to serve. (69)

After the birth of her still-born daughter she is in despair and feels she has failed. She says she feels female and flawed as if these feelings were two sides of the same coin. This is also due to the hype and hoopla created during her pregnancy. Even at that time her body is a spectacle. When she starts her menstrual cycle again after delivering the child she experiences mixed feelings about her body and expresses them in these words:

> Ordinarily, I feel relief and a sly pride that the cycles of my body are working as they should. But that afternoon I felt a bitter despair. It made me think of my baby whom my body had betrayed and I began to weep and inwardly curse the irony of a female physique that paid lip-service to certain but had fouled to perform the act with any competence. (269)

Anna succumbs to the stereotypical expectations and demands made on female body by patriarchy and it is through those blinkers that she views herself. At this juncture, she neither receives true support from her husband Martin Bates (engrossed as he is in creating an evolved species) nor from her lover Ingalls who only wants to exploit her body for his pleasure and to commercialise it. Ingalls, in his narrative titled *The Route Book of Judge Hiriam Percival Ingalls* observes in a very detached manner that "the giantess is overly fond of dainty accessories" (167). What he is suggesting is perhaps that it is that due to her complex regarding her large size she seeks a kind of compensation in "dainty accessories" to make her feel normal. He describes her breasts with a fetish-like attitude comparing them to mountains:

> I doubt if a mountain can compare in glory to a giantess breast. Where is a circle that seen from above looks like a temple of land with the blue vein over the heart running off the heights into the plain? (169)

The conflation of woman's body with nature is commonplace enough and these stereotypes are what Swan seems to suggest. Susan Swan uses parody as one of the main literary devices to problematize both identity as well as history, much in a postmodernist way. Discussing problems of identity, she writes in an essay titled "Desire and the Mythology of Femininity":

> I'm interested in the relationship between gender and individuality and how you shape an identity for yourself out of what your society hands you. While my female characters bump up against stereotyped definitions of femininity, they manage to survive by using these modes for their own ends. Perhaps I'm trying to suggest that character is more important than gender although where one ends and the other begins is a complex matter. (261)

Much of Anna Swan's experiences endorse this view of the author. Her struggles emanate from confronting stereotypes of both women and giants and trying to live by them. However, her diary entries show a different inner world of apprehension, ambivalence and sensitivity as much as any "normal" human being feels. It is this inner world that Susan Swan is trying to depict. She succeeds in showing the gap between perception and reality, as also the gap between reality and representation. Fighting shy of political doctrines she writes in the same essay about feminism:

> Feminism has meant to me the freedom to create and be heard in a new way. It doesn't affect my fiction directly, because I believe there are no conscious rules in art—only an intrinsic sense of right and wrong, a fascination with the interior life of the individual and the mysterious, enchanted world of the imagination. (262)

Susan Swan, using parody, questions the efficacy of conventional literary genres like the realistic novel, the diary and letters while reconstructing Anna Swan's life. She is self-reflexive in that she questions the very idea of biography and its claim to authenticity. She uses these very conventional genres in order to subvert them. Discussing parody, Linda Hutcheon in *The Politics of Postmodernism*, writes: "Parody works to foreground the *politics* of representation" (94). She further writes about its function in postmodernist works as being: "a value, problematizing, de-naturalizing form of acknowledging the history (and through irony, the politics) of representations." (94)

Swan, in presenting P.T. Barnum's and Ingalls' accounts of the giantess is trying to suggest that the interior life of a human being is vastly different from the way she is perceived, especially if she is a mythic figure. She is completely commodified, exploited and marketed by both Barnum and Ingalls for the representations of Anna Swan in their narratives are coloured by vested interests. This compels the reader to look into the politics of all representations rather than accepting them as neutral. Linda Hutcheon writes: "The politics of representation and the representation of politics frequently go hand in hand in parodic postmodern historiographic metafiction. Parody becomes a way of ironically revisiting the past of both art and history." (103-4)

While using traditional literary genres and conventions to tell stories or her stories, the writer unsettles the very conventions used, by subversion. Hutcheon observes that in a sense the writer of parody endorses the parodied: "As form of ironic representation, parody is doubly coded in political terms: it both legitimizes and subverts that which it parodies." (101)

Such devices become necessary particularly for women writers who write from within the Symbolic Order or the language of patriarchy. Parody, in this sense becomes a double voiced discourse.[8]

At the very outset Anna Swan adopts a self-deprecating tone and gives more weightage to others' views of her. Her tone is self-derisive and ironic introducing an anti-climatic mock heroic element thereby subverting the awe and wonder with which legends are begun:

> I grew *out* and up as does the BLUE WHALE, LARGEST IN THE SEA, and the AFRICAN BUSH ELEPHANT, LARGEST ON LAND. (1)

The capital letters serve to highlight difference and draw attention. After all, Anna Swan's story is that of drawing attention. That was her very source of livelihood. There is an official account of her Spiel No. 2 at Sunrise Trail Museum preceding Anna's own account of it. Her narrative is significantly titled "Real Time Spiel" and it is a more interesting account of the men in her life. She reduces them to their hand size: "experience has taught me that there is a correlation between the size of the hand and the size of what makes a man a man. Besides, men's hands have helped to shape my life." (5)

The juxtaposition of these two different narratives points to the clinical, uninteresting, monotonous qualities of official documentation as opposed to lively, flesh and blood first person narratives. A little later in the novel are testimonials given by Mary Johnson, Anna's aunt, Hubert Belcourt, the dwarf from New Annan and Janette Swan, Anna's sister. The testimonials have only one thing in common—they focus on Anna's size and are subjective and not always generous to her. The reader is given these, so as to not get too comfortable with Anna's own narrative and once again is confronted with other facts and perceptions. This serves to question the notion of a unified subject position and the absurdity of any attempt to search for "one true story" about any human being. Anna herself laments over her multiple selves in the aftermath of the destruction by fire at the museum in these words:

> And last of all, I wept for myself and the selves I was in my growth, including the AGORAPHOBIC VICTIM who cowered as the tackle ball broke the museum wall, the VICTORIAN LADY hauled like a pachyderm over the heads in the street, the GIANT ACTRESS who smiled as she was lowered to the roaring crowds and, finally, the BIG SURVIVOR who failed to convey her waters to the fiery wimbles until the festival was over. (145)

She has these thoughts while she urinates in fear, creating a flood almost drowning the ballerina. There are grotesque aspects of all the freaks in the novel. Anna's fluid secretions, in their hyperbolic descriptions arouse awe, incredulity and some disgust. The description of the museum fire is in her letter to her giant lover Angus McAskill contains a warning to him as well as the reader not to let her bantering tone fool him.

As the novel progresses Anna grows in self-awareness both of her sexuality and of men. She is aware of stereotypes of masculinity that she herself has believed in. After her sexual encounter with Apollo, she is graceful enough to acknowledge her own ignorance:

> It is silly to seek symbols of superiority in males. I have been as guilty of sloppy thinking as the normals who think the male is strong in all areas because he has strong muscles. What nonsense! A hole is not less than a rod; it is merely different, and it is a grave mistake to mythologize biological facts to prove that one sex is better than the other. (230)

She however, continues to give her own sexual pleasure a back seat, even in her relationship with Ingalls. When she discovers she is pregnant and Apollo wants to postpone their love-making, she tries to salvage her hurt pride by identifying with the prescribed role of giantess that goes with her body:

> He does not want to be the lover of the BIGGEST MODERN WOMAN! He does not know how fortunate he is that I find him desirable? I rose and coldly looked down at his popinjay dressed in the garish trousers of a Bowery tough. (233)

Her attitude to her bodily functions also changes to a certain extent, and this reduces her alienation. Taking a cue from Indian woman in a letter to her mother she gets aware of socialized feelings of disgust that a woman feels:

> The nerve of Indian women priding themselves on their bodies pleased and amused me. Why should we not celebrate the blood-letting upon which everything depends? Why should you, or any of us, Momma, refer to it as an affliction, although, I admit, I don't look my best when it comes. (270-71)

She has come a long way from the point where she feels betrayed by her body after delivering a still-born child. The body is problematized in that it becomes a take off point for suggesting other ideas. One such notion is that of "emblem fatigue" that giants suffer from. Angus McAskill tells Anna Swan about it. The notion of emblem fatigue brings into focus the fact of meanings and role expectations loaded on to any sign or emblem by dominant society. There is very little interest shown in the kind of people they really are. Anna points out the misconceptions people have towards giants and what appropriate behaviour towards them should be. One realizes that there is a wide gap between perception and reality as also the discrepancies in the truth claims made for legends. There is an inevitable gap between official documents and real life experiences and accounts of them found in marginalized literary genres such as letters and diaries. The writer seems to be suggesting her own difficulties in effectively reconstructing the identity of Anna Swan merely on the basis of official records. It is this self-reflexive nature of the novel that gives it a postmodern aspect. However, one should not get carried away by such seeming similarities and categorise it as simply a postmodern text. Feminist texts may employ these strategies for a different agenda and they have a definite message. Clarifying the point of divergence between feminism and postmodernism in *Feminist Fictions: Revisiting the Postmodern* Patricia Waugh writes:

> At the moment when postmodernism is forging its identity through articulating the exhaustion of the existential belief in self-presence and self-fulfilment and through the dispersal of the universal subject of liberalism, feminism (ostensibly, at any rate) is assembling its cultural identity in what appears to be the opposite direction. . . . As male writers lament its [the character/subject's] demise, women writers have not yet experienced that subjectivity which will give them a sense of personal autonomy, continuous identity, a history and agency in the world. (6)

Even as women are in the process of forging their identities, postmodernism sets about unsettling notions of 'self' and 'identity.'

The parody used by Susan Swan works on yet another level—that of foregrounding the inequalities in the US-Canadian relations. The body of the giantess is a metaphor for Canada—portrayed as feminized and helpless. Her body is described by Ingalls as terrain and her breasts as mountains. In 'Ingalls' Verse Warm-Up,' there are lightly veiled suggestions of the US-Canadian equation:

> Anna, your bridegroom
> is looking up from his cities
> smiling though his smoke-stacks
> and wearing a ginseng root in his teeth.
>
> See, the colossus
> is the man for your dimensions—
> a hill-billy gone citified
> a clay-eater among carpet-baggers (178)

The bridegroom being referred to is of course Martin Bates, the giant from Kentucky who marries Anna. The imperial intentions of "the giant" looking towards Anna (Canada) are unmistakable. In 'The Kentucky Giant's Hymeneal' to be recited by Bates are the following lines:

> Take me in, New World Wahine
> through your untapped vagina
> to more mountain-rimmed gardens
> where hot and cold airs
> run together and averages
> mean nothing. . . .
>
> Beloved—I will rise up
> in your empty heights
> and plunge through your
> regions of softwood
> to the end of your Atlantic
> depth once more
> your glass bowl
> will be exotic
> with tropical life. (182)

Apart from the sexual innuendo of these lines there is also the suggestion of a feminised Canada and a masculinised America waiting to rape the uncharted territories of the Northern neighbour. Anna's defiant reply in the poem titled 'Anna's Answer True' befits Canada's position. In a reworking of the popular song "Daisy, Daisy. . ." she sings:

> I'll be damned, Martin,
> if I'll be crammed
> on the seat of your
> imperial fantasy. (183)

Martin Bates, for his size and posturing turns out to be impotent. He is obsessed with genetic science and wants to create through Anna, an evolved species of giants. It is again ironic that he is unable to father any of Anna's children and she gives birth once to a still-born daughter and next to an infant whose sex is indeterminate and who dies. As Teresa Heffernan notes:

> Not only is Martin's thesis called into question by Anna's critique but so too is the entire tradition of scientific ("objective," "disinterested") documentation which has been used abused in attempts to illustrate "empirically" a hierarchy of value. (29)

These "scientific" theories have also fostered racist ones.

The relationship of unequals, however, is not a simple one. Just as Anna is attracted to the celebrity status she acquires after her New York performances, Canada is tied to the United States in capitalistic ventures. Anna is aware of being exploited inasmuch as Canada and as she records this:

> Although I recognized in Barnum face the crafty manipulator whom Angus had warned me about, at that moment I understood the extent of the opportunity Barnum offered—to escape the embittering experience of rural life, to spiel before approving crowds—Barnum's courtship of me could be a dream come true! (67)

Anna is quick to realize that Barnum is a manipulator but is lured by the opportunities of success and the wealth he offers. There is ample evidence within the novel to support this view as Anna writes in a letter to her mother about her relationship with Martin:

> I feel I am acting out America's relationship to the Canadas. Martin is the imperial ogre while I play the role of genteel/mate who believes that if everyone is well-mannered, we can inhabit a peaceable kingdom. That is the national dream of the Canadas, isn't it? A civilized garden where lions lie down with the doves. . . . Indeed, to be from the Canadas is to feel as women feel—cut off from the base of power. (273-74)

There is complete self-awareness of her position and irony. In spite of actually being taller, more popular and good natured than Martin, she is subjected to his tyranny. The critic Frank Davey, in his book *Post-National Arguments: The Politics of the Anglophone-Canadian Novel since 1967* notes that the technique of taking on board a feminist agenda and the nationalist one simultaneously is not unique to Susan Swan. He writes: "Discourses which conflate nationalist and feminist causes, like Anna's suggest that to be from the Canadas is to feel as women feel" (274), and these he implies represent a 'colonized' Canadian nation in the figure of the patriarchally colonized Canadian women have been a small but significant part of Canadian fiction and criticism since the 'ice maidens' of Margaret Atwood's *Survival* and the nationally troubled heroines of her *Surfacing* and *The Journals of Susanna Moodie*. (192). Anna does not succumb to feelings of being victimized and adopts a positive attitude towards the forging of an independent identity for Canada as much as she herself does within the limitations of her sphere.

The political perspective couched within the parodying of Anna Swan's gigantic body and the accompanying feelings of powerlessness, add an interesting dimension to the novel. The body becomes a central signifier and a contested site, foregrounding ambivalence towards it. In addition it also has metaphorical functions. The political message contained, however, does not undermine or diminish in any way the corporeality of the body itself.

NOTES

1. For a fuller discussion of Laurence's use of voices of irony and parody as expressions of Feminism, refer to Jill Franks' article, "Jesting Within: Voices of Irony and Parody as Expressions of Feminisms."
2. Mathew Martin traces a reversal of the Oedipal Complex and Oedipus society in *A Jest of God, The Fire-Dwellers* and *The Diviners* in the context of the repressed sexuality of the protagonists in an application of Freudian theory.
3. Brenda Beckman-Long examines Laurence's use of the first person or confessional narrative in the earlier two Manawakan novels and the subsequent shift to the third person narration in the later two novels and understands it to be a means of authorization of the text and adoption of an ideological perspective.
4. Ruth Panofsky sees a progression in the construction of the female subject from Adele Wiseman's *Sacrifice* (a male-centred novel) to *Crackpot* through a celebration of the maternal body.
5. For an elaborate analysis of Margaret Atwood's use of fairy tales as intertext for purposes of parody and subversion in her novels, refer to Sharon Rose Wilson's full-length study, *Margaret Atwood's Fairy-Tale Sexual Politics*.
6. Sonia Mycak's full-length study of Atwood's novels, *In Search of the Split Subject: Psychoanalysis, Phenomenology, and the Novels of Margaret Atwood* throws light on the fragmented subjectivities of her female protagonists and relates it to corporeality.
7. For an application of French feminist theories, (particularly Julia Kristeva's notion of the semiotic and Hélène Cixous' insistence on writing as resistance) to Laurence and Atwood refer to Christian Bŏk's "Sibyls: Echoes of French Feminism in *The Diviners* and *Lady Oracle*." The protagonists of both these novels are writers.
8. For a full discussion on the use of parody as a double-voiced discourse particularly used by Canadian writers, refer to Linda Hutcheon's *The Politics of Postmodernism*. This work yields a better understanding of how this particular literary device is used for subversion.

Chapter Three

Writing the Body

> For in the beginning of the body's history there is no beginning. There is a body folded inside a body wrapped around another body—all bodies breathing the body of language.
>
> Smaro Kamboureli in *A Mazing Space*

The writers studied in this chapter write the body in all its aspects openly and uninhibitedly. Their works demonstrate the need and capacity to get in touch with the body and write of its pleasures and pains. They are critical of the phallogocentrism that has dominated Western civilization and try to break away from it both in terms of the form and substance. In fact, they would want to break down such binaries of form and content that belie all conventional reader expectations. They experiment with genres as well in that, they disrupt literary ones by interpolating them with popular ones.[1] They also succeed in breaking down traditional boundaries between fiction and reality and problematise the very notion of reality by meshing together fact and fantasy. They need to break new ground in all possible ways for, as Shoshana Felman puts it, "The challenge facing the woman today is nothing less than to "re-invent" language, to re-learn how to speak: to speak not only against, but outside of the specular phallogocentric structure, to establish a discourse the status of which would no longer be defined by the phallacy of masculine meaning" (19). All the writers being studied show an interest in etymology and in exposing the gendered nature of language. As Dale Bauer lucidly writes, "Because all language is 'inherited' and because it is all socially and ideologically charged, the conflict of voices in a novel can reveal power structures and potential resistances to those structures" (674). However, there are individual variations among the writers' preoccupation with language per se. They are also informed by psychoanalytic, post-structuralist, and French feminist thought. This becomes more evident as one closely examines their works. They write intensely about female sexuality and the female body and often work within and from without conventional discourses and language. They have to do it, given the nature of female sexual pleasure. Irigaray says, "Woman's desire most likely does not speak the same language as man's desire, and it probably has been covered over by the logic that has dominated the West since the Greeks" (101).

The major French feminists such as Julia Kristeva, Hélène Cixous and Luce Irigaray are trained in psychoanalysis and work from that model either developing it or rejecting it. As Antoinette Fouque puts it, "The only discourse on sexuality that exists is the psychoanalytic discourse. Therefore the women's struggle must, of necessity, deal with the dialectical relationship between historical maternalism and psychoanalysis" (118).

3.1 Audrey Thomas—Bleeding Body of Desire

The writers being studied draw on memory, the unconscious and dreams. The first writer being studied in this chapter is Audrey Thomas. Her trilogy—*Songs My Mother Taught Me*, *Mrs. Blood* and *Blown Figures*—powerfully illustrates the manner in which women writers write the body. The aspects studied are her attitude to and portrayal of the female body and sexuality, the crucial link between the mother-daughter relationship and consequent problems with identity. Thomas, for most part, succeeds in exploring the hitherto hidden terrains of the female body; its pleasure and pain. Her exploration in the trilogy serves to foreground the ambivalent and conflicting attitudes that women often harbour towards their own sexuality. The first novel of trilogy, *Songs My Mother Taught Me* begins with a journey made by Isobel's family to Journey's End, her grandfather Harry's cottage, on the mountains. It is an account of Isobel's troubled childhood, the Cleary family's poverty and ends with Isobel as an adolescent planning to leave home and to go to Europe on a scholarship. Isobel's telling statement shows the attitudes to the body ingrained in her by her mother: "We lived the four of us, in a house where the body was virtually denied any existence—certainly any pleasant one. . . . Bodies were ugly, shameful things." (*SMMTM* 63).

Isobel's mother is a repressing phallic mother,[2] who is frustrated in her marital life. She is contemptuous of her husband's failure to be a provider and Isobel and her sister Jane begin to likewise see their father as a weakling. Their father figure, for temporary periods of time during their idyllic summer sojourns is their grandfather whose sense of power they bask in. Isobel often wants to disown both her parents and fantasizes about ideal parents. She is repulsed by her mother's body: "The sight of my mother's body filled me with shame and deep disgust. . . . I could not bear to think of her as having bodily sensations and functions at all." (64)

She internalizes the disgust with the body and even later as an adult, dwells obsessively on the body as grotesque. She learns to dissociate herself, that is, split herself off from her body, even as a young girl. These negative feelings are compounded by the social exclusion that she experiences due to their poor financial position. This reinforces the negative self-image already formed. Her mother calls menstrual periods 'a curse' and she is jolted when later Richard tells her that she has "cursed" his pajamas. Elaborating on her mother's attitude to the body and her fragmented view of it, she states: "Parts of the body and bodily functions had nicknames as well. A vagina was a 'tookie,' a penis (although rarely mentioned) a 'tea kettle' a bowel movement a 'grunter' or a 'daily duty.' It was all very coy and somehow dirty." (64)

She and her sister try their best to isolate themselves from their mother's fits of rage and hysterical outbursts. They find the constant quarrelling between the parents unsettling and emotionally disturbing. Jane escapes by having boyfriends and Isobel, after desperately seeking a job, lands one as an aide in a mental hospital. As an aide she has to look in the eye of all the deformities and body functions. Wanting to escape home she is faced with madness in the hospital wards but prefers that to the seeming sanity of home. She states wittily that, after her first day at the hospital, she lost her mental virginity. She obsesses over sex and finally loses her virginity to Kristoff from the hospital. The novel leaves her at a point where she is contentedly rowing a boat in circles, "like life." (177)

The second novel *Mrs. Blood* begins with Isobel being taken to the hospital for a threatened miscarriage and ends with her actually miscarrying. For most of the novel she is at the hospital and Thomas records her thought processes shifting back and forth from the present to the past. Emotions that dominate her are fear of death and an obsession with the body and the foetus within. The novel begins with an epigraph from Alice's *Adventures in Wonderland*:

> "But I don't want to go among mad people," Alice remarked.
> "Oh, you can't help that, said the Cat: "We're all mad here. I'm mad. You're mad."
> "How do you know I'm mad?" said Alice.
> "You must be," said the Cat, "or you wouldn't have come here." (9)

This circular, Catch 22 sort of answer, points to the chaos that Isobel is about to encounter in trying to preserve her sanity. It is also a pointer to Alice/Isobel's passivity and her need of an (Other) to define her. The allusions to Alice continue. In *Songs My Mother Taught Me*, when Isobel first enters the hospital she feels she is being thrown into a "rabbit hole." In *Mrs. Blood* she says, "I put a sign on my breast, "Eat me," and on my lips a notice, "Drink me," but only the mosquitoes came." (26)

Audrey Thomas although does not choose to wear the feminist label too obviously as she says: "You can't add 'feminism' to a story the way you can add vanilla to a cake, sticking your finger in and pasting." (*Goodbye Harold, Good Luck* XVIII). Her professed aim is not to make her novels mouthpieces of the feminist agenda but they do espouse feminist concerns with female sexuality and identity. Krishna Sarbadhikary, in her erudite study of Thomas's fiction, observes the significance of the epigraph in *Mrs. Blood* and writes:

> Thomas, in the epigraph at the beginning dedicates the text "To all the Alices, whatever your mothers called you," thus bonding heterogeneous female selves, as well as pointing to women's efforts to retain their sanity in an insane universe. (48)

The narrative in *Mrs. Blood* is split between "Mrs. Thing" and "Mrs. Blood" the two selves of Isobel. Mrs. Thing is the self rooted in the present, the more conscious, restrained and socialized one, while Mrs. Blood easily slips not just into the past but uninhibitedly expresses Isobel's desires, passions and fears. Isobel is conscious of this split identity. It is Mrs. Blood who remembers her adolescent body after a sexual initiation by Trigger, a life guard at the lake who remarks:

> "You've got big nipples. . . . You'll be able to nurse a baby really well."
>
> And I was flattered, you know, because I remembered Jessica ask at camp and how somebody said she wore an undershirt even though she was seventeen, and anyway her tits too were like rat bites—hadn't I ever spied on her in the shower? (36)

Isobel is judgmental about Jessica Ash's breasts and has internalized patriarchal norms assigned to the female body. The effect that the male gaze produces on her perception of the body is significant. The ambivalence she feels towards her body is expressed through the split selves—Mrs. Blood and Mrs. Thing. She uses a biblical allusion to refer to her body being offered as a sacrifice, Christ-like:

> All flesh is glass. This is my body, which was riven, my body which was roven—my flesh all scattered and tattered and torn, and Rosie is the riveter who nailed me there as a totem in front of the door. And he said why seek ye living among the dead. He is not here; she has risen. (59)

This is an image of a torn and alienated body offered for sacrifice. She projects feelings of victimisation onto her body. She also acknowledges her sexual needs, particularly her "lust" for Richard, her lover whose feel she says she carries "around with me like a birthmark or a scar" (66).

This section is followed by her memory of old women masturbating in the mental patient's ward she worked in, thereby portraying a deadened form of self-gratification. There are several references to her feelings of sexual frustration caused by her physical need for Jason, who forcibly restrains, tempers and often denies her sex. Women are socialized into suppressing and even denying their sexual needs. This fact constantly contrasted with the passionate abandonment which she experiences with Richard, causes her estrangement from her married partner Jason. It is again the Mrs. Blood self who can come to terms with these feelings. She conflates biblical and fairy tale allusions to express her anguish:

> And call out to Jason who has no ears, "This is my body" and fling back the sheets and cry out to him who has no eyes, "And this is my blood." And take his head between your hands and force it down, crying, "Drink this, eat this in remembrance of me. . . ." And cry out to Jason who has no hands, "Touch me, there and there, and don't stop, no don't stop. . . ." And the veil of the temple shall open and he shall see what I see and be consumed on my broken altar. (91-92)

There is an identification she feels with Christ and she is consumed by a narcissistic need for unconditional and complete love. The alienation of the body she experiences is expressed through her frequent references to "the traitor body."

As Mrs. Thing, she can more calmly analyze Jason's feelings from his point of view. However, she is overcome by an overwhelming sense of guilt again linked to her body, as she feels:

> I want to tell him I have been unfaithful to him, where and when and maybe even why. Yet I cannot. I am a victim of my sense of sin. It is not consideration for Jason that stops me but fear of the gods. I cried out to him that night "I am being punished because I didn't love my father." What if I am being punished because I was unfaithful? (103)

She feels guilt for not loving both her father and Jason, linking them in her psyche. These lines are also significant for they indicate that her own gods have failed her as she associates them with punishment and her fear of it. Her own guilt leads her to link her miscarriage and bodily pain to her sexual transgressions. The notions of the body as impure, unclean and dirty are imprinted in her mind by early conditioning. These ambivalent attitudes towards her body constantly make her swing from the need to be natural to the need to repress. When she compares sexual practices in "Other" civilizations as compared to the white, Western one rationally as Mrs. Thing, she concludes: "Our lust has been intellectualized into love between the sheets. . . . Nothing forced. All gentle, yet often this sham gentleness masks indifference, 'love' masks the absence of desire" (118).

She is of course thinking of her and Jason's habitual and restrained sex. She has memories of her first feelings of sexual arousal while reading the *Chinese Room* and repressing those feelings quickly after being summoned by her mother. The same repressed feelings come to the fore in her relations with Jason as she says: "Last night I woke up and wanted him and was ashamed. Why haven't we got between us the kind of honesty that admits of such a confession?" (168)

The guilt that follows her passion inevitably, forces her to go back in the past and dwell on the grotesque, aged female bodies at the hospital. These grotesque bodies continue to haunt her. Throwing light on women's need to suppress the body, Lillian B. Rubin writes in an article titled "The Sexual Dilemma":

> There's no gainsaying that through the ages of Western society, women's sexuality has come under attack, that there have been sometimes extreme pressures to control and confine it—even to deny its existence. (462)

This seems to be Audrey Thomas' concern as well as she tells an interviewer, "One must talk about forbidden subjects. That's the way in the end to defeat particular use of language" (Wachtel 67).

It is also useful to study Isobel's perception of the maternal body, both as in her mother and herself as mother. There is ambivalence evident in her perception of the maternal body as well, for she swings from alienation and disgust to narcissistic obsessive dwelling on its sensations and those caused by the foetus within. There is guilt that accompanies her feelings of not having fulfilled role expectations often echoing the presumed perceptions of people around her. This ambivalence is of course a reflection of the mother-daughter relationship and will be taken up shortly in this section. She found her mother unattractive and wishes that both her parents had been different. *In Songs My Mother Taught Me,* Isobel seemingly has no memory of seeing a pregnant woman as a child and as Mrs. Blood she wonders where all the pregnant women had gone or "Did my infant eyes simply accept protruding abdomens as part of the general view?" (*Mrs. Blood* 163) She has a very earthy, unromantic view of childbirth as well, at least as her Mrs. Blood self. She is hardly lyrical about the experience as is seen when she describes birthing, thus:

> They come out, if properly, head first and downwards, diving into life through the blazing red-ring of their mother's agony, as though through a hoop of fire. They are held up and admired and patted on the back as though they, and not the broken, spent thing lying on the table, were the heroes. (182)

She feels outrage at the violation of the body and thinks of the mother's body bleeding on the table, while all attention is riveted to the new born. The foetus and the newborn are often compared to various species of fish, a bird, a white dove etc. at several places in the novel. Referring to the mother who has just delivered the baby she says in empathy:

> And the bloody thing in the bed or on the table smiles and forgets the horror and the outrage and holds out her arms to receive her violator, her hero, her fish, saying "This is my body which was given for thee. Feed on me in thy heart by faith and by thanksgiving." (183)

A little later describing the birth of Mary, her daughter, she is more concise: "Consumed with pain consummated. That was at eight and the child was born at ten. Rip. Rip. And there rest in peace" (183). The experience of childbirth is described in its gory details without accompanying sentiments or glorification. And yet, she also feels "slack-bellied and proud" (184), showing her sense of achievement. There are once again contradictory feelings expressed. Through these ambivalent feelings she exposes the glorification and mythification of motherhood and childbirth. Patriarchy needs to circulate this myth to sustain itself. Monique Wittig rightly observes:

> instead of seeing giving birth as a forced production, we see it as a "natural," "biological" process, forgetting that in our societies births are planned (demography), forgetting that we ourselves are programmed to produce children, while this is the only social activity "short of war" that presents such a great danger of death. (179)

Patriarchy makes unreasonable demands on the woman's body. On the one hand, maternity is held out as the ultimate destiny to her and simultaneously shame and humiliation are attendant on the unattractive maternal body. The maternal body no longer is appealing sexually. This prospect further contributes to feelings of ambivalence to maternity that women do in fact experience. Isobel tries her best to understand Jason's distancing himself when she is pregnant with Mary and his "[o]bvious fear of her swelling body" (*Blown Figures* 215). She is intimidated by Jason's dominant and intruding mother at this stage and wonders whether "she had become for him once and for all MOTHER? Because her desires for the pleasures of the body should have been tempered or superseded by her concern with an absorption by the great mystery inside her?" (216)

The womb is an important image and ironically, instead of being an environment nurturing the growth of the child, becomes a life-threatening place. She plays on the word "child" in these lines:

> Cild>child. My cild was killed. My child was chilled. In my womb, the cild-hama, the child curled like a shrimp or a sea horse and clung to the slippery decks. (82)

This is followed by a newspaper report of a seven-year-old boy dying in an accident. Isobel has internalized the feelings of shame associated with the maternal body and feels the need to suppress her sexual desire. She craves for Jason to shower her with love in spite of her unattractive body after two children and a miscarriage but, as we are told, "[s]he was too appalled and ashamed of her body to ask—or want to ask." (341)

Referring to the institutionalization of motherhood, Jeffner Allen writes in an article titled, "Motherhood: The Annihilation of Women":

> The mark imposed by patriarchy on the bodies of all women compels all women to exist as mothers. The mark of motherhood inscribes the domination of man into women's body, making motherhood appear as a natural phenomenon. (380)

Thomas' account of Isobel's miscarriage outlining graphically the mental anguish at the loss of the child, feelings of guilt and the physical pain she undergoes, remains unique and one among few such descriptions in literature. This is one of the areas of women's lives that has remained shrouded in mystery and has been silenced. It foregrounds the complexity of the maternal body and women's attitudes towards it. In order to express the complexity of the experience, Thomas has to access the maternal of Isobel's "chora" referred to by Kristeva. As Ann Rosalind Jones in her article, "Writing the Body: toward an understanding of lécriture feminine" puts it:

> Women, for Kristeva, also speak and write as "hysterics," as outsiders to male-dominated discourse, for two reasons: the predominance in them drives related to anality and childbirth, and their marginal position vis-à-vis masculine culture. Their semiotic style is likely to involve repetitive, spasmodic separations from the dominating discourse, which more often, they are forced to imitate. (358)

Thomas uses a multiplicity of voices to portray her final mental breakdown and disintegration through the novels of the trilogy. She has to disrupt the neat, linear narrative and experiment in different ways with the form to achieve this purpose. This is necessitated by the nature of women's experiences that she is concerned with.

Thomas uses the disruptive strategies mentioned by Jones while remaining within the dominant discourse all the while. She does not seem to be concerned in evolving an alternative discourse as is suggested and practised by some French feminists, radical white writers and Québecoise writers to be discussed in a later chapter. She is not interested in evolving any exclusionary writing practice of the sort. The climax of Isobel's miscarriage is slowly built up and is narrated by Mrs. Thing. Her controlled panic is evident in her apparently calm verbal exchanges with Jason till the pain is accepted by her and she feels "I can cope: I am one of them" (*Mrs. Blood* 197). She is almost detached as if indulging in her habitual separation of body from mind as she begins to miscarry:

> So that when a part of the placenta comes away quite quickly and easily with about as much sensation as pulling off a large and rather stabber Band-Aid, I say calmly laying down my cards, "I think I'd better have a pill." (107)

Thomas ends the section with Isobel altering Hamlet's dying words to Horatio. This is followed by the third and final section of the novel in which Isobel's Mrs. Blood self takes over completely, signifying her eventual regression and final breakdown. Mrs. Blood's forays into the past in this section include the omens she has ignored, Isobel's near-perfect love-making with Richard, star forecasts for her zodiac sign Scorpio, the lurking fears of Africa, word play on "vulture" signifying death, her experiences when working in the mental hospital, biblical allusions suggestive of a wrathful god, her children's playful voices. Her thoughts disintegrate in the waves of pain till her mind, in its semi-conscious state, asks Jason for forgiveness for not being strong enough to retain the child. It finally comes to rest in the past, when Richard had cruelly asked her to get rid of their child once she had revealed the fact of her pregnancy to him. The section is replete with a plurality of voices, male and female running in Isobel's head and her linking the present miscarriage to her past abortion. Writing on the plurality of voices in Thomas' novel, Krishna Sarbadhikary elucidates: "The collage of shifting images, past memory, and past voices interspersed with present, announces a return of the repressed maternal, as the alter ego of Mrs. Blood, the body of maternal memory, takes over." (43)

The body brought to the centrestage at the end of *Mrs. Blood*, is a condemned and unclean one. Isobel sees herself as unclean in body and soul and the complex baggage of guilt she carries, snowballs. These feelings are evidenced in simple and seemingly disjuncted lines such as "I am so steeped in blood" (*Mrs. Blood* 217) and a little later, "everything that she lieth upon in her separation shall be unclean; everything also that she sitteth upon shall be unclean" (217). Thomas' uses of archaic words signify divine pronouncements. Her anguish increases in tempo as she cries, "Jason, my love, I have done a deed without a name" (218) and the cry emanating from deep within her soul as it were, "O friends come hither. I am so sated in the world, that I have lost my way forever" (218). She sees herself as paying for her infidelity and earlier abortion with her present miscarriage. In *Blown Figures*, the miscarriage situation recurs, this time for Delilah, Isobel's travel companion in her journey through Africa. She sees Delilah's predicament, as "a parody or looking-glass reversal of her own distress five years ago. The blood which links all women was linking them now." (479)

The maternal body with its baggage of guilt continues to haunt her in *Blown Figures.* This novel like the other two begins with the motif of journey. The journey, this time is to seek cleansing and purification in Africa. Her religion does not seem to offer redemption for her sin. The maternal body with its terrors, fears and memories of the past, dominates this novel. However, it is not an asexual body. The ambivalence towards the body persists as she sleeps with a Dutch boy on the ship. Thomas describes the functional body in scatological images, highlighting the foul qualities of the body. Isobel was made fully aware for the first time of the foulness we all carry within us, the reservoirs of pee, the huge sausage-casing holding back our shit (67). She soon dreams that night of having sex with the Devil who tells her that if the child she lost had grown up it would "have made a dreadfully ugly child." He tells her "Get away from me . . . you're unclean. The King could have you killed for that" (68). The repulsion Isobel feels for the body, especially her own is laden with guilt and finds expression in this dream. Later she muses on *The Scarlet Letter* with its themes of sex, adultery and punishment. In this manner, she is drawn to the body's scope of providing her pleasure and repelled by its foulness and pain.

The other related aspects are the mother-daughter matrix and the identity that emerges through the novels in the trilogy. The mother-daughter relationship is a crucial link between body perceptions and identity. It is also central to "writing the body." In Thomas' work, it offers a problematic and accounts for much of the ambivalence experienced by the subject in formation. The pre-Oedipal and Oedipal stages are identified by psychoanalytic theory as crucial to the construction of identity and gender formations. Healthy resolutions of these stages in the psycho-sexual development of the individual, are vital to the integrated identity to be achieved. There is a special significance for women as mothers in the successful resolution of these stages for, as Nancy Chodorow puts it, "[w]omen, as mothers, produce daughters with mothering capacities and the desire to mother. These capacities and needs are built into and grow out of the mother-daughter relationship itself" (7).[3]

Songs My Mother Taught Me deals with issues of growing up, adolescence and identity formation. Isobel, alienated even as a young girl from her peer group, develops a spilt identity—Isobel and I and posts cards to herself: "Dear Isobel, Having a swell time. Your friend I" (27). She has two rag dolls which she loses and they are significant as memories that resurface later. ". . . mother and baby, whom I called 'Me' and 'Mimi.' . . . Ten years later I came upon them by accident, bleached featureless by the wind and sun and rain. . . . It was like finery two small corpses; and I left them there, covered them up with pine needles and went away. For all I know they are still there in the forest. Isobel, perhaps they are your totems?" (19) It is interesting that in the last novel of the trilogy, *Blown Figures*, Isobel goes in search of her "buried" child to Africa. Chodorow, in her important study entitled *Reproduction of Mothering*, points out that "Good enough mothering" ("Good-enough" to socialize a non-psychotic child) requires certain relational capacities which are embedded in personality and a sense of self-in-relationship" (33). Isobel's mother herself does not have a good self-image and constantly feels ostracized by society. Isobel resists the feeble attempts her mother makes to induct her into her peer group but Isobel, "Loved the story of the Ugly Ducking and looked in the mirror and waited." (*SMMTM* 30). Isobel is haunted by two things: "death and the passage of time. Isobel, you are dying faster than the day." (33). These fears haunt her through adult life as well. She experiences ambivalent feelings of love and hate towards her mother triggered by her mother's inconsistencies. As she says: "My mother said terrible things and then changed her mind and wanted you to forget them, but how could you? Look how well Isobel remembers." (37-38)

The twin feelings of love and hate cause her to have ambivalent feelings later towards her own experience of motherhood. The repressed maternal surfaces later through the self of Mrs. Thing in the values she has internalized. Isobel has problems of the self-in-relationship as well. She often projects her feelings on to Jason, other people around her and her surroundings in general. Even her feelings for Jason are mercurial and often relate to her own state of mind and body. Writing on the development of narcissism Chodorow explains: "the infant's internalization of aspects of its relationship to its mother which are experienced as bad often results in splitting off and repression of that part of the ego involved in this bad relationship" (59-60).

Often she goes on to explain that, in an unsatisfactory environment, a "false self emerges on the pattern of conformity to, adaptation to, or else rebellion against, the unsatisfactory environment (60). Chodorow goes on to explain the position of the self or 'I' in the early stages of development where "the infant is cognitively narcissistic; its experience of self is an experience of everything else in its world. What is 'not-I' is libidinally and cognitively perceived as part of 'I.' Originally, the infant's lack of reality principle—its narcissistic relation to reality—is total" (61).

This is called stage of primary identification when there is a state of undifferentiation between the self and environment, mainly the mother. In *Blown Figures,* when Isabel experiences further disintegration of self and regresses, she comes to a point where she relates all the events happening around her and the things people say to her. She regresses in effect to this state of primary identification or narcissism. Thomas achieves this effect by making the narrative resemble the ramblings of a narcissistic psyche often juxtaposing her conscious thoughts, with dreams, fears, personal counselling columns' advice, advertisements, comic strips, biblical allusions etc. Isobel's growing inner chaos is reflected in the gradual fragmentation of the narrative with its empty chapters, one liners and seemingly random selection of news and things included.

Isobel experiences inadequacy as a mother and feels guilty on account of that. As Chodorow, explaining motherhood, puts it: "A mother identifies with her own mother (or the mother she wished she had) and tries to provide nurturant care for the child. At the same time, she re-experiences herself as a cared-for child, thus sharing with her child the possession of a good mother." (90)

Isobel feels "Maudlin tears" (*Mrs. Blood* 17) when she thinks of her children Mary and Nicholas while she is at the hospital. She plays on the word 'cope' thereby revealing feelings of inadequacy as a mother. These feelings are reinforced by the "ladies" who come to visit her and she often imagines them to be pronouncing judgments on her capacities as a mother. In *Mrs. Blood* her narrative is often self-reflexive and self-derisive. The split in the subject into Mrs. Blood and Mrs. Thing enables Isobel to be inside and outside of the Symbolic. It has been pointed out that Thomas speaks in an undifferentiated voice and Sarbadhikary points out in response to this: "it is a conscious strategy by which she explores and explodes boundaries of past/present, self/other, subject/object, signifier/signified, in the process of splitting and reconstructing the self, a process increasingly manifested in *Mrs. Blood* and *Blown Figures*." (23)

The plurality of voices serves to bring to life the chaotic world of Isobel's mind. In *Mrs. Blood* the image of a Japanese garden suggests order and daintiness. This is in contrast to the unruly, violent and mysterious Africa which reflects the dual forces of Isobel's psyche.

The other conflict ever present in Isobel is her attitude to 'victimhood.' She repeats in *Mrs. Blood* and in *Blown Figures* that there are no victims perhaps to salvage her feelings of guilt and yet feels victimized. Her mother's instability results in her feelings of abandonment which finds repetition in a hospital corridor when she follows a nurse and loses track of her. This experience is linked to feelings of terror at abandonment/loss that she experiences as a child when she loses track of her mother and follows a strange woman thinking her to be her mother: "And when I threw my arms around my mother's waist she was no longer my mother but a terrible voice which said, 'What on earth." And who wore the face of a stranger.' (*Mrs. Blood* 38-39)

Isobel re-enacts abandonment by her mother when she leaves her children behind at the hospital and later, the dead child's body in Africa. She is overcome by guilt and feelings of inadequacy. She experiences the split in herself once again when she is abandoned by Richard. She sees the "unreal" self following her "real" self as she walks the streets of London, unconsciously searching for Richard. These instances of abandonment bring fresh experiences of feelings of rejection:

Elaborating on the ideas of primary identification and undifferentiated identity, Chodorow writes:

> Most girls act in the world according to the reality principle and know cognitively that they are differentiated. In relation to their mother, however (and similarly, the mother in relation to her daughters), they experience themselves as overly attached, unindividuated, and without boundaries. Their conflict concerns "preoedipal issues, though it is replayed at a later time, informed by the development which has gone on and the conflicts which have emerged since the early period." (137)

Chodorow explains how girls, in order to achieve differentiation try in every way to be unlike their mothers. This could perhaps explain Isobel's sexual promiscuity, her infidelity, breaking of social norms and social isolation even in adult life.

Isobel's problems of identity also emanate from a weak father whose fears she has internalized. Isobel's mother instills her feeling of contempt for her husband in her daughter. Isobel is obsessed with death and yet fears it. This explains her concern expressed in *Songs My Mother Taught Me* about time running out. In *Blown Figures* she has visions of dying alone and waking up in a pool of her own blood (113). She fears that even then she would not go off quietly like a candle "but screaming, protesting, fighting. She would be dragged away into the other world calling Mother Mother. Mother" (114). Isobel's mindset is Persephone-like and yet the Demeter is also dominant since, "Like a someone in a burning building the child within her struggled to get out" (114). She then has a vision of dying "an orgasmic death" in the ocean (114). Feelings of the erotic are linked to the death-wish here. As she wants "To spread her thighs apart and let the warm sea enter and explore her with his milky fingers while tiny silver fishes swarm between her legs" (114). Life as Isobel sees it, is linked to sex and death in a continuum. This is expressed in a chapter in *Blown Figures*, which contains only three words: TUMMY TUMULUS TOMB (397).

This death-wish is a powerful force in Isobel's psyche as much as the need for life and sexual pleasure are. Writing on the suppression of female desire, Kadiatu Kanneh elucidates:

> She is socialized into an education which is imbued with the myths of witches and Medusas who claim the night, riding on the winds of desire and sisterhood, revelling in the self-lust whose impressive beauty, the 'masculine point of view' calls a terrible abomination. Women's huge wealth of desire is named a frightful and ugly depravity, a corruption, the fear of which woman has been forced to internalize. (138)

In Isobel's case, more than men, it is her Phallic mother who acts as patriarchy's agent. This results in Isobel's alienation from herself and others. Chodorow, discussing the infant's experience of fusion with the mother writes, "Qualities of the mother are introjected and become part of the self-image and qualities of the self projected outward" (73).

In *Blown Figures* the dual selves seen in *Mrs. Blood,* further multiply to include Isobel, Miss. Miller and I. There is further fragmentation bordering on insanity. Thomas again provides a rare glimpse into such an anguished mind. Accounts of women's mental breakdown from women's point of view are rare even today since this belongs to marginalized entities. Shoshana Felman writes:

> Madness and women, however, turn out to be the two outcasts of the establishment of readability. An ideological conditioning of literary and critical discourse, a political orientation of reading thus affirms not so much through the negative treatment of women as through their total neglect, their pure and simple omission. (11)

The narrator who is part of the split subject in *Blown Figures,* expresses concern in these words, "How to rescue Isobel without touching her, without becoming oneself an Isobel" (201).

The active and passive aspects are both present in Isobel and the active self offers a response to the dilemma: "Why did you always feel as though you needed to be rescued. . . . All your life you have been as passive as a princess in a fairy tale. Even this journey . . . what were you doing but waiting for signs and signals?" (218)

Yet, logic and rationality forsake Isobel and her superstitions and fears which are more deep-rooted take over. The pervading sense of guilt overwhelms her. Her religion offers her no solace and she seeks purification in African rituals. The sacrificial rituals appear in her dreams and continue to haunt her till she finally participates, partly in reality and partly hallucinating, in an African confessional ritual, which again offers no salvation. The narrative has switched to third person and is further distanced from the events even as the priest pronounces: "The end of being tired is death. It is too late, Isobel. The witches have eaten up your *kra*" (524). The people present at the ritual perceive Isobel to be a witch and legends grow around her and misfortune falls on the village after her visit. The narrative further collapses with the disintegration of Isobel's self as she dons the identity of a witch. She warns Mrs. Miller, her listening self, that there is no more twist to the tale. The novel ends with an address to time: "TIME! YOU MONSTROUS MOLE. WHY ARE YOU DOING THIS TO ME?" (547). Time has run out for Isobel with her having crossed the borders from "sanity" to insanity and life to death.

3.2 Tostevin's Subject-in-Process

Lola Lemire Tostevin's novel *Frog Moon* deals with the female body in equally interesting ways for she talks about the repressed body while emphasizing the need to connect with it. By forging a connection with the body Laura, the protagonist comes into her own as a writer. Closely linked to this is the mother-daughter relationship and the experience of the body by three generations of women in the novel. Laura's concern with retrieving her family history results in her narrative being 'polyvocal' with a plurality of selves taking centrestage at different times. Although this polyvocality is played out in shifting back and forth from the Symbolic to the semiotic, the Mother's presence is dominant.[4]

This dialogic relationship that Tostevin establishes between the Symbolic and the semiotic also enables her to explore both the "inner," domestic space of women and the "outer," geographic spaces men move in. The other issue that Tostevin takes up in all her works and does so in this novel as well is that of her relationship as a bilingual writer to her 'other'—Mother, the French language. The yearning caused by the absence or the loss she feels for this mother tongue is intense. Simultaneously, a crucial issue being worked out through the novel is that of 'subjectivity' or the subject-in-process (reflective of Kristeva's ideas). Tostevin is particularly concerned with this aspect as her subject is a writer. She subverts the traditional novel form by abandoning the conventional linear narrative, so that the maternal which is brought in by memory and is often repressed, can be foregrounded. These issues of gender allow her to experiment with the genre. It is difficult to locate a 'unified' self/narrator, since it slides constantly to enable other voices to emerge in the narrative. She uses the oral tradition of storytelling and includes myths and legends to eventually blur the distinctions between reality and fiction. The 'decent ring' of the self happens at several points in the novel, and this, coupled with her self-reflexivity, is often disconcerting to the conventional reader. However, it is a 'decent ring' done for a specific purpose, not necessarily in a postmodern sense. As Patricia Waugh puts it:

> If women have traditionally been positioned in terms of 'otherness,' then the desire to become subjects (which dominates the first phase of post-1960s feminist) is likely to be stronger than the desire to deconstruct, decentre, or fragment subjectivity (which dominates post-1960s postmodernist practice and poststructural theory). They have not yet *experienced* this 'whole' or 'unitary' or 'essential' subjectivity. (12)

Similarly, when these women writers use strategies like deconstruction, irony or parody it does not emerge as a postmodernist project. They have often been used as tools for their own agenda, which is often challenging patriarchal discourses. Linda Hutcheon observes: "Postmodern parodic and ironic representational strategies have offered feminist artists an effective way of working within and yet challenging dominant patriarchal metanarrative discourses" ("Incredulity . . ." 198).

Tostevin does this in her poetry as well as fiction. At an interview with Janice Williamson, when asked about her 'ironic mode of thinking,' Tostevin says: "I think I've always had a sense of irony about myself. As a young girl, I knew I was desperate being locked up in this convent for eight years of my life, but somehow it was such an absurd situation. . . . Philosophy doesn't have a sense of humour, so I took great pleasure in some of the poems in Sophie in injecting a certain humour into serious concerns." (273)

Tostevin seems concerned with the question of time since *Frog Moon* begins with Laura in the convent as a young girl and moves quickly to the present. Her story is quickly interrupted by the more distant past with her mother's narrative and then her father's stories intrude. It proceeds to Laura's introduction to literature and writing in the convent, then swings to the time she spends in Paris to write with the narrative coming back to the present. Various narratives get interwoven with the intermeshing of the past and present and there is really no closure to the novel with Laura's memories going back to the past but with a renewed or altered consciousness. Time in this sense is circular and spirals from the past to the present. What occasions the entire narrative is the annual Christmas dinner to which Laura's parents generally come. The occasion enables Laura to create her family history, weaving different stories she has heard all along, but she imposes her pattern on them and derives her own significance, from them. This is because she allows the subjects to speak for themselves so that there are shifting locations as well as points of view.

Laura's past is narrated in the third person illustrating her alienation and psychic distancing from it whereas the present is related in the first person. There is a silencing of the past in her psyche along with the reprisal of her body and sexuality in the convent. Even as she tries to join the choir, she is pronounced as being tone deaf and is asked to simply mouth the words without letting her voice be heard and visualize the sounds. The girls in the convent even eat in silence. When her friend Christine visits her, eleven years later, they giggle over their convent days and narrate the incidents to Louise and David, Laura's children: "Weeks, month, carved in silence. They give shape to those long expanses that would have been forgotten otherwise, each story as intimate as family or an old friend. That's the way it is with stories." (22)

Even as she remembers, there is a self-reflexivity and the reader is gently reminded that these are only her constructs. There is a blurring of the boundary between reality and fiction and a questioning of the 'truth' value of stories at the very outset.

Laura refers to herself at the convent as 'the young girl.' The girls residing in the convent are assigned limited spaces that offer them no privacy so that they have to contort their bodies even to change into their night clothes and they are instructed not to defile their bodies which they should regard as temples. The young girl fantasises about the convent walls being the wall of China and having tea with an emperor who lives in the Palace of the Moon. In the absence of words, images and fantasies become more active in her mind. She is haunted by superstitions connected with exposing her body to moonlight and turning into a '*loupgarou.*' Music coming from a nearby skating rink heightens her homesickness and makes her visualize people close to her. She experiences alienation for the first time as "This is the first time she conceives of herself as an image, the first time she visualizes everyone she cares for as a memory." (32)

Chimeras haunt her dreams as she tries to appease the memories of home. Her mother's voice and presence dominate her dream which symbolizes her separation from her mother. There is no speech in the dream "but the blanket of sound that maps her, curls inside her, is the familiar voice of her mother, a sonorous whoosh like a heartbeat. Body talk" (108). The dream is more sensory than verbal. She is haunted by superstitions surrounding the land of the Chimeras where:

> young girls are kept in boxes to prevent them from growing; their lips are slit to prevent them from speaking, their skulls compressed to keep them from thinking . . . when things go wrong in the land of the Chimeras, the she-monsters usually shoulder the blame. In the land of the Chimeras, the she-monsters are often sacrificed, a fate they willingly accept. For no matter how much their skulls have been compressed, their loneliness affords them a fuller understanding of these matters. (108)

The symbolism of the dream is quite telling in that, the she-monsters are capable of deep thought in spite of their bodies being repressed. The image of young girls in boxes of course brings to mind the restrictions of space imposed on the young girls. The young girl's daytime experiences of terror and fear find their ways to her dreams.

Due to the strictures imposed on the body and the resultant fear of and disgust with the body, young Laura develops anorexia:

> Even the taste of the Eucharist each morning nauseates her, the thin wafer made flesh, made bloody on her tongue before it dislodges from her palate, scrapes down her throat, along her stomach wall, towards the rot of her bowels. . . . She wonders: what morsel of Christ's body she is about to ingest. Which organ, limb, entrails or wound. Which mucus, marrow, semen. (127)

She is admitted into the infirmary for treatment when she comes across *Gray's Anatomy* where she discovers the names of female body parts. She feels each of the parts of the female genitalia and identifies them by their Latin names and discovers the sensations of her own body. She knows the names of the parts of the body but has no words for the sensations:

> In the process of naming parts of her body she didn't know she had, she is unable to find words to describe what she's feeling. She is bewildered by sensations to which she readily submits. A trembling on the verge of fulfilling a secret yearning. (135)

It is still an alienated sensibility that Tostevin is writing of. This is partly due to language, which distances the subject from her experience. On account of this alienation, Louis Dupré argues for a different kind of language in these words:

> And what can we say about her, the daughter, who is alienated from this language in which she can never recognize herself as subject, who sees herself cut off from her mother, who finds herself without a penis with which to identify with her father? In language she is always spoken about, she, a stranger to the act of speech. (27)

Since women are always alienated from the language of the Symbolic, Dupré writes that women need: "To affirm our women's language, de-centred, eccentric in relation to the symbolic, changeable, passionate, and linked to the semiotic chora." (Kristeva) (27)

The young girl takes a fistful of consecrated wafer from the chalice and puts them into her mouth to cure herself of her guilt:

> The body of Jesus will cleanse the rot of her bowels. She stuffs more wafers into her month. This is the rite through which unworthy daughters swallow the flesh of the Father and make themselves worthy again. Not only the Father's liver but his entire body, so the two of them, daughter and Father, are one. (136)

She conducts this rite of purification on herself wanting to rid herself of the guilt she feels after exploring her own body and getting acquainted with the names of her body parts. The notion of the body as impure is deeply ingrained in her. Earlier she is told by Soeur Lucienne that algebra and geometry are not of much use to girls. She is awed by the commanding quality of the equation:

> If A equals B equals C. The authority of the perfect triangle, like the Trinity. It knows everything, gapes from above the door of study hall and scrutinizes the bowel skulls it's about to penetrate. It invades playgrounds, bathrooms, refectories, prowls, dormitories, follows the small hand brushing against soft genitals or budding breasts under bedsheets. (99-100)

Math belongs to male domain and is as powerful as the all-seeing Trinity in the girls' eyes. Fear rules their lives and the worst fear of all was the fear of sin and the endless rites of penance for atonement and purification.

She describes confession in which the "Foreboding Eye" is replaced by the "Foreboding Ear." To the priest, the worst sins were sins of the flesh:

> Flesh, the soft parts of a mother's body, shhh. Bloody flesh, mucous flesh, entrails, organs shhh. Nakedness, buttocks, penis, vagina, menstruation shhh. Sex, shhh. The most doubtful parts of human nature, shhh. For these are the deadly sins that stain the soul, deface it until it caves in under the weight of its own decay, under the weight of its own flesh. (102)

Tostevin adopts a normal tone a little later saying "God's first language used to be Latin, but now it's French" (102). The young girl feels that when her venial sins do not lend her confession enough weight she has to invent bigger and better sins. Earlier she says in the three-pronged fork of the French Canada, the three prongs were English, the clergy and the Devil. In her mother's narrative is included the legend of Rose Latulippe based on the superstition, "Woman and her demon's gifts, because the Devil always entered a family's affairs through the female side" (51). The legend serves to show how the devil through his sexual attraction charmed his way to the young woman who had to pay for her indiscretion by either becoming a nun or an old maid. Religion had a powerful hold on women's bodies and this is symbolized by the Foreboding Eye and Ear. In the course of the novel Tostevin shows, how the strictures imposed by Catholicism controlled women's bodies over three generations. Laura's grandmother had borne seven children by the time she was thirty-three and worked herself to death and that made her "an angel." Laura's mother, a more pragmatic person, when called a Jezebel by a priest in public for dressing well, defies him. The priest, Monsieur Cure referring to women's body in his speech says: "Her body is a receptacle, a vessel for the sacred duty of motherhood, and as we all know, my dear parishioners, each woman's body is a symbol for the vessel that carried the Son of God. There is no greater honour than that." (58) Tostevin adopts a humorous tone in the narrative repeating the refrain, "Clickety-clack, Clickety-clack, break your grandma's back" (59).

In a chapter titled "carnal knowledge," Laura's father describes his life in a lumber camp as a young boy where he learned about sex in the context that women and the Devil went hand in hand. Just before Laura graduates from the convent she is paraded from class to class by the nuns dressed up in one of their habits. The nuns evidently want her to join their order. "The habit transformed her into something other than a powerless and fearful young girl" (175). For a time she thinks she has no choice but to become a nun or "lose her soul" (175). When she goes home for her holidays however, she falls in love with Geoffrey whom she later marries. This ends the convent's hold on her. As an aspiring writer much later in Paris, a strange encounter she has with a taxi driver who gets her in touch with her body. This is triggered off after an interesting exchange that they have on Picasso's paintings. Laura finds him physically revolting and thinks herself above the likes of him. Yet, when he caresses her, her body, as if with a will of its own, starts responding to his touch but after that he soon leaves. She sees an image of Picasso's painting which has heterosexual desire writ all over it with the intertwining bodies and their organs so topsy-turvy, that it is impossible to tell which one belonged to the man and which one to the woman. The commentary beside the image states "Art is never chaste" (209).

Laura starts writing after her brief but memorable sexual encounter with the taxi driver in Paris. Tostevin seems to suggest that it is the body's sensations that need to get translated into the text. That there is no substitute for real, lived experience for the writer, also seems to be suggested. Unless the strictures and inhibitions imposed on the body break down, she cannot become the subject of her own writing. She will always be written about. Tostevin, in a piece titled 're' writes:

> to speak the missing spoke that revolves around the spoken frame of reference ferret out what links in silence out of sight out of mind out of the corner of one eye the optical illusion (a ray of light?) which the text reflects. (42)

The writer has to move from being the silenced, suppressed maternal of the 'chora' to light and even that the lines seem to suggest may be only a reflection. Towards the end of the novel, Laura says:

> I am a middle-aged woman whose phantom body of old age hovers and dreams of the agility of its youth . . . the frog yearns to change its skin, pull it over its head like a dress, place it in its mouth, chew it, ingest it, so the fiction of that body is never lost. (215)

After having said this, Kaki (Cree for frog goddess), which is her childhood name, goes back to her childhood memories. The body enters the fiction and perhaps gets immortalized. In her interview with Janice Williamson, when asked about her series of erotic poems, the "Song of Songs" Tostevin says:

> I would like to write about heterosexual relationships in a way that isn't over-determined and predetermined. There's a great challenge for us to find new ways of relating to the other sex and new reciprocities to explore. . . . I didn't want to write heterosexual love poems where women are passive. It was very difficult. . . . I wanted to examine desire from a heterosexual perspective. I'm penetrating the language as much as being penetrated. It is also the penetration of the muse, who is herself erotic and looks for eroticism in the other; she is not passive but an erotic muse, a thinking

> muse, an emotional muse . . . the ('I') is not always the same woman, and it's not always the same lover. (274)

Tostevin, however is opposed to essentialism of any kind and to 'bipolar gender differentiation which culturally defines us' (277). She feels that writers like Genet and Barthes achieved this through homosexuality and heterosexuals should also "[f]ind their eroticism, their pleasure, outside the dichotomy of reproduction, of power over the other, and introduce women to pleasure that exceeds their traditional roles and as such displace those roles" (277). This is certainly what she is attempting in the novel.

Tostevin also unhinges standard notions of the maternal body as incapable of experiencing pleasure or as being asexual. Laura and her mother unsettle these notions. Laura's bonding with both her biological mother and the French language is strong and these rescue her from the repression of the body that she experiences at the convent. Laura's mother is a strong presence throughout the novel and has her own narrative as well. Laura unfavorably compares herself with her friend Christine, an artist, who lives in Paris and leads a bohemian life. As Laura sees it: "The children love it. . . . She exemplifies everything that I'm not; her artist's worldliness, clothes with just the right bohemian touch, her Parisian accent." (20)

This is in fact, Laura's self-image and her thwarted ambition of becoming a writer. And again when Christine relates stories about the convent to Laura's children, Laura thinks: "I suspect she takes great pleasure in reminding me, via the children, that I want always this lackluster model of domesticity and motherhood." (20)

This is a deprecating picture of motherhood and domesticity, which Laura has consciously chosen. The prospect of her parent's arrival makes Laura think of her losing touch with French and she is particularly troubled by her children's, particularly her son David's, resistance to the language. She gets into a flurry of activity cleaning the house in anticipation of their arrival and dreads her mother's censure as is seen when she says: "My mother always assesses a woman's worth by her floors" (23). She catches herself doing the same chides herself for still being her and thinks "mother's child" (23). Laura, however, cannot envisage Christmas or Christmas dinner without her mother and there is an image of Laura's mother Laura and Louise working together in the kitchen baking goodies. In a series of letters exchanged with Smaro Kamboureli, when Kamboureli expresses views resisting defining woman through the maternal, Tostevin clarifies her views on it in these words:

> To paraphrase Shirley [Neuman] in *A Mazing Space*, the symbiosis of the maternal and fetal bodies allows the maternal to write in a different rhythm, in order to recover control of both her maternal and sexual discourses. I agree with you however that motherhood cannot be the locus of her difference, otherwise she will be absorbed by it. (Kamboureli and Tostevin 23)

This very idea is espoused in Laura's discontentment. She needs to find herself as a writer, to be a whole person, and thereby be better integrated into her family once again. Tostevin is deeply influenced by Julia Kristeva's views on the maternal, the Symbolic and the Semiotic and the question of identity or subject-in-process. This is evident in her letters to Smaro Kamboureli, in which there is an animated discussion between them regarding these key concepts. Referring to the way Kristeva reconciles Symbolic with the semiotic, she writes:

> While she has always emphasized the importance of exceeding the Mother/Child relationship, she has also emphasized the importance of not suppressing it. The child cannot remain in the emotional or physical envelope of the mother, which exists in too great a proximity, so an 'imaginary father' is introduced as a loving third with which the infant-in-process identifies but not at the expense of the semiotic or the mother. This permits the investing of drives in the symbolic, and consequently the creating of a space of play and exchange between the semiotic and the symbolic. (24-25).

Tostevin moves on to that once the mother-child separation occurs. Perhaps the mother then turns to other things that she loves besides the child such as friends, lovers, creative work etc. She also feels:

> The difference between Kristeva and Lacan is that Kristeva puts more value on what happens before the mirror stage, before the Symbolic, which seems to prepare the mother far better for the space of exchange, interplay etc. (25)

These views of Tostevin find fruition in her poetry as well as fiction. In the novel, the semiotic in Laura's psyche often finds expression in the young girl's dreams and the myths and legends she grew up on. The Symbolic is the dominant mode she thinks in during her conscious state, and this involves a repression of her body and sexuality. The voices of the clèrgy, religion, superstitions and the all-seeing Trinity dominate her constantly. Yet, the semiotic, aligned with her mother, comforts her and finally rescues her. Memories of her mother offer her warmth and security. Her mother makes her feel special as if touched by an angel and tells her when she is still a child: "[O]n the night you were born an angel placed an index and a thumb on either side of your face and gave you dimples. A child with dimples. A child with dimples is marked for life, her mother said (36). Laura's very first memory is of her mother telling her stories. She repeats this at the end of the novel after she has begun to write. Laura's mother is however, not a stereotypical mother. She is described as having been beautiful and having used cosmetics. She defies the priest and does not think much of a religion that thinks of women as "vessels." She secretly buys the Junior Encyclopedia for her daughter and reads to her. Her illusions of her mother as having been as selfless as her own mother are upset when her mother tells her that she would save pennies over several weeks and buy herself small tins of salmon which she ate in hiding as a little girl so she wouldn't have to share them with her three sisters. Laura's perceptions about her, get clarified as she says:

> If, as with so many mothers, my mother's energy often seems limitless and unselfconscious, it is also often in conflict with her mothering role. It's not always practical to have children around. (78-79)

She is aware of the pragmatic qualities of her mother as she has always been the one to take care of mechanical problems with gadgets. There is an "unfeminine" side to her. Laura is not haunted by intense Matrophobia even as she realizes that she is growing to be like her mother. She admits to becoming "both fascinated and afraid of the new dimension" (79).

She knows stories in 'The Young Folks' by heart and recalls one of her favourites from *Heroes and Heroines*, "The Old Women and the Knight." Laura describes the old woman in the story as having "powers similar to my mother's, powers that would see her through anything, anywhere" (80). Her mother is her focal point. The answer to the question posed by the Queen to the Knight as to what was desired by women the most in order to save his life, is given by an old woman. The answer she gives him with which he saves his life, is that women wanted power over their lives, the power to choose what they wished to be.

The Knight passes the litmus test when he in fact has to accept the old woman as his wife and put himself in her hands allowing her to choose to do what she pleases. The Knight is rewarded with the old woman transforming herself into a beautiful, young woman. The crux of the story is of course that women must have the right to choose. The other mother that Laura is concerned with is her mother tongue—the French language, the loss of which she deeply mourns. For instance, once when she is exasperated with her children she thinks, "some emotions can only be expressed in the language closest to those emotions" (23). Similarly when she is about to re-construct her family history, piecing together the fragments of her parents' stories, she thinks that "living in a language that is not your mother tongue cuts you off from memory" (24). She is aware that much is lost in translation and this is the reason for her mourning the loss of her closeness to French. She refers to her plight in these words:

> The child who spoke French is no longer the adult who speaks English. She is the smallest doll in a set of nested dolls like the one Christine bought for Louise in a Russian gift shop, each doll living within another version of her self, as in a vault. (24)

Languages, when they are dead, can deaden a person's sensibility and can silence even an ethos. Laura understands the significance of her parents' yearly visit during Christmas and feels: "The re-creation of a small part of history through which some degree of relevance is restored, if only for a few days" (26). In celebrating Christmas with her parents Laura is re-enacting a traditional family ritual. She knows that through the loss of language her children are distanced from their roots. While negotiating the gap between her children and parents, Laura feels she has a hyphenated identity. Referring to her children she thinks:

> They will never experience how parents come to life again when, after a long absence, I hear them speak their mother tongue, I sometimes feel as if I don't belong to either my children or my parents. During those moments, when the mirrors of both languages crumble, I have the unsettling impression that I will always remain a stranger to myself. (25)

This points to the important fact of identity being linked to language and the alienation in Laura's life on this count. Tostevin writes about this crucial link between language and subjectivity in these words:

> Far from seeing clearly, writing also distorts and magnifies. The writer drawn to language, aware that language always draws its own designs but also aware that its sufficiency or insufficiency is irrelevant. Only in words can the writer apprehend what buzzes around her and in her head. Words—the natural habitat of the function of inhabiting and being. ("Working at Writing. . ." 40)

Laura's distance from her language is ultimately connected to the life she chooses. She expresses regret several times about not having stayed on in Montreal and realizes: "I had adapted my colours to my surrounding as protection but also to please" (146). It is significant that she does not begin to write till she is in Paris—the place where her language originated. She has to go there and convince herself that, "Paris has only confirmed that I don't belong there either" (214).

It is significant that she titles five of her chapters as "Babel Noel." Referring to the language issue she writes in an article titled, "Contamination: A Relation of Differences":

> Babel should have taught us no one language can impose itself on the world yet most of us continue to experience the passage from one language to another as essential loss. (14)

However, Laura is perceptive enough to understand even as she matures as a writer that firstly "Language is alive because it can die" (191) and when she is asked in Paris why she did not speak French with a Canadian accent, if in fact she was at all Canadian, she retorts, "I speak French in many languages" (202). Her identity when she is in Canada hinges on the French language but while in France, hinges on her Canadian nationality.

The third aspect to be looked at is the notion of subjectivity as understood by Tostevin. She works out this notion in the novel since it arises out of both "body perceptions" and language. Writing on Tostevin's poetry, Dawn McCance in an article titled, "Julia Kristeva and the Ethics of Exile" writes:

> In Tostevin's poetry, this 'alien condition' stems not only from the displacement of her French mother tongue, but from the excision of woman's tongue by a male monological system (32)

Tostevin resists this tendency in both her poetry and in the novel. Referring to the absence of woman's voice in discourse she writes: "I think it is significant that the only place in the Bible where woman speaks in her own voice is in 'Song of the Songs,' a text revolving around an amorous, erotic discourse" ("Contamination. . ." 14).

Her book of poems is titled 'sophie with 'Phil' absent and 'sophie present indicating male absence and female presence. It is a series of heterogeneous love poems, where the woman assumes the speaking subject's position. Describing the book she writes:

> The book revolves around women as absent in philosophy, attempts to displace contaminate the authority of philosophy through a woman's or 'sophie's point of view. 'Phil' is momentarily suspended, the suspension of his presence replaced by a small sign, an apostrophe, the presence of writing. As such the voice of truth, the virility of philosophy is contaminated by what has always been relegated to the lowest rung, the allegorical voice of a woman. (13)

Writers like Tostevin seek to re-store the 'Polyvocal' voice. She does this in the *Frog Moon* by developing polyvocality to include the male voice of Laura's father with stories suggesting male bonding in the lumber camp. She juxtaposes images of the men of the family watching a game together and three generations of women represented by Laura's mother, Laura and her daughter Louise baking bread. In her writing the semiotic and the Symbolic coexist as she thinks, "In any event, a father's stories shouldn't diminish a daughter's voice" (151-52) and then she give way to her father's narrative. She prods her father for his stories. She interrupts her father's narrative with statements as from an omniscient narrator giving her father whose name is Achilles, legendary qualities. Due to these intrusions, her father's account does assume mythic qualities. Laura assigns herself mythic qualities since she is named Kaki, a shortened version of Oma-Ka-Ki, second child of Oma-ma-ma, earth mother who birthed all spirits of the world, according to Cree legend. In an ironic tone, Laura reminds us that she was perhaps named as such not just because they were French Canadian but also because she was born in the month of June, the month of the Moon of Frogs. Laura says that while the other children born of Oma-ma-ma were endowed with magical powers, she was named "Kaki" after the croaking voice of the lowly frog, holding few magical powers except for the endless chore of controlling the insects of the world" (40). This mythic identity serves the purpose of expressing her feelings of being marginalized as a French Canadian and her name "associated with an element even less desirable than French Canadians" (40). Laura's father does not call her by this name in the presence of strangers and the name is retrieved when she is sent to the convent, "when the time had come for me to be proper" (40). Laura has to delink her identity from the name Kaki even as she has to discard her childhood when she enters the convent. She is reminded of the associations of the name in the convent when a nun asks her what it was she said and whether a frog had come out of her mouth. Laura relates a story of a time when "In the beginning was the Frog" (42) and how they emerged in the "shape of foul spirits from the mouth of dragons and false prophets." (42). Laura thinks that to the nun "Frog was just another word for swearing, another dirty word" (42). She imbibes all the negative connotations of the word. In an article titled, "Dialogue with the Other: The Use of Myth in Canadian Women's Poetry." Smaro Kamboureli, explaining the significance of myth in literature writes: "It is a repetition backwards, towards the roots of our perception, it is also a remembering forwards, towards the re-writing of the past, the revaluation of our present." (105)

Myths allow women writers to re/vision the past in order to re/fashion the present differently. It enables them to demythologize those other myths—the stereotypes that govern women's lives. They make strategic use of myths to engage the discourses of patriarchy. As Kamboureli puts it:

> The dialogic form that feminine experience tends to take in poetry enables women poets to demythologize the attitudes that have constructed that creative energy. Through the connotative use of myth, women poets engage themselves in an on-going dialogue with the world around them, thus re-locating themselves in a tradition that has both excluded and coerced their presence. Their dialogic discourse operates according to the principle of difference rather than the principle of opposition. (108)

Although the three writers studied in this chapter incorporate myths into different genres, the results are equally, startlingly different. Tostevin in the *Frog Moon* establishes a dialogic relation between the semiotic and the Symbolic writing Laura's psyche.[5] In the different narratives of different selves they sometimes run as parallel strands and sometimes weave into each other as in the case of the Rose Latulippe legend for instance, being woven into Laura's mother's down to earth narrative. Ultimately, the semiotic which is rooted in the female body's experiences, has to emerge as a more dominant voice for Laura to come into her own as a writer. In order to achieve this, the woman writer has to make a courageous effort in rejecting the false dichotomies imposed by patriarchy. Louis Dupré says:

> A matter of real urgency. To refuse the mask, refuse the double-play of language; the dichotomy of signifier-signified separated by a bar (Saussure), the dichotomy of the language-speech (Saussure) and competence-performance (Chomsky), the binarity of opposites. To give vent to a plural language that catches all the nuances of words beyond fixed definitions, that abandoned the order of the theological substantive of ownership. A language of relations of drift, alive with all our seedlings. (qtd. Godard 29)

Although Tostevin does not experiment with language in the novel as much as she does in her poetry, she exposes the binaries that Dupré refers to for what they are by privileging the oral over the written in the first place. She does this by also exploding the notion of a unified fixed subject. Hers is a subject-in-process in a Kristevan sense. Dawn McCance clarifies the Kristevan position in these words:

> While it is the case, for her, that there must be separation (of subject from object) and division (of conscious from unconscious) in order for a subject to posit meaning in language, the subject in language must nevertheless remain in a hyperbolic *sujet en process*: a subject-in-process on trial. This subject becomes itself as an unfinished production in language. It is thus a divided subject, placed on trial by its own otherness a subject, which posits its thesis as undecidable process between semiotic and symbolic. (29)

As an illustration of the points made above, the chapter titled (Babel Nöel) (ii) begins and ends with Laura's thoughts as a young girl at the convent. It contains Geoffrey's view of the Christmas preparations in the kitchen after he returns from a business trip and goes on to give his point of view on religion and his resistance to baptizing their children. This chapter ends with Laura as a young girl at the convent missing home, her parents and recalling images of their walk home after midnight mass. The narrative is in third person and yet the images are very sensory:

> Wet snow and the smell of incense clinging to her clothes, the moon caught in a network of winter branches, a benediction in which family, friends, strangers, and even nature collaborated. These images were once central to her life. How did they become too worn? (70)

A little earlier, in the same part of the chapter, Laura thinks of the Latin words of hymns they sang:

> For Laura, the foreign tongue of prayer yearns for a target that is seldom God. It pleads for the restoration of something that's been lost. A language prior to language when the world was but a dream. A language prior to splitting when a voice in the darkness uttered, let there be light, and speech was deemed as morning's gift. (70)

She is referring to a pre-Symbolic language, that of the sensory world. She seems to be lamenting the loss of such a language and the world of sensations—tactile and aural—that went with that. In the following chapter titled "Union" there is a shift to the first person narrative with descriptions of people in Ansonville, the town to which they return after a two week stay at her great uncle's farm. She goes into the etymology of the words "whore" and "Charity" and sees them closely allied. She examines the words with can be found suffixed to the word 'Cat.' Her mother's narrative in her own voice cuts in, further containing within it the story of "The Old Woman and the Knight" from *Heroes and Heroines.* Laura's narrative mingles with that of her mother and it resembles concentric circles of stories within stories with time always moving in a circular fashion. This chapter is followed by another titled "The Prophet of the Rand," her father's story-male discourse with descriptions of the gold rush. This is followed by a chapter titled "Confession" with the young girl's accounts of repression and her introduction to literature and passion through *Wuthering Heights*. In this manner, the division in the subject seeks expression through different 'selves' narrating different stories in both voices—male as well as female.

Even as she reconstructs her family history from the fragments of stories that her parents produce, Laura is aware of her role both as a writer and daughter in transmutation. She compares the writer to an "alchemist, practising the arcane art of transmuting elements of reality into the shining, enduring element of fiction. The daughter practising the magical art of transfiguration" (161). This self-reflexivity reminds the reader that the subject is also a writer coming into being. The writer in her can emerge only after the repressed material submerged in the 'chora' can come to the fore in the course of the dialogue of the semiotic and the Symbolic. McCance observes: "Tostevin neither identifies with the unitary subject nor suggests that women can withdraw into an asymbolic femininity. For her, a female self-identity can only be produced in process in language." (32-33)

The writer in Laura is aware of the blurred border between fiction and reality as she feels, "The more imagination a story teller had, the more he played around with facts" (163). She comes to the realization that, language being alive, changes and stories change as the world changes. The artist in her is impelled to further impose her own pattern and this is what she implies as she thinks while weaving a tapestry to make up her own pattern as she goes along. She realizes when she goes to Paris that just being in a location of arts will not automatically make a writer of her: "I'd been under the impression that I'd be able to gather my notes into stories here, but the moment I put pen to paper the stories empty themselves of all content, as if I've become inaccessible to myself." (197)

It is as if her imagination and creativity run dry. She comes to understand her own alienation from her body and the encounter with the taxi driver helps her find her body's rhythms which she subsequently puts into the text.

The fragrance of lilacs from bushes flowering in June has several associations for Laura. The perfume of lilacs also reminds her of her mentor Madame Wickersham, who introduced her to literature by giving her two important classics—Kafka's *Metamorphosis* and Ovid's *Metamorphoses*. She encourages the flowering of the writer in Laura by advising her with these words: "Gather your stories, your diaries, your fragments, your dictionary definitions, and put them into a book" (192-93).

Laura remembers these words years later when sets about becoming a writer. These words however, do not prove to be sufficient and finally her body's awakening to its eroticism and the message from another medium—the visual in the form of Picasso's abstracts of human bodies, nudge the artist lying dormant within her. Faced with the challenges of constructing the female subject by confronting the in-built biases of the dominant male discourses and its metanarratives, the woman writer also feels the compulsion to evolve new genres. Tostevin refers to this issue in her interview with Janice Williamson while she was still writing the *Frog Moon*:

> The fact that my novel will be divided into many stories already fragments the traditional view of what some people think a novel should be. I don't work within a framework of completion or closure, which will be a problem for traditionalists, or realists, whoever they may be: (278)

In this sense, some of the experiments with genre which are carried out by postmodern writers, resemble those by writers like Tostevin. Linda Hutcheon comments on the similarities between them with these words:

> In granting new and emphatic value to the notion of "experience," they [feminisms] have given a different angle on a very postmodern question: what constitutes a valid historical narrative? And who decides? This has lead to the re-evaluation of personal of life narratives—journals, letters, confessions, biographies, autobiographies, self-portraits. ("Incredulity . . ."190)

All these are called in for revising and simultaneously accepted as literary genres. Discourse, likewise becomes double-edged since many of the women writers use strategies of parody and irony. Tostevin is referring to the "upsetting" of genre as well as language talks about her idea of 'contamination.' She writes:

> I find the concept of contamination as a literary device rather appealing. Contamination means differences have been brought together so they make contact. It is from this point of view that 'sophie (and to a great extent all my work) was conceived. ("Contamination . . . 13)

This explains the preoccupation with language that Tostevin consistently shows as well. This preoccupation with language and genre seems to be prevailing particularly among women writers attempting to destabilize conventional notions, so as to break new ground and create new spaces to write from. They have to re/work language and breathe new life into "worn" images. Dupré expresses this view as she writes:

> Women who write are of necessity preoccupied with language, with form, since for them it's a question of subverting masculine language. A desire, therefore, to de-articulate the dominant discourse, to split open syntax, to let the over-flowing feminine into the signified, to reinvent its vocabulary, to reinvest it with new signified. ("The Doubly Complicit Memory" 30)

Tostevin, in her work does all that Dupré suggests and *Frog Moon* demonstrates the case with which she moves back and forth from the Symbolic to the semiotic.

3.3 Penn Kemp's Re/claiming the Body through Spirituality

Penn Kemp, a playwright and a novelist has to her credit seventeen books of poems and four plays which have been published. She is a 'sound' poet who 'performs' her work. In her own words: "Sounding can be a last resort for creative expression when words fail the enormity of the emotion. It is exciting to use the sound of human voices to portray the environment and inner space,"[6] Penn Kemp's works requires a slightly different treatment since they are informed by her spiritual experiences and vision. Mircea Eliade is profoundly prophetic about modern man when he writes:

> The progressive de-sacrilization of the modern man has altered the content of his spiritual life without breaking the matrices of his imagination. . . . A quantity of mythological litter still lingers in the ill-controlled zones of the mind. (18)

He then goes on to propose:

> These degraded images present to us the only possible point of departure for the spiritual renewal of modern man. It is of the greatest importance . . . to rediscover a whole mythology, if not theology, still concealed in the most ordinary, every day life of contemporary man. (18)

Penn Kemp's poetry celebrates the ordinary in everyday life, elevating it to the sacred. Although Kemp is a prolific writer, for the purposes of this book, the study has been confined to her books: *Animus* (1983), *Binding Twine* (1984), *Some Talk Magic* (1986), *Eidolons* (1988), *Throo* (1988) and *Four Women* (1999).

The frameworks offered by ecofeminism and spiritual feminism help us in understanding and contextualizing her poetry. Religion and spirituality deeply touch women's lives and feminists cannot afford to ignore these aspects. Religious symbols breathe fresh life into the otherwise profane lives of human beings. Goddess symbols in particular have led to women feeling empowered. Western thinkers have acknowledged that there has been a denigration of the female body expressed in religious taboos surrounding menstruation, childbirth, and menopause in women. Carol Christ notes that "while menstruating taboos may have originated in a perception of the awesome powers of the female body, they degenerated into a simple perception that there is something 'wrong' with female bodily functions. Later, menstruating women were forbidden to enter the sanctuary in ancient Hebrew and pre-modern Christian communities" (78). This denigration of the female body extends to childbirth as well. Feminists oppose these negative beliefs about the body. Western culture also does not hold menopausal and aging women in dignity. According to Christ, the Goddess symbol enables women to "rename" and "reclaim" the body and its cyclical processes. The different aspects of the Goddess symbol enable the empowerment of woman in all her aspects and stages. Christ says:

> the Goddess is celebrated in the triple aspect of youth, maturity, and age, or maiden, mother, and crone. The potentiality of the young girl is celebrated in the nymph or maiden aspect of the Goddess. The Goddess as mother is sometimes depicted giving birth, and giving birth is viewed as a symbol for all the creative, life-giving powers of the universe. The life-giving powers of the Goddess in her creative aspect are not limited to physical birth, for the Goddess is also seen as the crea-

> tor of all the arts of civilization, including healing, writing, and the giving of just law. Women in the middle of life who are not physical mothers may give birth to poems, songs, and books, or nurture other women, men and children. They, too, are incarnations of the Goddess in Her creative, life-giving aspect. At the end of life, women incarnate the crone aspect of the Goddess. The wise old woman, the woman who knows from experience what life is about, the woman whose closeness to her own death gives her a distance and perspective on the problems of life, is celebrated as the third aspect of the Goddess. Thus, women learn to value youth, creativity and wisdom in themselves and other women. (80)

This Goddess-centred view facilitates the acceptance of all stages of womanhood and re/claiming the body. Christ also refers to the new meanings that female bonding acquires in this context and, quoting Adrienne Rich, she writes:

> Adrienne Rich has pointed out that the mother-daughter bond perhaps the most important of woman's bonds, "resonant with charges . . . the flow of energy between two biologically alike bodies, out of which has lain in amniotic bliss inside the other, one of which has labored to give birth to the other," is rarely celebrated in patriarchal religion and culture. (83)

There is a revisioning of this relationship often through a retelling of myths like the Demeter-Persephone one. Christ points out that the Goddess symbol also has a special significance for the revaluation of body and nature and hence forms an important part in ecology movements as well (80). This perspective seeks to do away with dualisms of western thought such as spirit/ flesh and mind/ body so as to create reverence not only for human body but for the earth as a whole. It sees an interconnectedness in all creatures inhabiting the planet. Summing up the ecofeminist position Kate Rigby says:

> Indeed, for many, the Goddess is only a metaphor, personifying that animating and life-generating energy that flows through and interconnects all things. The symbol of the Goddess thus returns an aura of the sacred to the world of matter, and as such would appear to shape a spirituality that is not only feminist but also ecological in orientation, understanding the binary oppositions described within patriarchal monotheism (and, as others have pointed out, western rationalism) that have for so long contrived to make us strangers to ourselves and the earth. (26)

Ecofeminism sees a close connection between patriarchal domination of women and industrial exploitation of the earth. They would like reaffirming connections between women and nature which the liberal and socialist feminists sought to sever. Some feminists also see this link as a dangerous fallback into the hands of reactionary forces of patriarchy. Referring to Susan Griffin's influential early book *Woman and Nature* (1978), Rigby writes that "Reversing the common evaluation of the woman-nature connection, Griffin effectively redefines the feminist project as an emancipation with nature, rather than from it, as in the dominant Enlightenment tradition" (29). They are compelled to walk a tightrope in that the danger of falling into the traps of biological determination and nature-culture dichotomy always looms large. The ecofeminist spiritualist position sees a close link between woman and nature and assigns an important role to ritual. Rigby writes:

> Within ecofeminist Goddess spirituality, the conscious alignment of the self with nature is practised in the form of seasonal, solar and lunar celebrations and rites of passage, which affirm our bodily particularity, and attendant needs and desires, as the maternal locus of our earthliness and interconnectedness with others and, as such, as profoundly hierophonic, revealing the divine within the mundanity of our mortal flesh. (37)

Pointing the dangers of this position Rigby feels that it "could also lead to a narcissistic assimilation of all of nature to the self" (39). It also could lead to the marginalization of men. Nature cannot be viewed as static in idyllic terms since celebrating the cycle of seasonal change would mean something different when "the seasons themselves are changing under the impact of the greenhouse effect" (41). This position also seems to gloss over differences generated by race, class, culture and geographical location.

For poets like Penn Kemp, reclaiming the Goddess has also meant re/claiming the body as also the self. In other words, achieving wholeness away from the compartmentalization and fragmentation of life that western dichotomies often result in Kay Turner conveys as much in these words in her article "Contemporary Feminist Rituals" and says: "The suppression of the Goddess in our culture has meant the loss of images which identify personal and collective power in the female." (227)

This re/claiming enables these writers not only to empower themselves on a personal level but also in a collective sense. In the introduction to *Binding Twine,* Kemp mentions that her "task has been to transmute my personal experience into something larger, more accessible; to make my truth available, so that a correspondence is set up with the reader" (8).

Rooted in the sheer body experiences of the poet, *Binding Twine* tells the story of Kemp's custody fight for her children. However, as the critic Libby Scheier points out, while the direct use of experience in writing seems simple, "[t]here are several dangers. The writer may remain too close to the material to maintain her artistry. She might become too concerned about including all the details of what happened, rather than the core truth. Or she might simply sink into a well of emotion and write sentimentally or melodramatically" (17). Kemp manages to avoid these pitfalls. Scheier further makes a distinction between confessional poetry and personal poetry. Confessional poetry is liable to be self-pitying. "In effective personal poetry, the poet is able to put enough distance between herself and her experience both to exert, artistic control and to achieve an honest and ruthless contemplation of events. *Binding Twine* does this, and is the kind of personal poetry that is personal enough, hereby transcending limitations" (18). *Binding Twine* could very well be a novella. It is a long poem through which the reader who read with empathy can experience pain in the raw—the pain is physical and emotional. A combination of unhappy relationships, the pain of the custody battle coupled with separation from children is the raw material. Yet the seeds of transcendence are contained in it. The personal is universalized. Referring to patriarchy's suppression of the female, Judith Antonelli writes in an article titled "Feminist Spirituality: The Politics of the Psyche": "Patriarchy is based on fear of the female and the suppression of all 'female' qualities: woman, nature, the body feelings and emotion, instinct, intuition, and, finally life itself." (401)

This suppression is what poets like Penn Kemp seek release from in their works. Describing the qualities of the Anima or female principle inspiring her writing and appearing at "moments of transitions, moments of crisis and shock" in her life Kemp writes:

> Speech, 'la parole' is feminine, but words, 'le verbe,' are not. The ear is feminine, the shell, the curve of life emerging form the ocean. The cerebral-spinal fluid holds all our pre-conscious, pre-conception memories. Through the hydraulic flow and balance, we can access these memories of the etheric body and the soul. I listen to the sound of the sea-shell, to the voice of Anima. And recognize her song as my own, my deepest note. . . . Discovering my tone is discovering my self. ("A musing. . ." 54)

Certain themes such as the mother-daughter motif or self-reflexivity about writing take root in this book and remerge in later poems. She does not indulge in much word play in *Binding Twine* perhaps because she still was close to the experiences she was writing about. The poem, "The Last Time" is about her developing the ability to escape pain by developing the knack of leaving her body or separating her consciousness of self from her body:

> His hands closed on my neck
> The cord once again tightened.
>
> I flew out of body, a white
> Bird pealing, drifting
> out of bounds. (34)

In a poem titled "The Gift," Kemp addresses the other woman whom her husband began living with. The pain expressed is physical in its intensity and clearly she is mentally prepared to discard all the material wealth and the old life which she says she has grown out of:

> So you want to suck my marrow
> and strew my bones about the neighborhood.
>
> Who says you are dark?
> My bones collect themselves
> Into a new order. . .

And also:

> Take the man I ran from.
> Take the house I discard.
> Take that life. It is no longer mine.
>
> I shed a skin for you,
> The one I grew out of. (52)

The emotions in these poems are raw and arise out of her body as it were. The poems are filled with a recording of the abuses and names hurled at her including the label of 'witch' till she gathers herself to escape the negative stereotypes society tries to fit her into and empowers herself:

I let moonlight bless,
caress my huge belly,
swelling not with a
birth but old shit
and menstrual blood. (67)

Unable to fit into the ready-made moulds of patriarchy, the poet finds it necessary to forge new patterns of being. The experience of the children being taken away from her results in an anguished loss of purpose and identity she expresses· this poignantly in a poem titled "Un/Mother":

un asked, the barrage
of questions I need
no longer attend.

unanswered. Space
surrounds the ghosts.

who am I then with-
out them. Who. When . (72)

The loss of this role requires her to find new meanings in life and for her existence.

The old patterns need to be broken consciously and new ones created for her own sanity and survival. The raw pain she feels at the loss of her children is evident in the following lines from a poem titled "Passing":

We thought we were twenty
We wake up forty, Worn
with the weight of unlived
years. One morning we are
mothers by noon we are not. (96)

The loss of her children leads her to dwell on motherhood and the mother-child relationship, which is a recurring theme in her entire oeuvre. She is able to transcend her particular situation and move to 'The Great Mother' or the goddess she dwells on the maternal instinct as also her own need to be mothered and by doing this she encompasses the mother and daughter within herself.

The following lines from the poem "The Great Mother" express these feelings:

Our daughters cry out to us
as if we were mothers. Our
mothers cry out to us as if
we were daughters and mothers.

We can't answer till we know
we are mother and mothered.

Somewhere behind cerebral cortex

> rests another mother. (11)

She is helpless in changing the fact of loneliness that her daughter has to experience and the poem ends with a play on the words 'mother' and 'daughter':

> Mother daughter motheraughter
> mother ought. And then there
> are fathers. And sons. (11)

In a poem titled "Patterns" she contemplates on the established, age-old patterns of mothering":

> Giving and giving as women
> were taught by generations
> of mothers. Giving out of
> nothing. That is something
> only the goddess can expect
> to continue forever. (21)

The poem titled "My Mother Warns" reminds one of Demeter's voice with its stern warning to the daughter:

> Daughter, do not answer
> the faint cry—the one
> you almost hear
> through trailing vine.
>
> The mutter of the far-off
> bird, of the rotten
> tree: Ignore. (24)

The poet seems keen on breaking the conventional set patterns of mothering as she puts it in the following poem "Nonetheless":

> I push, push away the mothers'
> voice inside my head. (25)

By referring to it as 'mothers' voice' and not 'mother's voice' she seems to be suggesting the unison in which mothers have spoken through generations. The poet calls out to her daughter to listen along with her to "the low call/piping staccato, persistent./ Other voices./Other choices" (25). She wants to break the pattern but knows that she will come to follow her mother. However, she hopes that her daughter surprises her. The poet is referring to the entire lineage of mothers and daughters and the passing down of values. She has to conjure up ways of keeping the connection with her children and feels that the gifts she has given them are "memories and song." In a poem titled "The Dreams Multiply" she writes:

> Memories and songs from
> the middle brain act as refrain
> for you to repeat. There are

methods—This is conditioning.

Remember me. Remember what is
of value. I had so much yet to give. (43)

The mood that dominates the poem titled "The Last Presents" is one of impending loss of her children and on a Christmas afternoon, she has to break the news to her children:

Blue sky, deep snow and we lean
together against the broad trunk
Children's eyes, blue in white faces.
Their rosy cheeks. Their curious
hearts. This is our last present. (46)

The poems in *Binding Twine* convey emotion poignantly through their simplicity. The poet feels hurt by the ostracism she faces, and for being dubbed a "bad mother." Even worse was the subsequent court verdict which went against her. She is able to move from the role of mother to daughter and back to mother effortlessly and her poems contain both the voices, often running like parallel strains of music. The poem "Hand Me Down" speaks of mothers who perpetuate patriarchal values on account of their own conditioning. There is a subtle reference to the Demeter-Persephone myth in this poem:

The mothers are betrayed
into upholding traditions.
that keeps them in place.

The ritual rape of daughters
that mothers perpetuate.

And the daughters return
of their own accord.

Betrayed by the voice
in their head. The mother
speaks. The daughter

mouths the words as
her own, Compliant. (62)

There is a slight subversion of the myth in that the mothers perpetuate the ritual rape of their daughters. The poet takes on Persephone's voice in the poem "In Place of Persephone" where she revels in her eternal youth and voluntarily disappears:

I am the unfading flower
I disappear half a year.
They seek me out. Close
I am in. Closer, Closet. (65)

Persephone wants to free herself from her mother's hold. She is sought out and caught as it were. The mother's role is one, which seems to confine the poet as is expressed in the poems "Transmission" and "The Second of February." In "Transmission" she writes:

> The cord that fed me
> I feel the rest of my life.
> Wrapped around
> my neck. Cut off. (114)

In "The Second of February," the mother wonders why Persephone seems devoid of life spire of the festivities that surround her return:

> But why does the young one
> fall slack in the open arms,
> why is the purified one
> empty of essence, what has
> Possessed her, my daughter? (115)

The poet sees women progressing with each generation and feels that no shackles, not even the mother-daughter relationship, should bind women from moving ahead,

> I free you free me
> Liberation intertwined
> with a difference.
> The cycle of generation
> spirals once more. (119)

The ideas that germinate in *Binding Twine* get reworked and transmuted in Kemp's later poetry. She makes frequent use of myths particularly centring around goddesses. She claims even Anima to be an archetype. According to Ruth Falk:

> By discovering our true mythological roots we can demystify in spirit, and remythicize them; we can reclaim the power usurped by patriarchal control, we can begin to fill the overwhelming need for female models of strength and wisdom so lacking in contemporary culture. (qtd. Bella Debrida 142)

This surely is what Penn Kemp seems to be doing in reworking the myths revolving around goddesses in her poetry.

French feminists have amply endorsed and demonstrated the fact that the language of patriarchy is based on male presence and female absence. Bonnie Zimmerman writes summing up the French position:

> Woman cannot write herself in this discourse, she must create a new woman's language that will inscribe her/self. This controversial notion—that there is a Woman (what de Beauvoir and later Wittig disparage as the Eternal Feminine) to be written—produces fiction and polemics that are open, discursive, circular, fragmentary, punning and neologistical. ("Feminist Fiction. . ."185)

Penn Kemp makes ample use of word-play and circular and fragmentary structure. This is particularly evident in her long poem titled *Animus* which has six sub-sections titled: "Assent," "Formerly," "Psyche," "Descent," "By Name" and "Soundly." On the surface *Animus* could be read as a poem portraying the inner world of the woman as she falls in love, imagining that she will be perfect and whole an account of her relationship with her lover. The desire reveals itself to be illusory and realization dawns. *Animus* deals with the man-woman relationship but this time the poet is distanced from the experience. Entering and leaving a relationship is almost like a ritualistic dance with its own rhythmic pattern. One also senses a mixture of cynicism and humour in her handling of the theme of love. In this respect, it is very different in tone from *Binding Twine*.

The intimacy shared with a man has been so deep that he is a part of her psyche—the Animus within her. The layout of the verses resembles the shape of 'mandalas,' especially in the build-up of key lines to an ascent or crescendo. The rhythm of the sentence runs through them and emerging, as it were, from the unconscious, the poem transcends the personal, physical levels. As Carol Christ puts it: "Women's spiritual quest concerns a woman's awakening to the depths of her soul and her position in the universe." ("Images. . ." 329)

This is involved in every woman's reclaiming of her/self. This process is necessary for her further growth as Christ says: "Through awakening to new powers, women overcome self-negation and self hatred and refuse to be victims." (330) In this sense, Kemp deals with the relationship as devoid of feelings of self-pity or victimization, thereby marking her spiritual growth.

> Once there was a game
> he (who) would meet her—she must have been up that day
>   One step forward
> and entering into her field would for want of a better phrase fall in love
> Giant step forward. (*Animus* 30)

The moment involvement begins, separation is already on its way. It is inevitable and built into the bonding. The poet seems to say that this is the fate of all human relationships:

> One step together
> One step apart (31)

The rhythm gets broken. She is clearly referring to not just personal experience but the man-woman relationship in general. Seven years after the publication of *Animus* Penn Kemp, in an article titled, "Changing Subjects Changing Places," admitting the body's dominant role in her writing, explains, "so now I have reduced the relationship between male and female to the shifting balance of hormones. A new reductionism. My own shifting metaphor has ruled my subjects" (94). This of course is acknowledged with hindsight, perhaps after transcending certain commonplace human experiences.

The title poem "animus" (2) needs to be compared with the section titled "Psyche." There is an invocation to animus rendered in a chanting fashion. It is however, not an invocation in ordinary sense. It almost takes the form of name-calling. The word play goes from 'animus' to 'anonymous' to 'synonymous' to 'ominous' to 'misogynist enemy.' The poet throws a challenge as it were to the animus in her own psyche to emerge. It ends with Ms., apart from a break-off effect in sound, also signifies perhaps the feminists' preferred courtesy title. The concept of animus is Jungian and Coomi Vevaina sums up the framework succinctly:

> the process of individuation is an antidote to alienation. A dive into ourselves makes us aware of our fragmented state caused by false myths. By responding to archetypal figures which emerge from our own inner selves like the shadow (the dark, awkward side of our psyche), the anima or animus (the contrasexual side of our psyches), the mother, the father, the child, the Wise Old Man and the Great Mother, we become aware not only of our personal unconscious but also of our collective unconscious which, as mentioned earlier, is the psychic heritage common to all human beings and which constitutes the foundation of our psyches. (28-29)

The poet is trying to achieve wholeness in the process. As Carol Christ puts it:

> Women's new naming of self and world often reflect wholeness, a movement toward overcoming the dualisms of self and world, body and soul, nature and spirit, rational and emotional, which have plagued Western consciousness. ("Images . . ." 330)

Penn Kemp tries to overcome the dualism in her poetry and in the process transcends merely personal experience. She deconstructs sentences and words in such a conscious and well-thought-out way that it does not emerge as merely the postmodern play with surface, to achieve a kaleidoscopic effect. The poem reflects an entire philosophical system underlying it. At the same time, however, Kemp does not deconstruct language merely in keeping with radical feminist polemics. Her vision is broader than theirs and she touches the spiritual plane when language becomes redundant. The constant repetition of words and the overuse of language reduce it to a cacophony. She takes you to the point where sound tapers off and silence encompasses her very spirit. Louise Cotnoir, writing on the need for women to become "thieves of language," observes:

> We explode the dictionaries by the hypertrophy of the vocabulary used, we uproot words by suffixes made and by the invention of different words, we upset or ignore punctuation, we fracture codes and genres, we confuse pronouns. In short, it is by subverting the "thinkable" that we attempt to produce a new consciousness that is inevitably in contradiction with the society which uptill this point thought us and wrote us. ("The Marked Gender . . ."103)

Writers like Penn Kemp and Daphne Marlatt are propelled by this view as well. In the section titled "Psyche," following the direct address to animus is the line "Once having known you the certainty of seeing you moves sometimes through my body and always through my mind moves me certainly" (*Animus* 33).

This poem is written to create the effect of a 'mantra' almost with a gradual build-up from word to a whole line. Language, as it comes to the poet, is the act of creation, as it were. There is a build up of tempo imitative of the heightening of the experience itself. In the process the artificial boundaries of form and content are consciously ruptured. The form of the poem closely resembles the raw material or source of the poem. This line occurs several times and, while listening to Penn Kemp's reading of *Animus*, one can decipher at least three mental states during three different readings of the line. The first reading is rushed, full of intensity and passion—a woman in love. The second is almost unintelligible like the language of the psyche. The last one has sounds tapering off into calmness. Coherence and heightened awareness are reached through such effects. One can see the interconnectedness of the creative process and spiritual awareness. There seems to be a direct address to the radical feminists, and gynocritics in the words:

> my sisters you are voices
> in my head whispering
> "cast light upon him"
>
> but light is already cast
> he is no dark beast my sisters (*Animus* 34)

There seems to be an appeal to the radical feminists to modify their extreme stand. Kemp points to the pitfalls in their complete rejection of 'the male' and indicates that they are positing another equally oppressive system. As a result, we fail to recognize androgyny—the animus in each of us. Kemp sees them as being in danger of creating yet another stereotype:

> your thin voices
>   quaver
> like flickering shade.
>
>   I almost enter.
> when the future overcomes me
> you are off on your own
>
>   patterns'
> playback. (35)

At one level they are poems about love and being in love. In the first section of the book there are poems describing intimacy on a physical level. After this, the emotional plane of the relationship is dealt with. There is even at this stage, a separation of the 'he' from 'I.' The section "By Name" begins with a poem signifying a breakdown of coherence reflecting the limitations of language in general and syntax in particular to portray the poet's state of mind. A key line in this section is 'the spirit continues to move.' A clear shift to the spiritual plane is visible in this section. In the early part of it is still anticipation, a hoping for his return:

> I saw his shadow by
>   evening fire flicker
>   not knowing he lives
>
>   here at hearts' core
>   where self moves out
>   to other, my twin. (72)

This is not an actual person but the poet's shadow or doppelganger—a spiritual companion. And again:

a knock a voice
    at the door

    what calls you back?
    I'm busy writing you
    down. (73)

The distancing is already complete and the creative process set in motion. The male persona gradually assumes mythic dimensions:

on the first rise of the
Crescent
i belong to myself
I summon him within me
to me
stay
he comes he stands he will not sit he looms
he who appears   when the moon is full
to win moon magic from me
I know
his various guises
I know him
I ask him
To stay within me
my right side is his for the asking. (78)

The reference to the crescent moon in connection with the mental state of the poet places the male persona appears in a different dimension:

he looms
he who appears when the moon is full. (78)

These lines reinforce the mythic proportions:

with each full I am whole
i gain what the waning moon lost. (78)

This reminds one of the age-old links between the moon's phases, state of the psyche and a woman's body.

my right side
    goes quietly
        numb

animate it
    i charge you

i name you
animus. (79)

There is the invocatory tone when the poet calls on the animus in her to invigorate the anima, complement it and make her a whole individual. The artificial dualities created by patriarchy such as logic/ emotion, reason/ intuition etc. only lead to fragmentation of the self. Importantly both men and women are its victims.

In the section "Soundly," there is a return of coherence, reconciliation, a resolution but on a wholly new plane. The cycle is complete and harmony is achieved gradually. The section is suffused with the experience of the spiritual—a growth achieved through and rooted in experience:

bodies we have inhabitants a
self-enclosed totality wraps
we have shorn skins shed. (84)

The poet has now achieved a detachment from sensory experience and there is a suggestion of ethereality, which has replaced it.

a door opens a door closes in
that sudden lilt of silence (84)

New doors open when old ones close and these new ones draw the poet into silence, not music. This unusual juxtaposition is used to draw attention to the silence which is the result of self-realisation, of spiritual awakening.

As the section progresses, we come across an overtly spiritual poem in which the body-mind dichotomy is also dissolved in "the lovely rhythm of tai chi" (100). All dichotomies are unified in the old rhythm known to the poet. This is achieved through the rise and fall of energy through the spine which gives rise to "a parabola of joy" (100). The rhythm is of a different order, however, unknown hitherto since its "music is yet to be written" (100). The intricate pattern woven by the poet comes a full circle with the line "once having known you the certainty of seeing you move sometimes through my mind and always through my spirit moves me certainly" (101). The line takes on a new significance. The poet began with "once having known you the certainty of seeing you move sometimes through my mind and always through my body" (1). There is a progression from 'always through my body and sometimes through my mind' to 'sometimes through my mind all ways through my spirit' (101). There is a change from 'always' (time) to "all ways" (all paths included indicating the dimension of space). The intellect/mind is a few steps behind the spirit. Even that has to be subdued to reach 'nirvana.' These ideas are illustrated even in the layout of the poem. The performance of the poem achieves a tapering off effect unlike the way the first poem creates a quickening of tempo. The lines quoted from *Animus* have a mantric quality to them.

The collection of poems *Throo* has been called a "voiced collage. A vocal palimpsest" (appears on the jacket) by Daphne Marlatt. This is truly what it is. Demeter's wail for her Persephone heard in *Binding Twine* returns in these poems but Penn Kemp moves even beyond archetypes. The book has nine sections dedicated to nine goddesses namely Tara, Artemis, Hathor, Changing Woman, Venus, Hecate, Persephone, Demeter and Hera. The subtitle of the book is "Wise Cracking C'Odes from the Lunar Plexus." Referring to the subtitle, Kemp writes:

> I have just completed a manuscript, calling it "Wise Cracking the C'Ode of the Lunar Plexus." The lunar plexus I invented, have even positioned in the body. Its horns tip the two adrenaline glands. The crescent is in the back saddle. Now that it's been located, I'm sure scientists will discover its actuality and purpose. I'll leave that upto them. ("Amusing. . ." 56)

It is significant that a vital body part also identified by yogic practices, figures in the title. Sophie Drinker observes that Hat-hor, Bastet, Sarasvati, Bharati, Inanna, Artemis, and the Muses were all identified with "singing and dancing and the playing of certain instruments" (47). In her Tara poems, one can hear echoes of the idea of Adi Shakti (the Hindu Primal Goddess) who represents wisdom and creation on all levels, possesses diversity expressed through her ten forms (Dasa Maha Vidya), one of which is Tara. They reveal the inner workings of both the universe and the psyche once the veil of appearances is pulled down. As David Frawley points out, each of the ten forms of the goddess represents a particular approach to self-realization, to knowledge of that is within us and which transcends time and transient identity (72). Tara is the power of sound (shabda shakti). Dr. Frawley observes that the term 'Tara' means deliverer or saviour, from the Sanskrit root 'tri,' meaning 'to take across' as to take across a river, the ocean, a mountain, or any difficult situation (72).

Tara is the feminine form of Om or Om personified as a goddess. Tara is the unmanifest sound that exists in the ether of consciousness through which we can go beyond the entire manifestation. Since Om precedes all other mantras, Tara contains within herself all mantras, and only through her grace can one come to understand and use them properly. Tara is perhaps the most important goddess of mantric knowledge, the very personification of mantra Shakti. This seems to be the underlying significance of the Tara poems. The poet's reverence and humility before the goddess is brought out in the set of Tara poems. The goddess is manifest in the smallest particle of the cosmos. The goddess' play or 'leela' with her creation can be clearly seen as Shirin Kudchedkar observes in her article: "The Play of Line and Image in the Poetry of Penn(y) Kemp" (104).

> matter
> appearingreappearing
> manyonemany (*Throo* 10)

The above lines from the poem seem to suggest that the goddess is the essence of all creation appearing in manifold forms but is essentially one, seems to be the significance of the above lines. The monotheistic impulse is quite evident. Consciousness is manifested in through matter, diverse forms, and the poet seems to be stressing this. In the opening lines from *Tranceform* the poet writes:

> we are all your surrounding whose form is

of necessity feeling encoded in landscape. (*Throo* 10)

The ecofeminist spiritualist position on the goddess and nature is expressed by the priestess Starhawk in the words that "The goddess is manifest not just in human life, but in the interwoven chain of relationships that link all forms of life" (417).

Describing the concept of goddess and the position of the individual in the cosmos, she says:

> Each individual self, then, is linked by ties of blood and affection to a family, and by the bonds of love and trust to the coven, which in turn is a part of the large human community, the culture and society in which it is found, and that culture is part of the biological/geological community of Planet Earth and the cosmos beyond, the dance of being which we call Goddess. (418)

This is the position that Kemp seems to take with regard to the self in relation to the goddess and the cosmos. When the poet attempts to describe the spiritual experience of having a glimpse of the goddess, there is a breakdown of conventional syntax and language as a whole. The poet deconstructs language in a two-pronged way—to write and valorize the body and to express her spiritual experiences which also need a different idiom.

mother rock me
rock mother me
mother rocks me
rock smother me
rocks mother me
    mother
    rock.
    me
I am mothered I am mother I am moth mutter moth mother must

    might must
        night dust
    mother might
        mother must
    mother rock
        mother dust (*Throo* 11)

There is a movement from a vulnerable position "I am mothered" to "I am mother"—a position of strength. The play on the word mother has almost a lullaby effect when recited and the further break up of 'mother' to 'moth,' 'mutter, moth, mother, must' reminds one of the 'wild zone' of women's experiences or the pre-Oedipal language of the semiotic level being used to show how the poet needs to grapple with the limitations of language to verbalize an experience, not just feminine but also spiritual and therefore unique in itself. Penn Kemp expresses her thoughts on the need for a new idiom in these words:

> I have been interested in developing a language for the body so that I can be continually aware of its processes. But that language is direct and spatial, non-linear. Its form is that of a poem. I have

> become more aware of various forms of energies as I write, but they are kinesthetic and so by nature impossible to describe in words, except by analogy. ("Amusing . . ." 55)

Penn Kemp quite clearly wants to incorporate the body's corporeality and experiences into her spirituality and understands the fallacy of dichotomous thinking that creates an unnatural mind-body divide.

In *Throo* Kemp draws on goddesses from all ancient civilizations suggesting perhaps, their interconnectedness. The mother-daughter dialogue, a recurring motif in her poetry, reappears in *Throo*. She acknowledges that her writing got the impetus from her children talks and stories.[7] It is played out in complete anguish in *Binding Twine*. In *Throo,* it appears as parallel voices of mother and daughter in the collection dedicated to the Afro-American goddess-Changing Woman.

You round all night you clear	*see that sun up there?*
You call in the language	*Well, that's me.*
behind words	*the moon too.*
You say little	***A girl moon***
You say things	*When I move my head*
Things are	*clouds move*
what you light	*When I walk*
My lips serve	*they walk with me*
ecstasy	*When I run*
Place of panic	*they come too.*
Place of bliss	*Trees follow me around.*
one and the same	*All I have to do is move*
I spread	*my head*
dark	*to move*
blue	*everything (Throo* 36)

The child is in awe of the cosmos and her experiences of the world are characteristically sensorial. Concepts have not contaminated the purity of experience of the cosmos. Nothing is beyond her reach. It is perhaps the Zen way of not allowing language and logic to mar experience. In the second section, the child's voice has already imbibed the mother's words and reproduces it. In the section on Persephone, there is an attempt to make a connection with foremothers much in keeping, with the feminists' notion of having to establish their own literary foremothers and rewriting themselves into history.

> my feet no longer find my daughter by themselves
> I am almost normal
>   almost content
> grandmother where are you? (66)

There is an appeal to an older persona, "kind spirit guide" (60). The older spirit guides heals some of the pain of separation and the comforting takes place on a physical-cum-spiritual plane. The young one is drawn into her fold. Persephone's voice comes through effectively in

"Some Talk Magic" (*Throo* 67) for there is mixture of the plaintive, childlike, trusting archetypal Persephone qualities in it. Demeter's voice interposes—warning, protective, and yet aware that her daughter may not choose the well-trodden path of her foremothers. Penn Kemp writes that "Some Talk Magic" was partly written in amusement and partly in angst, as a record and an exploration of how language patterns are developed. "From listening to my children's language and imitating the way they constructed a world out of words, I became a sound poet."[8] Penn Kemp also writes that writing for her "is a process of changing . . . remembering the others in me" (92). She acknowledges the plurality of voices in her work and feels that "[e]ach voice writes her own concern. And then is recognized as singular when read back later" (92). In "Becoming," the contradiction between the need to protect and letting her daughter go is well expressed. There is a warning the mother issues against listening to the seductive call of the underworld in the use of the words "faint cry" and 'through the trailing vine' (*Throo* 69).

Later she warns:
And you will die if you
listen. We all will. (69)

These two lines link the archetypal situation to the condition of womanhood in general. By intertwining the mother's voice with the daughter's, she problematizes the mother-daughter relationship and brings out the contradictions that it is fraught with. Matrophobia—the fear women often feel about becoming replicas of their mothers and the resultant hatred of their mothers is well-documented by psychologists. The poet accepts her connection with her mother and speculates whether her daughter will be different:

My daughter's voice has not
changed. Maybe she will
surprise us. (69)

While reading the poem "The Second of February," one recalls the poet's personal anguish at being separated from her daughter for long periods. She is perhaps mourning her lost girlhood, the child-like innocence with which she perceived the world. Kemp is surely exploring the multitude of voices speaking 'throo' every woman. There is something decidedly individual in the tragic quality of each woman's experience. There is also sharing and bonding which is a consequence of shared experience, an echoing and a re-echoing of the mythic goddess' voices.

The section on Demeter is replete with nature imagery. Images of fertility and growth abound in the poems. The contrast between Persephone and Demeter are highlighted in "C'Loud":

The daughter has returned again
this spring to her mother.
goddess of grain, of harvest,
with a difference.

She hears with her the taint
of Experience, Queen now
of the Dead. She bears a false

promise of flowers for
unfulfilled fruit (*Throo* 78)

And later:

Not knowing what is happening
Gaia turns. (78)

Persephone, who is now tainted by experience and her acquaintance with the underworld, strikes a false chord in nature's harmony but the earth goddess continues her cycle, unaware of these changes. With a little imagination, one can understand what the poet is talking about womankind. Patriarchal control taints purity and richness. Earth however, is herself a goddess who continues her own course irrespective of the corruption that creeps in. The poet is perhaps referring to the staying power of woman. The Zen idea of how an eternity can be caught in a moment is expressed in the poem "Becoming" in the book *Travelling Light*. It is a meditative experience that reveals it.

Focus upon a single facet, peer through
its slate of coloured glass and you
will witness the scene you intend,
zoomed suddenly, sharply, close.
There do you see, can you hear?
    All events of our dear earth are
        In these facets, caught in that split
    between becoming and dissolution

One can witness eternity in a single
moment in close proximity.

And further:

Lies and desire
just cloud the perfect looking glass.
The body mirrors a pure receptacle.

The knowledge burns pretension off
    like lens in sun. Nothing left in
mind but the tremulous and sure
    attempt toward embodiment. (*Travelling Light* 34)

Lies and desire, which constitute the illusory world, cast a film on a "perfect looking glass" and the body is relegated to the position of being a mere "receptacle." Knowledge helps one get rid of pretension. One is reminded of 'jnana yoga' or the path of knowledge as one of the ways of attaining truth through a process of 'neti,' 'neti,' or rejection of all falsehood.

In the poem "Ends and Means" Penn Kemp achieves that perfect blend of the theme of spiritual growth and the creative process. It is a lightly structured poem and the poet, with a few deft strokes, can, through nature imagery, arrive at an important philosophical truth. She uses nature as a metaphor.

> The difference between flowers
> that fruit or not is only a nodule (*Travelling Light* 51)

She is here referring to the fruition of an idea that takes artistic form through creativity as well as the maturing of one's consciousness. This view can be supported by the last stanza:

> Patterns. How we toss
> to and fro still expectant mid-way
> through our lives. Almost mature, almost
> coming into our own. Seed potency
> bursting beyond hard casement
> through the boundary of design. (51)

The leap from experience to creating a work of art by imposing a pattern is what an artist struggles with. The potential within each one is waiting to burst out of the constraints. The poet seems to be saying that this is maturity. In one of the poems dedicated to Hecate in *Throo* she writes:

> I write to give this shadow
>   a mirror of herself
>   thru these reflecting eyes. (61)

These lines again demonstrate her self-reflexive writing. She refers to herself and the purpose of writing as being to write her/self. In order to be able to do this, language has to be turned upside down. In a poem dedicated to Hera called "The New Lectionary," she plays on the word Heraclites and creates a new one 'Hera clit (or) us' (89) and addresses the goddess as:

> Hera, who
> woos
> womb and
> woman (*Throo* 90)

These illustrations go to show that although Penn Kemp's work is predominantly spiritual in nature, she is deeply concerned about social issues as well. For instance, her concern about the mindless consumerism that is ravaging society, is well brought out in these lines from a poem titled "Night Orchestra":

> The sound of the perpetual
> twentieth century
> colonizing our future
> with a dominant beat, sales
> pitched for comfort, con-
> venience, reliance on

> appliance. (On Our Own Spoke)

The break up of the word 'convenience' suggests conning people into comfort and encouraging dependence on consumer products.

Her entire oeuvre reflects the body experiences of woman whether traumatic as in physical abuse recorded in *Binding Twine* or celebratory as in her later poems. The spiritual experiences either visionary or meditative emanate from body consciousness as expressed in one of her poems titled "Flux, Flash, Flood":

> A fever of estrogen deprivation confuses my cooling system. ("On Her Own Spoke")

Menopausal feelings are recorded but in a detached manner. The body again is only a take-off point. Kemp certainly goes a long way in breaking the body-mind barrier. She writes endorsing the dominant influence of the body in her writing, "Poetry has betrayed me. Metaphor has betrayed me. My body dominates me" ("Changing. . ." 93).

Again she writes of how the subject of her writing has been body-centred:

> My life has been changing the subject. A new explanation and my shape shifts again. My w(hole) definition of myself has been through birthing as creativity. While the metaphor holds, my body could not. I forgot to ask, birth what? At what cost? My pelvis split giving birth to my first child, and seven times since. In many ways that split reflects profoundly a change in self/shape from child/woman to woman with child who splits ad infinitum. Am I subject to objectification, that nothing is wholly good. And I object, but the subject shifts the shape around. (94)

There is however, a larger overriding vision that emerges through her work as in the long sound poem "When the Heart Parts" written to record her father's death. One finds a plurality of voices here—her mother's, brother's, father's, the doctor's, friend's, sounds of the life saving machines and the public address system in the hospital. What comes through this poem which is a mixture of prose and poetry, is mourning, grief and anguish but also acceptance of death and the love transmitted particularly through the female voices that keeps one tied to life till "ready for death." Life and Death coexist and the family rejuvenates itself with a new birth—that of her brother's child soon after the father's death. Only Love keeps the wheels turning. Love is needed for Life to sustain itself on the planet. Strength and life flow from the women who keep the heart in the "hearth," at home. The case for the spiritual worldview is put forward aptly by Judith Antonelli in her article "The Politics of the Psyche" when she writes:

> The essence of a spiritual view of politics lies in the perception that matter is a manifestation of energy, that material reality reflects and symbolizes psychic reality. An obvious example is that emotional conflicts often emerge in the form of physical illness. This is not to deny that material reality also gives rise to energy patterns—for life is a cyclical process, not a linear one, and therefore both can be true. (402)

This brings out the validity of both the worldviews. Penn Kemp's poetry seems to assert the validity of both aspects of reality. Her work is rich storehouse of memory of lived experience, whether it is a human relationship or meditation. She manages to trance/scribe and leaves us trance/formed through the genuineness of her work and the power of language. Word play comes easily to her but far from being mere surface play, she uses it as a device to deconstruct language and hit a core of truth lying beneath it.

The writers studied in this chapter seek to break free of the confines imposed by the language of patriarchy through etymology, deconstruction and word play but seem keen to expose the effects that societal strictures and taboos have on women's self perception and perception of their bodies. This, they tend to do by working within the Symbolic Order and sometimes succeed in breaking free of its shackles. The process of coming into their own as individuals and artists seems to be a rather painful one for most part.

NOTES

1. They also break down barriers between "high" art forms and popular forms. Audrey Thomas for instance, uses newspaper reports, star forecasts, advertisements etc. in her narrative.
2. Isobel's mother is a classic example of the Phallic or Terrible Mother in the Lacanian sense of having internalized patriarchal values to the extent of having become an agent of patriarchy herself.
3. For an in-depth analysis of the influence of mothering patterns or the process of individuation of the girl child in an extension and a reinterpretation of Freud's theory, useful for feminist analysis, see Nancy Chodorow's classic text, *The Reproduction of Mothering: Psychoanalysis and the Sociology of Gender.*
4. Lola Lemire Tostevin is admittedly influenced by Julia Kristeva's ideas of the 'semiotic' and her privileging of maternal space.
5. This dialogic relation between the Symbolic and the semiotic in Laura's narrative sets up a plurality of voices in the Bakhtinian sense and enables Tostevin to include the masculine discourse as well.

6, 7 & 8 are excerpts from Penn Kemp's e-mail to me, dated 14 May, 1999. (I would like to express my deep gratitude to Penn Kemp for permitting me to use excerpts from her e-mail dated 14 May 1999 and poems from *On Our Own Spoke* [Pendas productions, 1995]: Dialogue for and With Young Children and Mothers.)

Chapter Four

Writing the Body by Women of Colour

The ideas suggested by the chapter's title need to be problematized. "Writing the Body" or écriture au feminine refers to a mode of writing propagated and practised by French feminists as theorists and writers as also the Québecoise writers and some Anglophone women writers in Canada. Can this notion be extended to the works of women writers of colour? The second idea which needs to be problematized is that of "women of colour" or "the third world woman writer." Women of colour come from different races, and nations with varied historical experiences. In the context of Canada the term is used to refer mostly to immigrant writers. The concept of "the third world woman writer" need not refer to immigrant writers alone for it can also refer to writers located in the so-called Third World countries as well. "Third World" is again a misnomer for it bunches together people from different countries with different historical experiences. It is necessary to clarify these ideas at the outset. A similar problem occurs while referring to Western feminism/feminists." The idea of "third world women" is often used by the first world feminists as a means of homogenizing, vastly differing experiences for convenience than out of ignorance. As Chandra Talpade Mohanty writes in her influential essay, "Under Western Eyes: Feminist Scholarship and Colonial Discourse":

> An analysis of 'sexual difference' in the form of cross-culturally singular, monolithic notion of patriarchy or male dominance leads to the construction of a similarly reductive and homogeneous notion of what I call 'the third word difference' that stable ahistorical something that apparently oppresses most if not all the women in these countries. And it is in the production of this 'third world difference' that Western feminisms appropriate and 'colonize' the constitutive complexities which characterize the lives of women in these countries. It is in this process of discursive homogenization and systematization of the oppression of women in the third world that power is exercised in much of the recent feminist discourse, and this power needs to be defined and named. (174)

These words of caution are important for any researcher working on writers of colour to prevent her/him from falling into the trap of trying to dismantle the master's house with his own tools. This is especially useful when one is working within a theoretical paradigm such as "writing the body" which rose partly as a reaction to white, mainstream, liberal feminism. Facile applications of the theory to the works of coloured women writers are what one must refrain from. One also needs to guard against the stereotyping and homogenizing of the experiences of the women of the third world in the manner of some western critics studying women of the third world. This idea is aptly expressed by Valerie Amos and Pratibha Parmar:

> Feminist theories which examine our cultural practices as "feudal" residues or label us "traditional," also portray us as politically immature women who need to be versed and schooled in the ethos of Western feminism. They need to be continually challenged. (qtd. Mohanty 177)

4.1 Differences within Difference

There are a number of remarkable differences in the way women writers of colour write the body in comparison with the French feminists, or the Québecoise and white Anglophone writers in Canada. What immediately comes to mind is that writers of colour do not seem to be celebrating the body for its own sake unlike some white women writers who seem to do it. The body often serves as a site to play out their other struggles. The body becomes a metaphor to bring out instances of the triple bind they are in—of sex, race and class unlike the white writers who mainly pit their critique against the agencies of patriarchy; language being the foremost one. Even with reference to language, writers of colour are triply challenged in that they have to stave off not just its patriarchal biases but also those of race and class. In other words, there is a more significant agenda than merely celebrating the body they work from and which they tend to prioritize over the body. This is true of writers like Dionne Brand or Kaushalya Bannerji who challenge heterosexuality both through their writing and lifestyles. Expressing this view eloquently Kadiatu Kanneh writes in "Feminism and the Colonial Body":

> But it's not just in feminism that the bodies of Black people have been metaphorically invaded, analysed and represented by liberal, paternalist (or maternalist) principles. Where racial identity lies in the body, and its link to racism, culture and psychology has been endlessly documented by Western scientists, anthropologists, travel writers, photographers and journalists.. . . . Black female identities are not simply figurative or superficial sites of play and metaphor, but occupy very real political spaces of diaspora, dispossession and resistance. What is complicated is the simultaneity of suffering and power, marginalization and threat, submission and narcissism, which accrue to Black and women's bodies and their representation in racist cultures. (348)

The above lines clearly delineate the overriding concerns that dominate the works of black writers.[1] The necessity for 'difference' to be read in terms of not just sexual difference, is seconded by a mainstream writer like Lola Lemire Tostevin when she writes:

> It seems crucial . . . that the female subject writing herself into representation conceive herself not only through sexual difference and/or sexual preference but by a multiplicity of differences that cut across language, accent, race, class, gender, sexuality, form. . . . Differences between men and women, women and women, and perhaps more importantly within each woman. (223)

The mainstream, barring a few writers has notoriously ignored writers of colour or has subjected them to tokenism. This view is angrily put forth by well-known South Asian writer and critic Himani Bannerji. While referring to the attitude of critics in an all North American, white conference she says: "You are rendered invisible by the fact that there is no place for you in the mainstream, they will not organize a place for you, but they will make this little excursion into slum life." (23) The above lines bring to light the condescending attitude adopted by mainstream, white academia even towards established writers of renown. Similar sentiments are echoed by Makeda Silvera. When referring to white, Mainstream's response to the Black feminist movement she says: "It seems as if a Black radical feminist is too much of a threat to white feminists and to their protected literary world, a world which, I found, does not challenge racism or classism within society." (193)

In the same article Silvera points to the sheer indifference and callousness exhibited by white feminists towards issues concerning black writers and the black community as if racism was a problem that blacks had to deal with as she writes·

> For Black women this entails a day-to-day struggle against racism which is cast upon us by white feminists who remain blind to racism—to white skin privilege—and who continuë to see the world of women as a world without internal contradictions. We feel that if we do not deal with these internal contradictions we will end up with a world that is not radically changed. (194-95)

The objections that these writers of colour mainly have vis-à-vis white feminists are firstly, that they demonstrate complete indifference to the racial problems and other differences to be dealt with. Secondly, they harbour stereotypes about women of colour. These views are expressed by Himani Bannerji during the course of a discussion among writers of colour in the following way: "They talk about women as an empty category. They will not talk about women as class, about a particular type of woman, about women as race, so it leaves you very empty at the end." (10)[2]

Mainstream, white feminists also subscribe to stereotypes about women of colour. They too see them as traditional and male identified and feel that their struggles ought to be confined to the domestic sphere. As Makeda Silvera points out during the same discussion: "The latest issue has been how patriarchal our culture is and how male identified women of colour and immigrant women are. We are labelled male-identified every time we talk about struggling with Third World men to end racism and imperialism." (12)

All this goes to show that not only do the concerns and agenda of the women writers of colour differ vastly from mainstream white feminists but also that as writers, the strategies and modes they adopt consequently differ. Claire Harris in an article titled "Working with/out a net" throws light on this aspect:

> For it is the quest for an authentic black sensibility, for the reclamation of the black self, and the placing of that self casually, and truthfully in Canada which is seen as vaguely threatening. Not surprisingly. Such reality-based writing is bound to challenge the peculiarly Canadian myths of tolerance and humane objectivity. For the artist, self-definition is of primary importance. But unlike the self-definition of men, everywhere accepted as the particular illustrating the universal, the self-definition of the black woman is seen as both self-indulgence and irrelevant. (74)

The notion of the body as conceived by French feminists is extremely problematic for marginalized women who accuse them of essentialism and biologism. This protest has been eloquently expressed by Brenda Carr in her analysis of M. Nourbese Philip's work in the following lines:

> Until recently, the most prominent academic discourses, even within feminist practice, through which the social subject and her body have been through were psychoanalytic and semiotic. But are jouissance, desire, and codification the only modalities that our theorizing can register and account for? What of "the practical body," the "useful body," "the intelligible body"? The pained body? (75)

The body experiences of women of colour have been significantly different from their white counterparts and this is surely reflected in their writing their bodies as also in their use of the body as a metaphor. Informed by this awareness it would be more meaningful to study their works as these issues are likely to find expression in them.

Maxine Baca Zinn and Bonnie Thornton Dill propound the notion of multiracial feminism in an attempt to resist monolithic categories like "third world" or "women of colour." They write:

> First, multiracial feminism asserts that gender is constructed by a range of interlocking inequalities, what Patricia Hill Collins calls a "matrix of domination." The idea of a matrix is that several fundamental systems work with and through each other. People experience race, class, gender and sexuality differently depending upon their social location in the structures of race, class, gender and sexuality. For example, people of the same race will experience race differently depending upon their location in the class structure as working class, professional managerial class, or unemployed; in the gender structure as female or male; and in structures of sexuality as heterosexual, homosexual, or bisexual. (327)

These lines foreground the complexities involved in writing the coloured female body. They go on to say, "Multiracial feminism, in our view, focuses not just on differences but also on the way in which differences and domination intersect and are historically and socially constituted. It challenges feminist scholars to go beyond the mere recognition and inclusion of difference to reshape basic concepts and theories of our disciplines." (329) The works of these writers need to be studied keeping these complex issues in mind.

Theorists like Barbara Smith and bell hooks have proposed the need for different theoretical tools to study this literature due to the different space that these women write from. Smith advocates the need of evolve a different methodology. In her influential essay "Toward a Black Feminist Criticism," she opines that the black feminist critic must begin with a "primary commitment to exploring how both sexual and racial politics and black and female identity are inextricable elements in black women's writing; she would also work from the assumptions that black women writers constitute an identifiable literary tradition" (163). She goes on to show how the critic would have to be familiar with this verifiable tradition. Of course one has to remember that Caribbean writers in Canada like Brand and Philip have lamented the lack of this tradition for them and have felt that their writing would perhaps have been different had it been in the United States. As first generation writers in diaspora they are in the process of putting down these roots. This however, does not invalidate Smith's advocacy of the need for a different paradigm for the critic to work from. bell hooks is critical of much feminist theory, in that it has become elitist and merely a preoccupation of academics. It does not seem rooted in reality. She is critical of French feminist theory for the same reason. Referring to the recent linguistically oriented theories, she writes in *Talking Back*:

> While such work enriches our understanding of gender politics, it is important to remember that this is not a universal discourse, that it is politically and culturally specific, and emerges from specific relationships particular French feminist scholars have to their political and social reality. Two thinkers whose work immediately comes to mind are Luce Irigaray (*Speculum of the Other Woman*) and Julia Kristeva (*Desire in Language*). Although this work honours the relationship between feminist discourse and political practice, it is often used within university settings to establish a select intellectual elite and to reinforce and perpetuate systems of domination, most obviously white western cultural imperialism. When any feminist theory is employed in this way, feminist movement to end sexist domination is undermined. (40)

hooks therefore feels that much of the prevailing theory has no touch with reality and that is seen as an unhealthy trend that robs the feminist struggle of its vitality. Writers like bell hooks are equally against the tendency to get ghettoized. Since oppressed groups constantly seek new strategies of resistance they seek strategic engagements with other contemporary theories. For example, she looks at the postmodern critique of identity and finds its "critique of essentialism as it pertains to the construction of identity" (26) a significant point. Within the black community she advocates a plurality of voices and subjectivities. Similarly, she finds the postmodern deconstruction of "master narratives" useful, as the narratives of marginalized groups have been silenced. bell hooks has also problematized the notion of sexuality and this thought is reflected in the works of black writers in the US and Canada. hooks points out that race and sex have always been overlapping discourses in the United States since slavery. She writes in an essay titled, "Reflections on Race and Sex":

> The black women's bodies were the discursive terrain, the playing fields where racism and sexuality converged. Rape both right and rite of the white male dominating group was a cultural norm. Rape was also an apt metaphor for European imperialist colonization of Africa and North America. (57)

Theory is grounded in the materiality of the body. Violence, in terms of rape and slavery, has been the dominant experience of the black community. Sexuality is linked to power in this context. hooks writes in the same essay:

> Sexuality has always provided gendered metaphors for colonization. Free countries equated with free men, domination with castration, the loss of manhood, and rape—the terrorist act re-enacting the drama of conquest, as men of the dominating group sexually violate the bodies of women who are among the dominated. The intent of this act was to continually remind dominated men of their loss of power; rape was a gesture of symbolic castration. (57)

hooks also points out that there is no psychosexual history of slavery that studies the multidimensional aspects of this domination, even the physical one. She laments that black intellectuals have unquestioningly accepted the use of these gendered metaphors and have themselves internalized the very same ones. The tendency to see race and class as separate issues undermines the resistance and splinters the black community. hooks is therefore against the promotion of an either/or competition between the oppressive systems. Language conspires to splinter the community with its in-built gender biases centred around the sexual nuances of meaning as hooks sees it. She likewise calls for a rethinking of aesthetics. She acknowledges that in their artistic products as in other aspects of their lives, black artists have to address/confront the dominant discourses. As a critical black theorist, she is aware of the plurality of experiences and artistic productions coming from her community and wants complete freedom for that. This view is expressed by her in these words:

> There can never be one critical paradigm for the evaluation of an artistic work. In part, a radical aesthetic acknowledges that we are constantly changing positions and locations, that our needs and concerns vary, that these diverse directions must correspond with shifts in critical thinking. Narrow limiting aesthetics within the black community tend to place innovative black artistry on the margins. (111)

For the black writer the margin as a location, becomes a strategic point from which to speak. It becomes a space created from which one gets a different view of reality—the outer and the inner. More than anything else, according to bell hooks, it becomes a place one chooses to be located at as a space of resistance. This enables one to perceive the centre-margin paradigm differently. She writes:

> I am located in the margin. I make a definite distinction between that marginality which is imposed by oppressive structures and that marginality one chooses as site of resistance—as location of radical openness and possibility. (153)

These ideas lead to a more sensitized understanding of the works of women writers of colour.

4.2 Writers in Diaspora

Equally strong challenges to mainstream theories of "writing the body" come from Black women writers in Canada such as Dionne Brand and M. Nourbese Philip. These women writers are now to be considered in this section. The Combahee River Collective, a statement made by the Black Feminist Movement in 1977 makes their stand towards men adequately clear in the following words:

> Although we are feminists and lesbians, we feel solidarity with progressive Black men and do not advocate fractionalization that white women who are separatists demand. . . . We struggle together with Black men against racism, while we also struggle with Black men about sexism. (213)

They are therefore, not on a confrontation course with Black men, nor want to live in a utopia, devoid of men. The statement also goes on to reject notions of biological determinism as being antithetical to its survival and further questions the adequacy of ideas of lesbian separatism. It feels that issues of sex cannot be separated from those of race and class since these oppressions are experienced simultaneously by Black women in their daily lives. These issues have not been addressed or acknowledged by even the radical, white feminists. They recognize the need to evolve their own agenda, find their own voice and evolve a new idiom as marginalized people. Audre Lorde puts forth this view eloquently in her influential essay, "The Master's Tools Will Never Dismantle the Master's House" in the following lines:

> Those of us who stand outside the circle of this society's definition of acceptable women; those of us who have been forged in the crucibles of difference; those of us who are poor, who are lesbians, who are black, who are older, know *that survival is not an academic skill.* It is learning how to stand alone, unpopular and sometimes reviled, and how to make common cause with those other identified as outside the structures, in order to define and seek a world in which we can all flourish. It is learning how to take our differences and make them strengths. For the maser's tools will never dismantle the master's house. (99)

What one understands from the above lines is that unlike radical feminism which celebrates and revels in difference, there is the notion of using difference as a strategic tool simply out of necessity arising out of the fact of being on the fringes of society. The lament of not being understood by mainstream feminists is echoed by Gloria Anzaldua when she writes: "The lesbian of colour is not only invisible, she does not even exist. Our speech is inaudible. We speak in tongues like the outcastes and the insane." (165)

She assigns a very significant role to writing since only when women of colour write can their authentic stories be heard. And they need to write to avoid erasure. She says: "The act of writing is the act of making soul, alchemy. It is the quest for the self, for the centre of the self, which we women of colour have come to think of as 'other'—the dark, the feminine." (169)

It is quite evident that even their practice of writing they would differ vastly with this deeper, underlying concern. She advocates writing about all that is close to women's lives assuring that nothing is too trivial and that the danger lies in sacrificing the particular to the universal. She advises women in these words:

> Write of what most links us with life, the sensation of the body, the images seen by the eye, the expansion of the psyche in tranquillity: moments of high intensity, its movement, sounds, thoughts. *Even though we go hungry we are not impoverished of experiences.* (172)

She however, points out in the same essay that writing is not always simple or comfortable and is beset with dangers:

> Writing is dangerous because we are afraid of what the writing reveals: the fears, the angers, the strengths of a woman under a triple or quadrulpe oppression. Yet in that very act lies our survival because a woman who writes has power. And a woman with power is feared. (171)

In this powerful essay, Anzaldua clarifies that the lesbian writer of colour has a special and risky mission. Similar views are echoed by Dionne Brand about writing poetry in an interview with Eva Tihanyi:

> Why I think poetry can be dangerous—and that's different from being dangerous, I suppose is as Adrienne Rich says in one of her essays, that poetry is the least commoditized art. That is, one can not sell it really. It resists markets, commercialism. And perhaps in today's world it can offer an alternative to the unrelenting idiocy of corporate culture. (9)

Brand is very clear about her purposes. She says in the same interview that she writes about the world around her and that writing is a potent act: "So if writing can stir us to think about who we want to be, it can stir us from repressive ways of thinking and oppressive ways of being, then I want to keep writing." (9)

Her poetry espouses these aims. In her poetry it is difficult to disengage the personal from the political. Her collection titled *No Language is Neutral* contains both in ample measure for there is a continuous engagement of the personal with the political. Several people have been critical of the multicultural policy of Canada, in that it seems to be a convenient cover to maintain ethnic boundaries which inevitably lead to compartmentalization and even ghettoization. Dawn Thompson, one of its vehement critics, writes: "The tenacious idea of a mosaic was an aesthetically appealing metaphor for passive tolerance that did little to change a radically unequal situation." (56)

Thompson, in the same article, demonstrates how identity politics works hand in hand with multiculturalism as a policing process. Similar views are expressed by Trinh Minh-ha as she writes that those in a dominant position want "a difference or an otherness that will not go so far as to question the foundation of their beings and makings. [They seek the *unspoiled* African, Asian or Native American, who remains preoccupied with his/her image of the *real* native—the truly different—than with the issues of hegemony, racism, feminism and social change." (88) This attitude often leads the dominant community into tokenism which is resented by these writers. These larger concerns and issues preoccupy women writers of colour like Dionne Brand, M. Nourbese Philip, Beatrice Culleton, Shani Mootoo and Joy Kogawa and some of their works are scrutinized in this section.

Dionne Brand and Marlene Philip also evince a keen interest in the issue of language since it is so intricately tied to subjectivity and representation. Their works are performative texts which exhibit these concerns in form and substance. *No Language is Neutral* is a text illustrative of the crucial issues that engage women writers of colour in the Afro-Caribbean diaspora. Dionne Brand exhibits the ambivalence of identity and place typically experienced by this community. Brand is from Trinidad, a place which Claire Harris documents in her article titled "Poets in Limbo" as being "colonized earlier and more deeply than any other part of the world" (116).

4.3 Dionne Brand and the Politicization of Language

Dionne Brand uses the body as a metaphor to write about the theft of language just as Marlene Philip does in the poem "Discourse on the Logic of Language." In the poem titled "Return" she shows how some things never change while some others do. The poet returns to her homeland and the associations of the place with memories of slavery come crowding back to her. That the colonizer has left an indelible mark on the Caribbean culture and language is indicated with the puns on the word "white washed." The heat and the place itself bring associations of the past, colonial as well as personal. It is however, not nostalgia of a conventional kind or for its own sake. Poverty and exploitation are the unchanged facts even in the postcolonial scene. They are now under different masters but the exploitation continues. These views are contained in the lines:

> bare-footed hot, women worried, still the faces, masked in sweat and sweetness, still the eyes watery, ancient, still the hard, distinct, brittle smell of slavery. (10)

Memory and re/covery of history are overriding concerns of the poet throughout the text. Philip assigns a very crucial role to this memory as having potential for subversion and writes that it "has a potentially kinetic quality and must impel us to action" (20).[3] Brand, in the lines mentioned above is trying to recapture images of the work worn bodies of slave women. These are different kinds of bodies that require to be written about for her own self and for posterity.

The poems addressed to the women rebels Phyllis and Jackie, have a tone of respect and admiration. Heroic qualities and their strength are portrayed. The tone suggests the familiarity enjoyed by the poet with these women and her bonding with them. Although both are public figures, there is a personal note in these poems. In "Phyllis" she records an endearing image of the imprisoned revolutionary in these lines:

> Phyllis, I remember your laugh, luminous and bubbling in the flaming dark evening and the moment after, your eyes serious, searching for your glasses. (12)

Phyllis is evidently a woman with a sense of humour and fun, not a stereotypical, intellectual revolutionary figure. The last few lines give her an almost legendary quality:

> Phyllis, they said you defied the prison guards and talked through their shouts to be quiet your laugh clanging against the stone walls your look silencing soldiers. (13)

These lines show the courage demonstrated by the leader in Grenada in defying the authority of the repressive regime. In the poem titled "Blues Spiritual for Mammy Prater," Brand's anger is a controlled one. The anger is shown as if it resides in Mammy Prater in the following lines:

> she knew that if she had the patience, to avoid killing a white man that I would see this photograph. (17)

The poet is perhaps referring to the pent-up anger in black women after experiencing centuries of exploitation when any number of them could have taken revenge. It would however, have been suicidal since they would not have survived to tell their stories to the future generations of black women. They were denied their language and education and could not write their histories. But Brand says, "she took care not to lose the signs to write in those eyes what her fingers could not script." (19)

It is left to the poet and to black women in general to decipher the past from her eyes in the photograph that speaks volumes and re/write their histories. This is the reason why black and native writers assign a crucial role to the oral tradition. The poet feels as if Mammy Prater had waited patiently for a century to be discovered by her daughters. Brand conveys a lot of emotion through this simple poem describing the still portrait of an ex-slave.

In *No Language is Neutral*, there are memories of slaves being brought in irons. Language runs parallel to history and carries vestiges of past experiences. She refers to the strict rigours of Standard English as she writes: "language here was strict description and teeth edging truth" (22). In an interview with Beverly Daurio, when asked about the title of the book, Brand's response was:

> It's based on a line from Derek Walcott's "Midsummer": no language is neutral/ the green oak of English is a murmurous cathedral/ where some take umbrage and some take peace/ but all help to widen its shade." Walcott and I come from different generations and different genders; the English language that he wants to claim is not the same one that I want to claim. The one that I want contains the resistances to how that language was made, because language was made through imperialism, through the oppression of women. As women and as peoples of colour we write against that language. The more power we acquire to speak and act . . . the more we change that language. I write to say something about the world. The language that I encounter as a response to me in the world is no more neutral than mine to it. (15)

She expresses this very idea in her poem. She finds that she is restricted in her "navigation" by the "swift undertow" meaning the limitations of Standard English, which she finds is racialized and genderized so as to reflect only white, heterosexual male experiences. She uses transferred epithets like "malicious horizon" to express her bitterness. Her slave ancestor had to fight odds to survive and improvise ways of communication as they were ripped apart from their culture and language. She brings these ideas out in the following lines:

> The malicious horizon made us the essential thinkers of technology. How to fly gravity, how to balance basket and prose reaching for murder. (*NLN* 23)

The only sounds they hear are those of rolling chains and copper gongs as the slaves move in rows and the falsetto sounds of whips being cracked. They are forbidden to communicate so that "talking was left for night and hush was the idiom and hot core" (23).

Brand has to recover the life story of Liney, her great grandmother. For this she has to force details out of her ninety year old uncle Ben. He recollects through tears that her mother was a "sugar cake" (24). Referring to Liney she writes:

> This time Liney done see vision in this green guava season, fly skinless and turn into river fish, dream sheself, praise god, without sex and womb when sex is hell and womb she to pay. (25)

She seeks to escape from her body. The body is not something affording pleasure and sex is described as hell, suggesting that it was forced and painful resulting in unwanted children. Liney, the marginalized woman can never be the centre of her story. Liney's story only emerges in patches and is expressed in both nation language and Standard English. She expresses this idea in the lines:

> In between, Liney, in between, as if your life could never see itself, blooded and coarsened on this island as mine, driven over places too hard to know in their easy terror. (26)

Brand can identify with Liney's quality of life since Liney's life also had been touched by colonization. Teresa Zackodnik, in her article, "I am Blackening in My Way: Identity and Place in Dionne Brand's *No Language is Neutral*, referring to the following lines in the poem, writes: "between me and history/ we have made a patch of it, a verse still missing you/ at the subject" (26). The problem posed by language in creating the subject is further elaborated upon in these words:

> To choose between Standard English and nation language is to cut off a branch of one's experience, thus forcing one into a liminal space. Brand argues that her great grandmother's history does not lie between her experience as subject and as colonized object; rather it lies in her experience as divided subject, "in between." (202)

Even as the poem runs through the gamut of generations of colonial experiences of Liney through her mother to herself, her struggle with the in-built biases in Standard English in regard to race and gender continue till she evolves a different language arising out of lesbian body experiences. In this sense, it is a polyphonic poem. She recalls that her mother could not find a way out of the double bind:

> A woman who thought she was human but got the message, female and black and somehow those who gave it to her were like family, mother and brother, spitting woman at her, somehow they were the only place to return to and this gushing river had already swallowed most of her, the little girl drowned on its indifferent bank. (27)

Brand is not comfortable with nation language either, since it has, in its own way silenced black women with its sexist ideologies. These views are endorsed by M. Nourbese Philip in her article, "Making the House Our own: Colonized Language and the Civil War of Words." Philip writes about the limitations of Standard English and says that it psychically colonized those of Black African descent "through a language that was not only experientially foreign, but also etymologically hostile and expressive of the non-being of the African" (43). Brand realizes that parts of Liney's life story can be erased due to her own selective process as well. She also feels that perhaps she cannot look straight at the facts. "Sidelong glances are my specialty" (26). Having borne several children, Liney's body has seen a lot of wear and tear. Her story remains half told. Brand refers to the erasure from official history of marginalized people like those belonging to her race. History is manipulated by the powerful. In a few lines, she simply and beautifully traces the connection between Liney, her mother and herself:

> History will only hear you if you give birth to a woman who smoothes starched linen in the wardrobe drawer, trembles when she walks and who gives birth to another woman who cries near a river and vanishes and who gives birth to a woman who is a poet, and, even then. (26)

"Even then" refuses to give closure thereby suggesting the continuity of experiences of racism and sexism by these women. She describes her own flight from home to Canada in these lines "Five hundred dollars and a passport full of sand and winking water" (28). This is how she reaches the alien country so far from home, having left the warm, familiar and lush green tropical Caribbean island behind. She is overwhelmed by the experience of the western, urban landscape with its cold and concrete structures, commercialization and the anonymity of big city life. The immigrant's first experience of culture shock and racism is poignantly expressed in the line:

> you the
> thin mixture of just come and don't exist. (29)

There is a description of her and her cousin Pearl trying in vain to recapture the spirit of Christmas back home. Even the food does not taste the same. She points to the dilemma faced by the immigrant of leaving home for something better, yearning for home and not yet arriving. In the alien, cold environment even nostalgia rings false. She writes:

> Well, even
> our nostalgia was a lie, skittish as the truth these
> bundle of years. (30)

However, she is compelled finally to break her twenty years of silence. The dilemma faced by people in diaspora between a materially better but soulless existence is what Brand is attempting to get at. In the same interview when asked about her life in Canada which seems much less concerned with how one is "in the soul," her reply is:

> I guess what the statement about living in the soul meant that when one arrives in a rural place like Tobago (I go there more than I go to Trinidad) one is called to account for being human. Nobody knows me, but they *know* me. In this way of being they say, "You can't be in our presence and act as if you are not. (Daurio 9)

In her poems she refers to the lack of freedom to be oneself in an alien country. Even nostalgia is suppressed. Even as she writes, she realizes the potency of language and the very act of writing. She knows that it makes a statement: "Each sentence realized or dreamed jumps like a pulse with history and takes a side." (34)

She knows that her writing is informed by race, class and gender and that it determines her very subject position. Teresa Zackodnik, in her article understands Brand's subject position as being divided and polyvalent with a purpose:

> The voicing of subjectivity as a dialogue of differences privileges the dialogue between self and other in herself; rather than attempting to overcome division, Brand embraces difference. (206)

Zackodnik points out that this is exemplified in the following lines from the poem:

> What I say in any language in cold in faultless
> knowledge of skin, in drunkenness and weeping,
> told as a woman without matches and tinder, not in
> words and in words learnt by heart,
> told in secret and not in secret, and listen. (34)

This position of awareness enables her to move beyond nostalgia, forge her identity and find her own voice, even if in an alien country. In "hard against the soul" there is evidence of a new language in formation. This is a language Brand evolves with her lesbian lover. The attempt is evident in the following lines:

> these warm
> watery syllables, a woman's tongue so like a culture,
> plunging toward stones not yet formed into flesh,
> language not yet made. . . .
> It signifies the birth of a new
> language, more authentic and
> truthful to her experiences. Like an
> epiphany it dawns on her
> with her lover by her side that:
> . . . we must make a sense here to living. (39)

Referring to "hard against the soul" in the interview with Beverly Daurio, Brand says:

> That poem is about my first lover, but it is also about recognizing I was a lesbian, and why. I looked at ocean earth, and I thought, that's right, I love that, there's something about the fecundity of it, the richness, that somehow verified my love for women. (16)

Before this experience, she admits that her work had been political. She finds that her life as a lesbian has had a positive impact on her work. She says: "Much of my work before didn't deal with sexuality as political; somehow I've gotten deeper, more honest sense of myself since coming out." (16)

She feels it is time to voice her experiences, breaking her long silence. She realizes that she has to make her life in the new place meaningful. The years of silence have to be broken and for this she has to evolve a new language and articulate such experiences.

This language is created by the erotic lesbian pleasure with the bodies erupting into the text. Elizabeth Meese writes in *(Sem)Erotics: Theorizing Lesbian: Writing*: "The lesbian writer seeks to intervene in language, reinvent, or better, re-work its texture, to produce an exploratory language through which we can find ourselves as subjects and (of) desire" (14). This is what Brand attempts even as she and her lover share the immigrant experience of alienation from their environment. This attempt will involve her establishing her subjectivity by negotiating her split self. She has to do this with her lover's help: "I heard her navigate the thick soil of who we are. Her boundless black self rising." (41)

In an article on Brand's poetry, particularly "hard against the soul," Meira Cook observes:

> The collapse of the body positioned in terms of inside/outside metaphors vis-à-vis the text, results in a curiously evasive subject, a subjectivity constructed at the intersection of the hidden and the revealed. . . . Because of the blurring of the distinction between the viewer and the specular body, there is similar conflation of the lover with the beloved. (90)

This however, does not mean that Brand abandons her larger social concerns as she writes:

> do not think that things escape me,
> this drawn skin of hunger twanging as a bow.

> this shiver whistling into the face of white capital. (42)

Her overriding concern is society at large and her work is at the core Marxist in orientation. She points to the power that socialization has over us. We internalize social values, standards of beauty and gender expectations laid down by society and shaking off these shackles is the first step to take towards liberation.

It is easy to see in Brand's poetry a growth from immigrant nostalgia to a complete affirmation of the self. This becomes possible only by getting in touch with her body with her lesbian lover. The experience proves to be liberating. Only after this does it become possible for the poet to shake off the heterosexist bind, in order to evolve language âfresh. As Cook affirms in her scholarly article:

> Brand's writing constructs the female body as a site of performance, whether of the gaze or of the voice, the embodied/ enacted textual body, the body constructed by language, the writing body as contaminated by her position in language, since there is no outside of power, no pure place outside the desire of the text. (91)

Thus in the final analysis, discovery of identity, subjectivity and language are intertwined with the body and its experiences. At the same time, there is no self-indulgent, narcissistic obsession with the body. This is due to the fact that in Dionne Brand's work, the personal and the political are inextricably interwoven.

Women theorists/writers of colour contest the notion of the ahistoricized, non-cultural specific body. Writers like Hélène Cixous has come under attack for her use of the metaphor the dark continent of Africa, to suggest the female body as also for her call to ignore differences of race, colour and national boundaries in an attempt to create women into a Utopia.[4] In response to Cixous' ideas pertaining to the body in her influential essay "The Laugh of the Medusa" the theorist/critic Kadiatu Kanneh writes:

> For black feminists there can be no easy separation between blackness and womanhood, just as there cannot be a simple slicing apart of white racial identity and womanhood. This reality informs a black feminist approach to the body, sensual pleasure and political language. (144)

Kanneh, in her essay titled, "Love, Mourning and Metaphor: Terms of Identity" goes on to point out:

> Sensual pleasure has as much to do with cultural identity as it has to do with physical sensation, and the articulation of the erotic for black women is the marker of a certain socio-historical belonging as it were for white women. (144)

Hence when one studies the works of women theorists/writers of colour, there is no denial of the body as such but there is a need felt to contextualize and historicize the body. Simultaneously a great need felt to resist the essentializing of women's bodies or the experiences.

Trinh Minh-ha is not averse to the notion of writing the body at all, but she delves into the complexities of the theory and practice of it. She also points to subtle distinctions between:

> "write yourself," write your body and write about yourself, your body, your inner life, your fears, inhibitions, desires, and pleasures. The first refers to a scriptive act—the emergence of a writing self—the second, to a consolidation of writing from the self. The two often overlap, but the type that consistently inundates the market is without doubt the second one: write-about biographies or novels, through whose stories the woman author constitutes an identity. (28-29)

She advocates the reconnection with the body but is against its compartmentalization in any respect. She suggests this idea in these words:

> We write—think and feel—(with) our entire bodies rather than only (with) our minds or hearts. It is a perversion to consider thought the product of one specialized organ, the brain, and feeling, that of the heart. (36)

She however, cautions against falling into the trap of getting caught in the discourse of sexuality for its own sake and suggests that it would simply be a step in the direction of being heard.

4.4 The Black Female Body in Exile and Alienation

It is unfair to treat all the Black women poets in Canada as a monolithic group saying the same things for there is a wide diversity socially and historically among them. The black people in Canada come from diverse backgrounds. The earliest migration was in the latter part of the eighteenth century with slaves having escaped from the US. Even as early as the American revolution, free Blacks came to settle in Canada. In the Sixties, there was an influx of immigrants from the West Indies and Africa. These came from different ethnic groups. The most vocal of them have undoubtedly been the women poets from the Caribbean islands like Lillian Allen, Dionne Brand, Claire Harris and M. Nourbese Philip. Their experiences as first generation black women poets have been quite different from those of other black women. They have often expressed resentment at having to carry the burden of representing entire communities and even their race. As Makeda Silvera puts it:

> And why is the same group of Black women called upon time and again to speak for thousands of other Black women, as if we are the Black women in the world? ("How Far. . ." 71)

They have put up strong resistance to homogenizing tendencies within the feminist movement and have dealt with problems of ghettoization both in the academia and in the publishing world. Consequently they have had to deal with the issue of how to reach their audience and have had to resort to performance and other means to sidestep the elitism of the literary world. Lillian Allen, in her essay titled, "A Writing of Resistance, Black Women's Writing in Canada" in *Women and Words* foregrounds the problems Black women writers face in publishing their works:

> When a Black/minority/ethnic writer submits work to publishers, they don't have the tools or the frame of reference necessary to make a proper analysis. Serious confrontational writing is considered neither serious nor writing. Publishers most comfortable with the song and dance routine within a recognizably British form or with the kind of Naipaulian consciousness where you hate

> yourself and reinforce ideas of your inferiority while using a skill with technical brilliance in the same way the oppressor does, thus forever trapping yourself within his form and dialectics. (64)

Writers like Silvera are blatant in their criticism of the white feminist literary scene as well. She writes:

> I then moved into the white feminist literary scene where I thought I could now create and publish words, but I found the doors of the feminist publications tightly guarded, even shut. It seems as if a Black radical feminist is too much of threat to white feminists and to their protected literary world, a world which, I found does not challenge racism or classism within society. (*How Far*. . .70)

Black women writers in Canada lament the lack of a tradition unlike their counterparts in the United States. It is left to writers like Allen, Brand, Harris and Philip to forge this tradition and theorize along the way. They also resist attempts at sweeping them under an umbrella term like "women of colour" and keen to point to the differing historical experiences and concerns of writers of Asian origin. In her interview with Coomi Vevaina, M. Nourbese Philip astutely observes:

> The Asians in the Caribbeans had a psychological advantage over those from Africa as they did not have their culture taken away from them. Culture as you know, really roots you, gives you that grounding. (21)

It is for this reason that Black writers show more concern with the issue of language than their Asian counterparts. Their deconstruction of language and their attempts to create their own, should not be confused with the efforts of radical white feminist writers like Daphne Marlatt. They work from a different perspective towards different goals. The body that erupts into the text of Black women writers is a very different from that in the works of white writers and the literary texts that emerge are likewise different.

The conditions of exile and alienation are as predominant in Philip's work as they are in Brand's. These emotions are time and again being grappled with and it is exile in a deeper sense arising out of the African diaspora and early memories of slavery, than simply that which can be found in the works of first generation immigrant writers. M. Nourbese Philip herself puts it succinctly in these words:

> Many-faceted and many-layered, this condition of exile is the legacy of colonialism and imperialism that first exiled Africans from their ethnicity and all its expressions—language, religion, education, music patterns of family relationships into the pale and beyond, into the nether, nether land of race. From this exile there would no relief, no recourse, no return. (*Frontiers* 10)

This is an underlying current in Philip's entire oeuvre. It is not something as simplistic as nostalgia for the country left behind. Memories of loss and exile emerge as it were from the collective unconscious. She assigns a crucial role to memory for the retrieval of the Black voice and identity as she writes in the same essay: "I am also arguing for a subversive role for memory, that memory's more than nostalgia—it has a potentially kinetic quality and must impel us to action." (*Frontiers* 20) This idea as mentioned earlier is dramatized in her poems like "Discourse on the Logic of Language," "Questions! Questions!" etc.

Black women writers feel that the policy of multiculturalism has not solved their problems and in fact serves to camouflage the racism that seems to be inherent in Canadian society. In an essay titled "Why Multiculturalism Cannot End Racism," Philip writes:

> multiculturalism, as we know it, has no answers for the problems of racism or white supremacy—unless it is combined with a clearly articulated policy of anti-racism, directed at rooting out the effects of racist and white supremacist thinking. (*Frontiers* 185)

These writers, therefore continue to struggle against racism, which still works in invidious ways and against sexism displayed by white, patriarchal society as well as their own men. As Philip writes in an essay titled "Who's Listening?," this multiplies their alienation several fold:

> Scourges such as racism and sexism can also create a profound sense of alienation, resulting in what can best be described as psychic exile, even among those artists who are not in physical exile. (*Frontiers* 28)

The task for the Black woman writer is therefore a daunting one where she has to confront these realities and constantly use unique strategies of subversion which require her to constantly collide with dominant discourses, consciously disengaging from them and engaging them. Philip admits this to be a tough task indeed as she writes in an essay "Journal Entries against Reaction: Damned if We Do and Damned if We Don't":

> The challenge today for Black women writers is to subvert those restrictions that subtly, and not so subtly, suggest we should only write about certain topics, in certain ways; we will have to find new ways of including our wholeness in our work while maintaining our integrity as Black women writers. (64-65)

The writer positions herself in a unique location and assumes tremendous importance under these circumstances. On this count black women writers have subverted the centre-margin paradigm and revolutionized and creatively used the notion of the margin. In an interview with Barbara Carey, Philip elaborates on her concept of the margin, saying:

> For me, as a Black woman writing here, that boundary or margin beyond which there seems to be "nothing" is not only out there—it is also within me. . . . I feel I'm constantly pushing against some kind of margin, beyond which I don't know what there is. (18)

She is more definite about the positive attribute of this location in her essay titled "Father Tongue":

> I do position myself on the margin in the sense of the word meaning "frontier." By so doing one's relationship to the dominant culture immediately changes—what was the mainstream immediately becomes hinterland with all that that connotes. (*Genealogy* 128)

This is not to say that Philip is indifferent to the dominant community or oblivious to its reality. She does acknowledge certain basic commonality in women's situation as she writes:

> we must acknowledge there is a basic common denominator of female experience—in all cultures and in all classes—has been the fact that our bodies have achieved a universal negative significance; bodies which have become palimpsests upon which men have inscribed and reinscribed their texts. ("Who's Listening?" 44)

At the same time she is averse to the ahistorical, ageographical manner in which female identity has been conceived of and is being manipulated, sidelining issues of race and class. The body may be a common denominator but the exploitation and violence committed on the coloured body has been carried on an incomparable scale as compared to the objectification and commodification of the white woman's body. The Black slave woman, stripped off her roots, language and culture, forcibly brought into the New World had nothing but her body and Philip writes about this in a powerful piece titled "Displace—The Space Between":

> The Black woman comes to the New World with only the body. And the space between. The European buys her not only for her strength, but also to service the Black man sexually—to keep him calm. And to produce new chattels—units of production—for the plantation machine. (*Genealogy* 76)

The Black female body had a different role to play in the capitalist-imperialist project. Philip puns on the word "Displace" as meaning "this place" or the genital area of the female body the Caribbean in the demotic, as also the displacement the black woman was subjected to in order to serve the aims of imperialist. This is only one illustration of how Philip uses the father tongue or Standard English and mother tongue or the 'demotic.' She uses it in a double-edged way. It is amply clear that the Black female body is a different signifier as she admits in an essay titled "Gut Issues in Babylon: Racism and Anti-Racism in the Arts":

> My body and its body intelligence—I include the mind in this concept—are deeply involved and implicated in the practice of racism—against me and others—even though I personally may never be physically attacked. Remembering—I have never forgotten!—that it was for our bodies that we were first brought to this brave New World, the irony of this observation does not escape me. (*Frontiers* 212)

She refers to the body's intelligence and the mind as a part of the body rejecting the mind-body dichotomy of Western thought. In fact, she interestingly subverts Cartesian logic in the following manner in "Journal Entries against Reaction":

> We bleed, therefore we are. In opposition to the cogito ergo sum of Cartesian philosophy, which would have us believe something as simple and reflexive as thinking proves our existence. (*Frontiers* 66)

Before embarking on a close study of M. Nourbese Philip's collection titled *She Tries Her Tongue, Her Silence Softly Breaks*, it is fruitful to examine how Philip perceives this particular collection. In the essay titled, "The Absence of Writing or How I Almost Became a Spy," she writes:

> There was a profound eruption of the body into the text of *She Tries Her Tongue.* This represents a significant development for me as a poet. The manuscript has become a blaze along a poetic path.

> In the New World, the female African body became the site of exploitation and profoundly anti-human demands—forced reproduction along with forced abduction and sale of children. Furthermore, while the possibility of rape remains the amorphous threat it is, the female body continues to be severely circumscribed in its interaction with the physical surrounding space and place. How then does this affect the making of poetry, the making of words, making of I-mages if poetry, as I happen to believe, "begins in the body and ends in the body?" *She Tries Her Tongue* is the first blaze along the path to understanding and resolving this particular conundrum. (24)

In the above paragraph, she clearly delineates the link between the body, place and language. This link which she establishes is evident in all her works and particularly in *She Tries Her Tongue*. This view is endorsed by the critic Brenda Carr in her article, "To Heal the Word Wounded: Agency and Materiality of Language and Form in M. Nourbese Philip's *She Tries Her Tongue Her Silence Softly Breaks*," Carr writes:

> Philip's poetic praxis activates theoretical questions circulating around the crucially interlinked concepts—body, memory, history, and materiality. Bringing the site-specific body of Philip's text into dialogue with body-relevant theories, particularly feminist, postcolonial and new historicist, enables a practice of historicizing the body and its relationship to language in a race accountable way. (73)

Carr's analysis proceeds to do as promised. Carr problematizes the notion of the body and 'jouissance' as posited by body-centred feminist theories arising out of psychoanalysis and semiotics.

The notion of the body itself acquires nuances never before thought of in the works of writers like M. Nourbese Philip. In her works, the body, text, history and memory are interlaced to re/cover the splintered self of the Black female subject.

The opening section in *She Tries Her Tongue* contains a series of seven poems titled, "And over Every Land and Sea." In this series, Philip evokes the Ceres-Proserpine myth of the mother's search for her abducted daughter. The poems work on several levels and contain the twin voices of mother and daughter, often in turns. It has opening quotations from Ovid's *Metamorphoses* suggesting the use of the traditional myth for subversive purposes. It is significant that the opening poem, "Questions! Questions!" begins in the middle of the mythic story with the mother searching for her daughter over land and sea. There is no reference to the idyllic past in it. She uses the demotic in the opening lines: "Where she, where she, where she/ be, where she gone?" (28). The reader is immediately drawn into a different ethos and its accompanying sensibility. The landscape visualized is Caribbean with the flora, fauna and colours of the islands. The anguish of loss is brought out in the lines, "grief gone mad with crazy—so them say" (28). The next poem titled, "Adoption Bureau" contains the voice of the daughter seeking the mother. The images evoke the anguish of loss and innocence. The imagery is physical with references to "skin," "hair," "heart" and "beat." The innocence and eagerness with which the daughter seeks the mother is depicted in the question, "tell me, do/ I smell like her?" (*STHT* 29) The reference to colonialism is implicit in the words "blow of the

North East trades" (29) and the resultant loss. Carole Boyce Davies, in her book *Black Women, Writing and Identity: Migrations of the Subject* perceptively notes:

> Mother-daughter tensions are right at the centre of the rewriting of home. In any writing of home by women writers in patriarchal or matriarchal cultures, the challenge to the meaning of the mother attains symbolic importance in terms of definition and redefinition. (127-28)

This is endorsed by Philip herself in an interview with Janice Williamson where she discusses the poem "Questions! Questions!" When questioned about mother/ daughter genealogy and the particular connections she makes in her writing, she says:

> The first poem where Ceres and Persephone play their part, "Questions! Questions!" was conceived when I went back to Tobago for the first time after many, many years. Given the fact that I was born there and only spent my first eight years in Tobago, it plays a very important part in my writing life. I think that is where my writing comes from, and what set the poem going was some memory of losing that place. There's also, I believe, some personal stuff within my own experience around the emotional loss of my mother, which I believe many women experience. I think those two experiences came together in that poem. On a still larger level—beyond the personal—is the leitmotif of seeking and returning to the mother as in the motherland, Africa, that continually plays a part in almost all the writing by New World Africans. (228-29)

The juxtaposition of the introductory lines from the mythic story in Standard English and the dramatization in the poem that follows in the demotic, sets up a tension within the text which reminds the reader constantly that Philip is recontextualizing the myth in a new way to convey new truths. She intends this effect as she writes, "The excitement for me as a writer comes in the confrontation between the formal and demotic within the text itself ("Absence of Writing . . ." 18).

The poem titled "Dream-Skins" (32) is filled with sensuous body imagery and contains an account of the goddess' travels to the very interior caverns in search of her daughter. The poem has a dream-like quality and blurs distinctions between reality and visions. The images are also gory in that a lizard-headed, half human being suckles the young one. There is an image of this head being severed off and an image of a plant sprouting from the mouth with the release of silence. This finally climaxes with the act of naming and the acquisition of voice. The lost daughter is found but wounded and in need of healing by the mother. This enacts the loss and acquisition of a voice of a different kind, however damaged it might be. Philip writes of this painful process in her non-fiction as well:

> For the many like me, Black and female, it is imperative that our writing begins to recreate our histories and our myths, as well integrate that most painful of experiences--loss of our history and our word. The reacquisition of power to create in one's own i-mage and to create one's own I-mage is vital to this process. ("Absence of Writing" 25)

This is in fact, the major challenge faced by the Black woman writer. Philip acknowledges, however, that in the absence of language and culture, the relationship of her community with the dominant group turns out to be extremely complex and strange. She writes:

> We need now, however, to be m/othered by those very societies and cultures which have destroyed our cultures, enriched themselves on our exploited labour, and who would now banish, if not destroy us. ("Echoes in a Stranger Land" 23)

This complex and painful relationship with the dominant culture finds repeated expression in her works. The series of poems titled "Cyclamen Girl" (38-45) contains an account of a young, black girl's initiation into the Christian religion and has several references to the rituals involved in the induction. This is the religion of the white, dominant community and there is evidently again a clash of cultures and religions as dramatized in the poems. The clash is often between the tenets of Christianity and the old, goddess-oriented religion of Africa. Brenda Carr in her article notes that in the poems:

> Diverse cultural discourses are also invoked and recontextualized: missionary, scientific, educational, literary, and historical. Philip's "cross-cultural montage" of parallel literary, non-literary, and social texts as a strategy of transforming the "discursive dilemma" for the Afrosporic subject is loosely resonant with a new historicist method. (81)

Carr, in the same article, examines the postmodernist features of Philip's creative strategies. However, it is not a practice of postmodernism for its own sake or because it happens to be trendy. There is a far deeper philosophy at work and Philip elaborates on this in an interview with Janice Williamson and says:

> One loses sight of the Caribbean and the New World, which for me represents massive interruptions for different people—for the aboriginal peoples, whose time was permanently interrupted, for the Africans and Asians who were brought there, and even for the Europeans who came. I never seem to be able to write anything through from start to finish without interrupting it somehow by some other discourse. Some other voice is continually interrupting. That's the historical and social matrix from which my writing is partly coming, it's in touch with or resonating with that historical material. (230)

The poem "The Catechist" (38) describes a young, black girl's first communion. The communion becomes a context to describe, her first exposure to Christian ritual. It also foregrounds her body poised as it is between girlhood and womanhood as well as to expose the stereotypes of the female body. The very opening lines are suggestive of this with their reference to her "early-blooming brown legs" (38), of cyclamen girls being "early bloomers in the heat of it all" (38) and even a reference to "the lurking smell of early pregnancy" (38). There is a suggestion of the clash of cultures in the juxtaposition of the demotic word "massa" and its Standard English equivalent "master" and the cyclamen girl caught between the two. In the poem "Eucharistic Contradictions" (39), there is a further development of the Afrosporic female subject "double-imaged" (39) or "doubly imagined" (39), "dubbed dumb" (39). The subject is trapped in the labels/abuses assigned by the dominant group namely, "mulatto, dougla, niggerancoolie" (39). Catechism is presumed to answer questions of faith but the contradictions remain unanswered for her—those of god, doubt and dogma. The poem is aptly titled "The Catechism" (40), in that, it again deals with the contradictions confronting her by way of religious tenets and the realities of her life. Guilt is internalized by her and she is socialized into this both by the imperialist, racist discourses like Victorian sexual mores of "no sex before marriage/ no love after" (40) and sexism which is transmitted and institutionalized by women of her own community—"the code of mama" (40). They present her with societal expectations and norms of beauty and alienate the body. These social dogmas are to her mind a more complex restriction than even religion. Like a trapeze artist, she is constantly compelled to swing between these moulds prepared for her and all social institutions, including religion, seem to conspire in the attempt. She is really referring to the humiliation, shame and guilt loaded on to the female body and sexuality. The poem titled "Vows" (41) paints the picture of the properly attired girl ready for the vows to be taken during religious confirmation. It is significant that white is the colour of her ribbons, socks, shoes and the Book of Common Prayer, her dress and her very soul. It requires her to deny what she really is and the things that signify her—"sunshine/ black skin &/ doubt/ (in that order)" (41). The reality of her black skin is something that overrides all other things. In the poem, "Transfiguration" (42)—a process where one's appearance is altered to make one look better, there is an act of "naming" being looked at. The process is reversed by Philip so as to enable her to get to her real African self. The dominant, Western religious discourses have sought to "name" her but the poet resorts to memory of the African goddess "Oshun" (42) and evokes the grief of loss of her childhood, "the childhood" of her community really, which is also a fleeting memory, resonant with the sound of African "Rhythm!/ Song!/ Drum!" (42). She has to delve into this collective memory to re/surrect I-mages of the past so as to re/cover her lost self. Philip, in this pöignant poem is evoking the grief of the loss of the past, so as to rouse the black, female subject from amnesia caused by the imposition of Western, imperialistic discourses. In the essay titled, "Absence of Writing or How I Almost became a Spy" she writes:

> It is perhaps, ironic that New World Africans, descendants of cultures and societies where the word and the act of naming was the focal point and fulcrum of societal forces, should find themselves in a situation where the word, their word and the power to name was denied them. (21)

This is precisely what Philip seems to be tackling in the poem.

The poem titled "The Communicant" (44) again refers to the associations that the girl has when she receives communion. The scepticism is contained in the line, "or so they have been told" (44). There is doubt which she feels about whether Christ really sacrificed His life for her lot since there seems to be no salvation from the scourges of racism and sexism. In the poem "Epiphany," which ends the section, there is a portrayal of the psychic journey the girl has to make. This involves the reworking of memory to attain her true self and a return to her African past evoked by an image of a goddess—"The great stone-bird mother" dropping her daughters from her "open beak." (45) This enables the cyclamen girl to return "to her own" (45) essential being. This realization or spiritual journey is implied in the title, "Epiphany" (45) with its dual meaning. The original one refers to the Christian festival on January 6 commemorating the visit of the Magi to Bethlehem to see baby Jesus. Philip reverses the significance of the title to mean an attainment of psychic wholeness by a return to the African self by the Black, female subject in diaspora. This is the kinetic quality of memory impelling one to action that she refers to in her essay. The poem "African Majesty: From Grassland and Forest (The Barbara and Murray Collection)" (48) describes the feelings evoked on seeing an African artifact in a museum collection. It again speaks of feelings for the loss of culture and roots. The artifact seems to have captured a petrified past. Philip adopts an ironic tone when she refers to "the wisdomed wood/ stripped of reason/ restored to living proof" (49) of primitive aesthetics: "the African influence" on—/ Bracque, Picasso, Brancussi" (49). African art was dismissed as primitive and yet has influenced modernist painters like Picasso. The poem laments the loss of art, along with culture due to the systematic destruction of both by colonialism. In the poem, "Meditations on the Declension of Beauty by the Girl with the Flying Cheek-bones" (52), there are simultaneously issues being raised—one of language and the other of norms of beauty laid down by the West. By asking the question in parts and repeating them in different sequences, Philip shows the hesitant tone and apprehension with which it is asked. Language, with its in-built racist and sexist biases has led to the very erasure of the black, female subject. She writes in "The Absence of Writing. . .": "The English language merely served to articulate the non-being of the African, over and above her primary function as a chattel and unit of production." (16)

She also asserts the beauty of the girl with the flying cheek-bones, her broad nose and black skin as also the man with the "full-moon lips" (53). Black people have been dubbed by racists as having "kinky hair" and "thick lips." In this poem, Philip moves into the realm of the language issue. Her search for a language, stripped of racism and sexism is a path-breaking one and the series of poems beginning with "Discourse on the Logic of Language" deal in depth with the issue.

The poem "Discourse on the Logic of Language" (56-59) has several voices. The centrepiece speaks of English as a foreign language creating unspeakable anguish. The poet calls English the father tongue and laments the absence of a mother tongue which results in silence: This silencing has occurred over the centuries. To the right side of the page in italicized print, is an edict which asks every slave owner to ensure that his slaves belonged to different ethnolinguistic groups so that they would not be able to communicate to one another and foment rebellion. To the left of the margin is a short story of the mother holding the newborn child close and tonguing the child's body clean of the "creamy white substance" (56) coating it. This is in order to cleanse it of the influence of the whites and breathe new language into the child. On the adjacent page, are contained the theories of two scientists—Doctor Wernicke and Broca (57). Dr. Broca set out to prove that white men of the Caucasian race were superior to women, Blacks and other peoples of colour. Philip shows how the discourse of science has run parallel to the colonial project, reinforcing the myths and beliefs it used to sustain itself.

The poem continues with the lament of being silenced by having a foreign language imposed and the anguish that English has been for colonized people. There is a plea to the mother by the child as it were, to be mothered and given a language. The right side of the centrepiece contains an edict threatening the removal of the tongue if any slave were caught speaking his native language. The edict further threatens the offender with the public humiliation of having his cut-off tongue being hung in a public place. The short story of the mother and child continues in the margin with the mother prying the mouth of the child open and touching her tongue to that of the child and blowing words into her daughter's mouth. The adjacent page, in mimicry of scientific data collection, has a multiple choice questionnaire which establishes the crucial importance of the tongue to the human body. Referring to this poem, in her interview with Janice Williamson, Philip says:

> What I was mainly concerned with in "Discourse on the Logic of Language" was the colonizing experience—how what we call a mother tongue, in this instance English, was, when you traced its lineage, really a father tongue, in that it was the white male colonizer bringing us language. In that sense there are parallels with the feminist project of delineating a 'patriarchal' language. (228)

In the same interview she discusses the eruption of the body into the text:

> The body appears throughout the poem: tongues, penises, blood, you name it. It seems to me the only time that we—as women—legitimately take up space physically is when we're pregnant. The fat woman is still not seen as quite legitimate. (239)

She also says that she felt a keen desire to take up more and more space and the poems did get visibly bigger. Referring to *She Tries Her Tongue,* she says in the same interview:

> When I finished that manuscript, I could identify the area of my body—the right side of my abdomen—where the poems had come from. . . . That experience or sensation was very important to me because it really rooted me in the body in a very important way that hadn't quite happened in the two earlier books of poetry. (239)

Talking about the erotic, she says:

> the Black female body—at least for me—is still trying to get out from under the oppressive weight of various myths—highly sexed Black woman; matriarch Black woman; asexual Black woman; castrating, ball-crushing Black woman. (240)

Philip is as much concerned with the undoing of these stereotypes and the material realities of the Black woman's life as she is with detoxifying English. When one reads "Discourse on the Logic of Language," a little closely, one is tempted to improvise and extend the Lacanian notion of the Mirror stage further to explain the fragmented, Black female self. In the very layout of the poem, it is obvious that the mother-female child exchange is marginalized, pitted as it is against the powerful edicts emanating from the white, patriarchal Symbolic Order. The confusion and ambivalence of the unformed, Black female subject robbed of the mother tongue and alienated from English, the father tongue is the centrepiece. The mother tongue's alienation from the Symbolic Order results in the anguish felt by the daughter and it is finally the mother who has to breathe new words into her daughter's mouth, after detoxifying her of the "white, creamy substance" (56)—the vestiges of colonialism. This is perhaps, the only way for her to create a positive self emerging from a positive identification with the mother, poised as both are, on the margins of the social order.

In the poem "Universal Grammar" (62-67), there is a parody of the universality of grammar as known to the logocentric West. In the act of parsing, there is a breaking up of the sentence, disintegrating it into parts. The sentence parsed is significant, in that it speaks of memory, of the race contained in the human body—"The smallest cell remembers O" (62). 'O' is the first syllable of the name of the African goddess of the river—O/shun. She ends the exercise in grammar by asking how one can lose a language when the smallest cell of the body remembers. The answer is contained in what follows—violence and coercion practised by the white male colonizer. She ends this piece with a tip from "Mother's recipe on How to Make a Language Yours and How Not to get Raped" (67) in the process of creating a new language. What needs to be done is reject all that is oppressive and restraining:

> Slip mouth over the syllable; moisten with tongue the word./Suck Slide Play Caress Blow—Love it, but if the word/ gags, bite it off—at its source—/ Spit it out / Start again. (67)

Brenda Carr writes commenting on this poem:

> With this textual play, reminiscent of Héléne Cixous, Philip specifically remembers the superimposed scene of sexual and linguistic violation for the Afrosporic female subject and re-performs it as one where she has the power to fellate or castrate. (79)

Philip is interested very deeply in the language issue since she is aware of the power that it wields and has wielded in the past often resulting even in the erasure of civilizations. Black humour and bitterness are rampant in all these poems with their textual play on language excercises. She is equally committed to the evolving of a new language inasmuch as deconstructing the old. These twin tasks are by no means easy as she writes in her essay "The Absence of Writing. . .":

> The language as we know it has to be dislocated and acted upon—even destroyed—so that it begins to serve our purposes. It is our only language, and while it is our mother tongue, ours is also a father tongue. (19)

In the poem "The Question of Language is the Answer to Power" (70-75), she takes up a lesson in phonetics and in the process of providing practice in vowel sounds, gives us the account of slaves being brought to the New World. The lesson becomes an occasion for Philip to ponder over the evolution of a new language with its own semantics and sound and more pliable to the use of her people. It also leads her to wonder about the loss of language and whether words collected historical responses in the piece titled ("Helpful questions and commentary" 74). Brenda Carr, analyzing strategies used by Philip notes:

> Through her emphasis on language, Philip also puts pressure on various discourses that legitimize and materialize colonialist and neo-colonialist practices: education (grammar lessons), religion (catechism), nineteenth century scientific racism, documentary (history and the museum archive). In several sequences, she stages counter grammar and voice lessons to denaturalize them as part of an educational apparatus used to construct the "non-being" of the enslaved African as the condition of possibility for the Western imperial subject. (78-79)

In the poem "Testimony Stoops to Mother Tongue" (78-82), she seeks the release of the "walled tongues" (79) and wants to destroy the restraining, logocentric aspects of the father tongue, English. She evokes the image of a black mother breast-feeding snakes that threaten to multiply and in-breed. They develop new heads like Gorgons when she chops them off. With regard to the question of her mixing of standard English and the Caribbean demotic in her works, she writes:

> If you work entirely in nation language or the Caribbean demotic of English you do, to a large degree restrict your audience to those familiar enough with it; if you move to standard English you lose much of that audience and, along with that loss, an understanding of many of the traditions, history, and culture which contextualize your work. ("Who's Listening?" 37)

This is often a dilemma that writers like Philip, Brand and Harris are faced with. The choice would also affect their subject matter, thought patterns and images in their works. The experience of having been uprooted from their culture has resulted in them subverting and twisting the language at hand to make it serve their purposes. Philip writes with regard to this aspect:

> The havoc that the African wreaked upon the English language is, in fact, the metaphorical equivalent of the havoc that coming into the New World represented for the African. ("Hurrying on Up" 49)

In the title poem, "She Tries Her Tongue, Her Silence Softly Breaks" (84-99), she writes of this very experience of being uprooted from culture and family. The Black woman was dragged into the new world, with nothing to call her own. The adjacent page to this poem contains a tip from "The Practical Guide to Gardening" (85), which explains that uprooting and transplanting are painful processes for plants. We are left to imagine the havoc it wreaked on an entire race. The poem continues with the Black female subject seeking and searching for root words from her own memory. Having suffered amnesia such meanings are difficult to come upon because of ages of "unuse" (86). The adjacent page contains details from "Facts to Live by and Die" (87), describing the anatomical location of memory. More significant than the location is the fact that memory is what makes us human. Whatever is stored in long-term memory is linked to our emotions. She inserts excerpts from scientific, rational discourses as interruptions of her own discourse to bring to the attention of the reader, the vital links and collisions of these discourses. It is significant again, that the vital process of re/membering is rooted in the body.

The poem continues by stating as a matter of fact, how in the absence of roots and the mother tongue, the Black female subject's "harsh husk of a future-present begins" (88). The adjacent section contains a humorous account of the story of the three little pigs and their attempts to keep the intruder—"the big bad wolf" (89)—out.

The Black female subject continues the struggle to re/cover the lost sounds and words from memory. Again, the adjacent page describes the vision of Christ coming back to the apostles and being able to understand all languages. This signifies the hope and promise that

Christianity always holds out for oppressed people. The poem continues with acknowledging the basic experiences being expressed universally in all languages in these words:

absencelosstears laughter grief
in any language
the same (92)

These experiences are however, magnified for those who have a

blackened stump of a tongue torn
out
withered
petrified
burnt
on the pyres of silence (92)

She is referring to her own race, condemned to silence by the stump of tongue, torn out of their bodies, withered and petrified and of no more use.

The adjacent page states, as a matter of fact that even the mother abandons the child and refuses to nourish it if it is touched by strangers. This is what in fact, happened to the black people brought to the new world. They were abandoned by their mother, Africa, tortured into silence by the colonizers and forced to deny their roots and abandon their languages. It is in these circumstances that English was imposed on them. This was bound to lead to a problematic and ambivalent relationship with the master's tongues. Philip expresses this very idea in these words in "Absence of Writing. . .":

> The paradox at the heart of this acquisition, however, is that the African learned both to speak and to be dumb at the same time, to give voice to the experience and I-mage, yet remain silent. That silence has had profound effect upon the English-speaking Caribbean artist working in the medium of words. (16)

The poem is followed by an ironical prayer to the patriarchal Christian God asking for forgiveness for the inability to sing hymns in the absence of voice and verbal crippling that has occurred. The adjacent page has lines from "The Book of unCommon Prayer" (95) ironically titled. She ends with a poignant rhetorical question: "Is it in the nature of God to forgive himself—For his sin?" (95)

God's sin having been to put a people in the position of losing everything and being forced into an alien land stripped of their dignity and culture. She also questions whether God's mercy is only reserved for the white, affluent people. It is indeed an uncommon and unique prayer. The questioning does lead Philip to certain hard conclusions and truths.

Memory is what the black female subject has to fall back on. It is memory that will serve her in her attempts to forge her identity and evolve a language. She valorizes the role of memory even over history that is centred as a master narrative. She delves into etymology to seek the meanings of words like "history" and "memory." Since history is narration or "learning by inquiry" (97), and memory is "to care for," "be anxious," "think," "consider" and "remember"

(97), it precedes history both as a process and in value. She draws on traditional sources like *Klein's Comprehensive Etymological Dictionary of the English Language* (97) to arrive at the foregone conclusion that without memory there can be no history. Posing this as a rhetorical, self-explanatory question creates more impact.

This long and painful search enables the poet—a Black, female subject, to come to acquire new language. This new language emanates from body rhythms:

> That body should speak
> When silence is,
> Limbs dance. . . .
> That body might become tongue
> Tempered to speech
> And where the latter falters
> Paper with its words
> The crack of silence. (98)

Since the African woman was allowed to come to the New World with her body alone, it is left to the body to render her with speech and break her centuries of silence, so that the poet is empowered like Philomela to sing and come into her own being with her own new language—"pure utterance" (98). She is now able to re/trieve the ancient, lost wisdom of her tribe, which had known how to live as a community and in harmony with nature. It is significant that the book ends with a narrative from ancient, African tribal culture finally interrupting the intrusion of Western, dominant discourses into her writing. Throwing light on the Black female sensibility, Carole Boyce Davies writes:

> In the same way as diaspora assumes expansiveness and elsewhereness, migrations of the Black female subject pursue the path of movement outside the terms of dominant discourses. (37)

The collection of poems traces the trajectory of the poet's epic journey from the fragmentation of self and cultural identity arising out of the colonial experience through the pain and trauma of loss to the achieving of wholeness and integration and language of expression. This is made possible mainly when the poet is able to move likewise, from alienation from her body resulting from racist exploitation and abuse to getting in touch with her real, black female body which yields a new language through its memories of sounds and rhythms of the past.

4.5 The Coloured Body and Ambivalent Identity

The role of the body with its ramifications for identity formation is portrayed in the novel, *In Search of April Raintree* by Beatrice Culleton.

The novel deals with low self-esteem and negative self images rooted in perceptions about the half-breed status of the Métis. This is most obviously manifested in internalized negative images of the characters' perceptions of their own bodies, particularly their skin colour. Culleton's novel is replete with references to light and dark skins and the social status that goes with them.

At the very outset, April begins with physical descriptions of her sister Cheryl and herself—Cheryl as having inherited the father's Indian looks and she herself as being light skinned like her mother. It is amply clear that the sisters are marked out for different destinies merely by virtue of their skin colour. April adopts a "white attitude" towards her own sister and does not want to be associated with the Métis. She is vain about her light-skinned mother keeping the cleanest house, envies the rich, white kids she encounters, aspires to be like them and identifies "boogeyman" with a black person. In this way, she sets herself apart from the rest of her people and this proves to be the cause of her tragedy.

April's first exposure to sexuality is predictably linked with negative images of her community. As a child, she witnesses a man masturbating and her mother having sex with another man, all in one night. These negative images which she forms of her own people are reinforced later at her foster home. As Janice Acoose in her article "The Problem of Searching for April Raintree" observes:

> The word "halfbreed," which connotes a product of animal husbandry, is used consistently by Mrs. DeRosier and her children who shamefully dehumanize April. (231)

When they mete out physical abuse constantly, April develops a passive attitude, a survival strategy. Hope is always held out to April that she would eventually be reunited with her family. Later this heightens the feeling of betrayal even more. She dreads the word "halfbreed" and feels betrayed by faith as well since the Christian virtues taught by the Dion family do not stand the test of the trials she is put through at the DeRosiers'. Long before Cheryl writes to her about the Métis leader, Louis Riel, her mind about her community is already made up and she feels "anything to do with Indians I despised" (42). When she notices her own tan, she pities Cheryl for not being able to pass off her brown skin as a tan. She desperately wants to change her ethnic identity for by then she has clearly internalized all the negative stereotypes about herself and her people.

Margery Fee, in her article, "Deploying Identity in the Face of Racism" writes about the problem of identity:

> The difficulties that these people have in identifying as Aboriginal are compounded by a lack of cultural background and by pervasive racism in the surrounding culture. They lack both the "purity" of ancestry and the cultural knowledge that might otherwise support an identification as Aboriginal. (215)

Cheryl, who goes into a more emotionally nourishing environment, forms a positive identification with the Métis. April's ambivalent feelings towards her parents resulting from their inconsistencies, result in her own ambivalent identity. Cheryl's positive identification makes her defiant and, as children, both of them suffer the ultimate humiliation by having the DeRosiers chop off their hair. It is prisoners who have their hair cut off. This serves to physically disfigure and humiliate the girls. In the article titled, "Abuse and Violence: April Raintree's Human Rights (if she had any)," Agnes Grant makes the following observation:

> Hair was a particular preoccupation of European colonizers; dominant groups have long performed rituals which involve shearing the hair of subordinates. Cutting hair is found to be a key part of rituals of cross-cultural domination all over the world. (242)

Access to and control over the body of the dominated becomes a sure sign of domination for the oppressor. This has been evident, particularly in racial domination practised throughout the world through times immemorial. Later, the episode of rape described in graphic detail, shows that racism at its worst is behind the violence practised on April's body. Grant observes something similar as she writes in the same article:

> April's self had long been lost; though physically more traumatic, the rape was a further episode where her rights were violated and she had to cope as best as she could. (244)

The rape is not just a demonstration of power over her body (as all rapes are) but a double humiliation of her coloured body by the white rapists. This is traumatic for April whose self-definition is rooted in his pride in skin colour. When Cheryl visits her at the Radcliff home, she thinks: "As a matter of fact, we could have been almost identical twins, except for our skin colouring. No wonder I had always found her so beautiful. My pretentious way of admitting my own beauty" (106). Ironically, she is later raped on the mistaken assumption that she is Cheryl. It is significant that once she realizes during the trial that Cheryl was the intended victim, she stops the ritual baths she takes to cleanse her body after the rape. The violence and degradation represented by the rape is mainly linked to race, both from the rapists' perception as well as that of April, the victim. Margery Fee perceptively notes this link in her article, in the following words:

> From April's perspective, "she" was not raped—Cheryl was, and implicitly deserved it—so April no longer has to accept the imposition of Nativeness on her and can overcome her sense that she somehow deserved this degradation. (221)

The long lecture given by Mrs. Semple becomes crucial in different ways for the identity formation for both the sisters:

> and you girls are headed in that direction. It starts out with the fighting, the running away, the lies. Next come the accusations that everyone in the world is against you. There are sullen, uncooperative silences, the feeling sorry for yourselves. And when you go on your own, you get pregnant right away, or you can't find or keep jobs. So you'll start with alcohol and drugs. From there, you get into shop lifting and prostitution, and in and out of jails. You'll live with men who abuse you. And so on it goes. You'll end up like your parents, living off society. In both your cases, it would be a pity because Miss Turner and I knew you both when you were little. And you both were remarkable youngsters. Now you're going the same route as many other native girls. If you don't smarten up, you'll end up in the same place they do. Skid row! (62)

With this damning analysis, she almost seals the fate of the two girls. The negative images quite explicit in her talk, are stored in their subconscious. April's whole life is geared towards proving her wrong and in Cheryl's case it becomes a kind of self-fulfilling prophecy as she herself mentions later in the novel. This speech strikes a death knell at any shred of dignity or positive self-image they may have had. This also makes April internalize the racism she is constantly subjected to in white society and she in turn, practises it in subtle ways towards Cheryl. She avoids spending time with Cheryl and chooses to be with her white friends as she admits to herself in these words:

> To ease the guilt I felt for not choosing Cheryl's company, I told myself that I had to start making my life, for me, and that both of us should have friends of our own, not always relying on each other. I wrote Cheryl a hurried letter to tell her all this. (85)

She later learns during Cheryl's outburst of anger that she had been aware all along of April's condescending attitude.

Culleton seems to be pointing to the inadequacies of both April and Cheryl's ways of being. Both the alternatives deny a part of the reality of existence. Cheryl's identification with the Métis, although a positive one, is built on fragile foundations and not based on lived experience. She wants to return to an idyllic past and says as much to her sister about her plans to go and live like her community used to amidst nature. She imagines her father to be tall and straight like an Indian warrior of the past. Her images are based on books she has read and on account of this she is cruelly shattered out of her illusions when she meets her father. This becomes the turning point in her life and consequently her dreams for herself and her community turn sour. Yet she tries to remain proud of her Métis identity and stands up to their white friends at the Radcliff residence. One of them tells her:

> "Oh, I've read about Indians. Beautiful people they are. But you're not exactly Indians are you? What is the word for people like you?" one asked. "Women," Cheryl replied instantly. "No, no, I mean nationality?" "Oh, I am sorry. We're Canadians," Cheryl said smiling sweetly. (107)

At this point, Cheryl is the more perceptive of the two sisters; self-aware and courageous. She refuses to be ghettoized or locked in. As Margery Fee observes:

> She does not take the bait of the exclusionary question, but asserts that the similarities between her and her racist questioner are important as the differences, and she demonstrates that identity is a tool to use in negotiating ever-changing social relationships, rather than a trap or a fortress. (218)

The sisters perceive their community differently. April rightly observes, "I knew that Cheryl saw their quiet beauty, their simple wisdom. All I could see were watery eyes, leathery brown skin-uneducated natives" (158). April has clearly internalized the white colonizer's perceptions of her community while Cheryl's pride and strength are rooted in her perception of the past of her community. When Cheryl learns that April is to marry Bob Radcliff, she makes perceptive observations about him which later turn out to be true. She points out to April that she is not likely to be ever satisfied till she accepts that Métis part of herself and this time too is proved right. April too acts in the interests of her sister but her desire to protect her sister from the reality of her parents' condition and their abandonment of them proves to be the cause of the rupture in their relationship.

The rape episode is significant in several ways. Although it gives a graphic description of April's body being violated, the tone is one of clinical detachment. When the rape is occurring, she thinks, "Inside my head, I screamed long and loud, trying to block everything out" (130). Later, during her ritual bath, she thinks of her ability to separate her mind from her body and feels that it was perhaps that which kept her from snapping after the assault. Even as a child, in DeRosier's foster care, April's survival strategy, while being physically assaulted by them, is to separate her mind from her body.

The rape episode also seems to coincide with the two sisters exchanging their very souls as it were. April's first step towards asserting her identity and re/covering herself is when she reports the rape to the police and seeks justice. A further transformation sets in when they go to the Friendship Centre and an Old Thunderbird Woman reaches towards April and puts her hand on hers. She communicates a deep wisdom through her eyes and touch. Cheryl's death ironically restores April to life. When she smashes the glass bottle drawing blood from her hand, she is finally able to grieve for her parents, Cheryl and her own people, with the words, "I hate you for what you've done to my people." (194)

April gets acquainted with the sister she hardly knew through her journals and the letter and goes on to raise Cheryl's son. She remembers Cheryl as having once said: "All life dies to give new life" (207). Tragically, it had cost her Cheryl's life to realize her true self and accept her Métis heritage towards the end of the novel, as she says, "the denial had been lifted from my spirit. It was tragic that it had taken Cheryl's death to bring me to accept my identity" (207).

Like many Native narratives, the text is not a linear one. It starts with the present, goes to the past and comes back to the present with the reader and narrator at a higher level of awareness. It contains several voices which can be heard at times directly and at times through April's consciousness. As Helen Hoy observes in her article, "Nothing but the Truth: Discursive Transparency in Beatrice Culleton" Cheryl's voice is represented through various discourses. Referring to Cheryl's voice, she writes:

> She is represented in a variety of discourses: the stumbling and (unlikely) letters of a pre-schooler; subsequent letter; academic speeches and essays on Métis history; oratory written for a university newspaper but in the end delivered orally at a powwow; dialogue most centrally; and, posthumously, diary entries. (276)

Cheryl's subjectivity is a constructed one, both by April's narration and the reader's understanding. The reader is also led to the question of the authenticity of the narrator's account of events. April is herself in a state of 'becoming.' It is possible to locate selves instead of a unified identity. As Helen Hoy points out in her study:

> In place of the bounded and unitary self, *In Search of April Raintree* creates permeable and melded selves. The narrative voice is fluid and inclusive, neither hermeneutically singular nor neatly bifurcated. (281)

This reflects the ambivalent identity of April as well as throws up the question of perception and authenticity. The plurality of voices also makes us aware of the internal dialogue and the questioning taking place within the text. Also central to the text is the notion of difference, which constitutes an ongoing debate within feminism. Heather Zwicker, in her article, "The Limits of Sisterhood" writes, "Taken metaphorically 'sisterhood' describes a well known—and fraught—trope for feminism" (324).

Sisterhood or the need to create a community of women in spite of difference is a daunting task for feminists. The novel goes to show how given their ideological differences sisterhood is difficult to maintain even between biological sisters. With April and Cheryl, as Zwicker points out, "race becomes a constitutive element of their gendered identity early on." (325). Their responses to history even at school are different. April is the assimilationist and Cheryl adopts identity politics. Zwicker observes: "as feminists we desperately want Cheryl's uncompromising political vision to triumph over April's quiescence" (328). Her death therefore, seems unfair in the face of the politics she adopts since her stance seems absolutely correct. April, true to her liberal stance, feels that as Zwicker puts it:

> The only option she has is to ignore the differences between them, trying to adopt an ethos of forgiving and forgetting that does not allow for narratives of pain and betrayal to be admitted and worked out. (331)

This approach adopted by liberal feminists is often resented by feminists of colour as being the mainstream's attempts to co-opt and dilute their agenda. The novel seems to suggest that the need for a community of women is a crucial one, however difficult that might be and for this dialogue, honesty and mutual respect are essential. This point is put forth eloquently by bell hooks in *Feminist Theory: From Margin to Center* in these words:

> Women of colour must confront our absorption of white supremacist beliefs, "internalized racism," which may lead us to feel self-hate, to vent anger and rage at injustice at one another, or lead one ethnic group to make no effort to communicate with one another. (57)

This is the challenge that feminism faces at present. The insensitivity that white, mainstream liberal feminism has shown towards the issues confronting women of colour, has led to the splintering of the movement. There has also been difficulty encountered in women of different ethnicities comprehending each other and coming together even on a minimum agenda. Poverty and the lack of affluence have rendered a lot of women of colour invisible. These are also the issues the novel seems to address at a metaphorical level.

4.6 'Transgendering' and Liminal Identities

When one reads Shani Mootoo's *Cereus Blooms at Night*, one is struck by the craftsmanship of the writer who succeeds in foregrounding issues of gender and the immigrant experience without making the polemics of these debates too obvious and without compromising the aesthetic value of the work or the high drama it contains.

The novel is essentially the story of Mala Ramchandin who does not narrate her own story but whose life is pieced together through multiple narrations. She and her sister Asha become victims of their father's battering and sexual abuse after their mother Sarah runs off with Lavinia, her childhood friend whom their father Chandin had always loved. There is a curious love triangle between the two women and Chandin. Being the son of an indentured labourer, Ramchandin from India is uprooted from his family and religion for financial betterment. Thus the saga of the family encompassing three generations unfolds. Chandin is made to take up residence with Reverend Thoroughly's family and grows up cultivating their manners and culture only to give it all up in the frustration for not being able to marry their daughter, Lavinia.

Lavinia is sent to a place called the Shivering Wetlands (evidently England) on the pretext that most of their relations resided there. Chandin is hurt and humiliated and marries Sarah on the rebound but never gets over his love for Lavinia. Lavinia, on her return to Paradise, a town in Lantanacamara, where the novel is set, develops a lesbian attachment to Sarah. Although both Lavinia and Sarah love their children, they are compelled by circumstances to elope abandoning Asha and Pohpoh as Mala is affectionately called. Mala is suddenly catapulted to the role of mother and protector of her sister Asha. She has to submit her body to the sexual abuse of her father who expects the daughters to come to him in turns. Mala's manipulations are designed to keep Asha out of his sight. Thus comes the horrifying end to Mala's childhood. Asha makes her escape out of Paradise in her teens and this leaves Mala to face the brunt of her father's sexual attentions and battering. The only ray of hope in her young life is her love for Ambrose Mohanty or Boyie, her schoolmate. Ambrose is sent to the Shivering Wetlands to study theology. He rejects the central premise of Christianity that man is the centre of the universe and returns to Paradise, having abandoned theology for entomology. Back home he begins to renew his relationship with Mala. The two of them have always enjoyed a camaraderie in protecting insects and birds from the bullies of the school. A while later they are caught making love by Chandin who attacks them and gets killed by a door slammed on him by Ambrose. Ambrose abandons Mala, as he cannot digest the fact that Mala has been the victim of her father's sexual abuse. He later regrets abandoning her, but she goes insane in the meantime. All that he can offer her by way of love, retribution and remorse is to leave food at her doorstep each day, making his son Otoh carry it to her house. The past with its drama is brought back by the incident of Otoh's discovery of Chandin's decaying, dead body in Mala's house. It was there for years after the house had been burnt down. The story begins with Mala being brought to a home for the aged. Tyler, a male nurse gets to know her story in parts from his grandmother. Ambrose sleeps for long periods, not being able to face himself and is brought back to life as it were by his son Otoh wanting to reunite his father with Mala. In the process he discovers his homosexual love for Tyler. Love is held out as the only possible healing force in the novel.

The ideas of home and the definition of self are connected. Mootoo problematizes both these concepts in the course of the novel. Anglophone literature in Canada has been preoccupied with home more as a state of mind than as a physical place. The idea is highlighted by Joanne Saul, in her review of the novel:

> In an age of globalization, transnationalism and mass migration, definitions of home have become more and more complex, particularly for those whose homelands have been colonized. Recent his-

> tories of colonization and displacement have meant that writing 'home' is not always innocent and idyllic but often a practice fraught with ambivalence and conflict. (par.1)

This becomes a major determining factor in identity construction. Homi Bhabha, in an essay referring to the problem of hybridity, discusses the need for creating a 'third space.' This is where an immigrant can carve out a unique identity for himself. Mootoo herself was born in Ireland, raised in Trinidad, studied visual arts in University of Ontario, relocated in Vancouver and now shuttles between Vancouver and San Francisco. In her novel, Mootoo unsettles romantic ideas of home as is seen in the novel when Elsie Mohanty says to her son Otoh: "You grow up here and you don't realize everybody in this place wish they could be somebody or something else. That is the story of life here in Lantanacamara." (237)[5]

The novel questions the very idea of 'border' by collapsing a lot of categories like home and the world, outside and the inside (that space which is supposed to be a haven of peace and security), sanity and insanity, man-woman, child-adult, and the insider-outsider.

Lantanacamara, a lush green, mythic tropical island, and tropical and (ironically named) Paradise in the novel, is in fact hellish for Mala and Asha with its claustrophobia associations and the physical abuse they undergo. The inside of the house signifies decay with rotting corpse of Chandin while the outside garden which is teeming with insects and birds gives Mala solace. It is the outsider Tyler who re/constructs Mala's story whereas the insiders have abandoned her. The narrative technique with its telescoping effect of narrative within narrative, and the plethora of gradually emerging voices, corresponds to the writer's concerns. Therefore, what constitutes home is examined by Mootoo in ironical terms. Contrary to belief about home being a place that evokes a great deal of nostalgia for the immigrant writer who often romanticizes a fossilized idea of home which he left behind decades ago, the place is seen as a trap. The fragments of Mala's past which Tyler pieces together do not contain an idyllic childhood. She has to confront the reality of her mother's lesbianism in the midst of her parents' marital discord. The intimacy of that lesbian relationship is fixed like still photographs in Mala's childhood memories. One is reminded that by training Mootoo is a visual artist. Chandin captures one of those poignant moments in a photograph he clicks on the beach. There is again a distancing effect for the reader this time through the camera lens. This is an important symbol in the novel, in that it is a piece of family history. It continues to haunt Chandin and Mala in different ways. The Shivering Wetlands hold out the promise of educational uplift and social mobility but it also signifies alienation from one's origins and this is an ambivalence the immigrant writer needs to confront. Canada, the country Asha finally migrates to, is held out as a space of further liberation from her past. She, in turn offers Mala the prospect of migration as security in her letters.

There are autobiographical elements in these parts of the novel since Shani Mootoo was a victim of child abuse herself. It took her several years of therapy and a relationship with a sensitive woman to confront the fact. She was abused between the ages of 2-13 years by different people, so much so that the rage was reflected in her paintings. An art critic, Jack Shadbolt, reports that Mootoo admits as having said that she was not going to be able to paint anymore unless she checked out what was eating her up inside (Sherman par. 4). In an interview she admits how it affected her very sense of well being with Barbara Sherman, "It was as if I wanted to run away from myself, leave my body behind and just escape" (par. 16) (there is an interesting parallel between her and Penn Kemp in the sense of wanting to leave the body behind as a result of abuse). She, like Kemp, turned to Buddhism and would chant to centre herself. Like Mala in the novel, she found comfort and safety in the garden and wished that some day something good would come of all that was happening to her and that she would be able to use it in some way. She says in the interview with the visual artist, Sarinder Dhaliwal, that she fell in love with art in her earlier youth because "of its possibilities for ambiguity of metering out, not spilling what was inside of me" (par. 2). She turned to writing much later but for precisely the opposite reason Mootoo says, "I find writing to be a form in which I can delve more deeply into a subject than I have been able to do in video or visual art" (par. 2). In fact, literature provided her with an escape route in early childhood: "I started reading everything I could, all kinds of books and I disappeared in them. I got myself lost in words." It is after she visited the Stave Correction Centre and talked to the offenders that she could address the problem of abuse. Strangely it has not made her bitter towards men as she says in the same interview: "It's just that women act out mostly on themselves and men seem to aggress on other people that are less powerful than themselves" (par. 2).

These views are expressed in her sensitive portrayal of male characters like Tyler and Chandin. Except for the central romance of the novel—that of Ambrose and Mala, the rest of the characters are of unconventional gender preferences. Mootoo subverts traditional conventions of narratives by making Tyler, a liminal subject, the narrator of the piece. He is constantly apologetic about bringing in his own story (which highlights his marginality in the narrative itself) but he knows that it is necessary to establish his presence. To his misfortune he has internalized the social ostracism he faces as a result of his sexual preferences. It is important for him to narrate Mala's story since she reaffirms his gender identity and accepts him. Professionally, for him she is the first resident entrusted fully in his care thereby marking his success as a nurse. Tyler feels compelled to 'prove' himself since it is a female-dominated profession. Till then he had been given only menial and lesser jobs to do. Summarizing Monique Wittig's views on discourse, Judith Butler writes: "Discourse becomes oppressive when it requires that the speaking subject, in order to speak participates in the very terms of that oppression—that is, take for granted the speaking subject's own impossibility or unintelligibility." (116) This is perhaps the very dilemma Tyler faces but ultimately a genuine concern and compassion are what lead him to the truth of the story. Butler, in elaborating Wittig's position says further:

> Women, lesbians, and gay men, [Wittig argues] cannot assume the position of the speaking subject within the linguistic system of compulsory heterosexuality. To speak within the system is to be deprived of the possibility of speech; hence, to speak at all in that context is a performative contradiction, the linguistic assertion of a self that cannot "be" within language that asserts it. (116)

Wittig here points out that in the discourses of dominance, liminal identities can never become speaking subjects. Mootoo, by making Tyler the narrator of Mala's story, makes it possible for him to narrate his own story in the interstices and thereby come to his own as a speaking subject as well. Tyler, earlier in the novel, mentions being a survivor and seeing Mala's fighting spirit creates an instant bonding between them. Both of them face ostracism and put up a fight by refusing to play by socially prescribed rules.

Sexuality plays a crucial role in the formation of identity and the subject position one adopts. Tyler perceives himself in the following way:

> Not a man and not ever able to be woman, suspended nameless in a state between existence and non-existence. (77)

Ironically Tyler is born a man but has the psyche of a woman and Otoh, born a woman has the mental make up of a man. Through these characters Mootoo seeks to collapse the sexual norms given by society as also the tendency to see gender as a biological given. The physical description of Otoh suggests an ambivalent sexual identity. Mootoo describes him as seen by Tyler in the following words:

> At one glance he had the angularity and sprightliness of a girl reluctantly on the verge of becoming a woman, and at the next the innocent feyness of a young boy who would never quite grow into the glove of manhood. (100-1)

This is Tyler's view of Otoh. Tyler of course is enamoured of Otoh's beauty and a little later the reader is given a glimpse of the turmoil created by sexuality and its ambivalence as experienced by Otoh:

> He held the nipples between his fingers, squeezed and rubbed them until they puckered into little squares, trying to imagine what Mavis might have felt like when she lay next to him and touched his shirtless body. He was grateful for such small breasts. As long as his tightly belted trousers were never removed he had nothing to worry about. (141)

A little earlier with Mavis by his side Otoh experiences pleasure but it is more autoerotic as it seems to have little to do with his partner. Otoh's sexual identity is more ambivalent than Tyler's. Towards the end even while his mother expresses doubt about marriage with Mavis, he still seems to be in denial of the body he/she is born with and feels that he has to take a final decision about his sexuality which would determine his identity.

In spite of such ambivalence, it is Tyler and Otoh who show capacity for love and compassion in uncovering Mala's past and in caring for her. Mootoo makes a studied effort to unfold the humane qualities of these two characters who would be considered "freakish" by social standards.

Mala's body, aside from portraying the trauma of sexual abuse in childhood, is a central metaphor for playing out various power struggles. Feminists have recognized ages ago that rape is not just forced sex but the assertion of power over the victim and all that the victim represents. Chandin uses Mala's body to vent his impotent anger and humiliation caused by his wife, Sarah. Chandin's is a fractured ego, one of the remnants of the postcolonial subject's experiences in the Caribbean. He is sent to Reverend Thoroughly for Western grooming and education and loses his roots. In the final analysis he emerges as a victim of the 'brown sahib' mentality. These are the mimic men who perpetrate the colonial mindset. They give vent to their frustrations resulting from an inability to get accepted by the dominant community and/or accepting their worldview by oppressing their own kind. This issue highlights Mootoo's concern with the postcolonial condition as a theme parallel to the theme of women's oppression and sexuality. Ambrose is a more aware character than Chandin since he abandons the dominant Christian worldview. Also, he returns to Lantanacamara unlike most people who stay on in the Shivering Wetlands and marry foreigners. Ambrose is, however not courageous enough to stand up to his convictions or be supportive to Mala. His ultimate act of betrayal is turning his back on her after he kills her father. Mala drifts into insanity when she is abandoned once again by a loved one while Ambrose takes to sleeping his guilt off.

Mala's body—the daily recipient of sexual abuse and battering by her father, develops its own defence mechanisms for survival. She learns to shut out the pain by numbing her body to its daily dose. As long as her romance with Ambrose is there, her body even yearns for him and she experiences desire and pleasure when they make love after his return to Paradise. She revels in the physical sensations of pleasure and pleasant fragrances in her sexual encounters with Ambrose in contrast to the ugliness of forced sex with her father. It is she who is the eager partner. Even during their childhood's brief sexual episode, she focuses on her own pleasure and leaves him unfulfilled. Her body learns to experience desire for the male body and pleasure in spite of its early trauma of sexual abuse. She is keen to prove to herself that it can be pleasurable: "She used this hardness to arrive at her intended destination before he could even unbuckle his belt." (96) She leaves him confused, humiliated and unfulfilled. She has to later deal with her father's advances and she is already mentally and physically preparing herself for that.

When Ambrose betrays and abandons her, she has to develop psychological defences for her survival. She loses touch with reality to avoid its glaring cruelty and acquires a split personality. She is Mala, the protector, adult and nurturer as also Pohpoh, the vulnerable child who needs protection. She does this through regression. Regression enables her to become her own mother in the absence of her real mother. Mothering comes naturally to her as she has early on been compelled to be a mother to her sister Asha and a substitute wife to her father. Mala is the archetypal nurturer, the mother to humans, animals, birds and insects. Mootoo uses irony very deftly in the plot: Mala, who never really had her mother, has to be a mother not just to her sister but in a sense even to Ambrose, whom she is protective of and takes great pleasure in feeding varieties of large portions of food. The love she feels for him is not romantic but more complex and deep.

Strong shades of ecofeminism and the 'womanist' position are presented by Shani Mootoo in the novel. Qualities which are labeled as 'feminine' by patriarchy such as compassion, nurturing and protection are held out as essential for the preservation of the planet. Mootoo shows in a sensitive manner that these qualities are not just the prerogatives of women but that men like Tyler and Otoh also possess them in large measures. Mootoo succeeds in 'transgendering' for she goes beyond the category of gender in her sympathetic portrayal of Tyler as a homosexual and in her attempts to understand Chandin's violence. The sympathy for homosexuals reminds one that in the early phases of the Lesbian movement there was a strategic coming together of lesbians and gay men, a political position that was abandoned later.

Mala imparts her love for plants and insects to Ambrose while at school and both of them make it their mission to protect snails from the school bullies. This stance is a definite departure from the concerns of mainstream feminist writers and their treatment of male characters. Mootoo seems to be reiterating that men are victims as much as women in terms of the oppressive institutions of patriarchy in general and the colonial experience in particular. The colonial experience proves to be as traumatizing psychologically to the male and female characters as is the exploitation of the female body. Even while Mala is being victimized she justifies her victimizer, thus proving that the victim becomes part of the pattern of abuse. Body sensations for Mala get compartmentalized and a means of escape from the psychological injury. Curiously there is an almost prosaic and economic rendering of Mala's first molestation by her father. This is perhaps due to Mootoo's own problems in confronting it. However the pain and trauma are more poignant in their understatement than a hysterical rendering would have been. Mala allows Ambrose to touch her as a means of escape: "But they were children and she had let him, not because she felt any love for him but because she wanted the ticklish feeling and moments of escape the act gave her." (193)

She divorces her body sensations from her consciousness. This process is however, not simple because the body's memory cannot be erased. As Mootoo describes in the following lines:

> She began to feel what she normally was oblivious to: her face and neck, wet with sweat and tears, bruises on her legs, skin that felt as though it had been torn off her back in thick chunks. Her lower stomach ached. Fear was breaking her, was unprying her memory. She was reminded of what she usually ignored or commanded herself to forget: her legs being ripped apart, something entered her down there, entering her and then scooping her insides out. Her body remembered. (174-75)

The trauma experienced is a very powerful memory stored as it were by her body and let loose by different associations. Mala is not just a protector and nurturer of nature but seeks solace in it. She severs all human contact after Ambrose deserts her. Mootoo writes:

> Mala's companions were the garden's birds, insects, snails and reptiles. She and they and the abundant foliage gossiped among themselves. She listened intently. With an ear pressed to the ground she heard ant communities building, transporting food and breeding. (127)

In the absence of and longing for her mother she turns to Nature, the mother from whom she gets security and cover. These she never gets from her human mother when she is distraught. In highlighting of this relationship with nature, Mootoo portrays the beauty of Caribbean flora and fauna in its entire gamut. Significantly there are sketches of the most unique insects through the pages of the novel.

Given the child Mala's bewilderment at the lesbian relationship of her mother, one can see that there is no glorification of the relationship. This is very unlike what one finds in the Québecoise or some black women writers' works. Mala's is a mortifying jolt into sexual awakening. The Lavinia-Sarah relationship is suggestive of the 'butch-femme' roles, which continue to be a raging controversy in lesbian communities even today.

Beginning with gender, there is a collapsing of various other culturally-constructed categories. Mootoo does not wish to be pigeonholed into categories like Indo-Caribbean, lesbian, South Asian etc. but all these groups are claiming her.

One of the strategies she uses for transgendering is to use one liminal identity to speak for another. This is discussed elaborately by the British critic Coral Ann Howells in her article, "A Shared Queerness: Liminal Identities in Shani Mootoo's *Cereus Blooms at Night*." Tyler, a homosexual, speaks for Mala who is othered by virtue of being old, supposedly insane, single and a suspected criminal. Although the lesbian relationship is not glorified, the children are happier with Lavinia and Sarah than with their parents. It is Mala's communion with nature that forms the symbolic ideal in the novel. This is a latent utopian vision but this undomesticated space would also allow for fluidity in sexuality and gender identities. The womanist stance seems to be more relevant and wholesome to the entire species today with the planet being endangered as it is. The stench of decay permeating the place does not make Mala flinch. She identifies with the insects which she protects but this causes the decay of her own existence. Nature allows death to sustain life. The novel touchingly records the story of her own slow death to free others like her mother and her sister. Cereus, the central metaphor in the novel, is symbolic of hope and redemption through love. Rare and beautiful as the flower is, it is akin to love and compassion—the only redeeming factors of an otherwise sterile human existence. Cereus is a metaphor for Mala herself for there are several images of flowers hanging limp and like Mala's body and spirit. Just like the fleeting moments of happiness in her life, they bloom with an intoxicating, heady perfume at moments in the night. Even while the house burns down with all its vegetation and insects, Otoh rescues a small cutting of the cereus plant (which is a cactus) to be given to Mala at the end of the novel. Love is seen as a healing force both in its heterosexual and homosexual manifestations. The reworking of the category of gender is important to Shani Mootoo, given her Indo-Caribbean background as well.[6]

The humiliating position of women is portrayed powerfully in the novel. Chandin rages when he discovers his daughter is with Ambrose. This is because he feels that another man has stolen his daughter as if she is his property. On discovering his daughter with Ambrose, he rages:

> "What the ass. . .?" he mumbled "A man tiefing my baby? He brave even to try. I ent go to let nobody tief my woman again. No man, no woman, no body go tief my property again. I go kill he. I go kill she too, if it comes to that. I go kill myself too. I sharpenin' my cutlass tonight." (220)

She is his property in the most literal and crude sense and so is Asha. Sarah is subjected to a loveless marriage. Elsie Mohanty is similarly caught in a loveless marriage with Ambrose who dwells in his past. She gets respite from his clutter, his demands and mainly his talk only when he sleeps for long periods of time.

There seems to be a subversion of the Sleeping Beauty fairy tale with reference to Ambrose's love for Mala who wakes him, with the help of the efforts of his son Otoh. The other border that is sought to be demolished is that between sanity and insanity. Feminists have pointed out that in the Freudian paradigm the hysterical woman is really one who does not conform to patriarchal roles. Mala, in her act of defiance, also goes insane and this results in her further alienation from society. The postman refuses to deliver Asha's letters written over several years. The letters might have rescued her from a total breakdown. Time is a continuum in which for her, the past holds more reality than the present. The narration is cyclic, beginning and ending with Tyler's story. Referring to his narrative, Tyler himself tells the reader that he is about to "fashion a single garment out of myriad parts" (105). His marginal identity helps him to align himself with Mala and this enables him to re/cover her story and helps her perhaps to re/cover sanity uttering her first words in public—the first word being 'Pohpoh,' her own name. This signifies her movement towards integration after having suffered a split identity and living in the past. She links the name Pohpoh with associations of her father's use of it. In the early part of the novel, she utters the name as if it were that of a pet animal or bird showing that she has blocked out the trauma of the past. There is evidence of her consciousness returning as she has tears in her eyes when Asha's letters are read out to her, much like Nettie's letter to Celie in *The Color Purple*. The epistolary is woven into the narrative to signify the distance and the promise of new beginning in a new place. One is also reminded of Jean Rhys' *Wide Sargasso Sea*, with the centring of the insane protagonist and the re-telling of the story from the point of view of one with a marginal identity. The familiar Caribbean trope of the burnt down house suggestive of purification and renewal is present in this novel too. The narrative with its build up of mystery and suspense which climaxes with Otoh's discovery of Chandin's corpse in the interiors of the house, has Gothic overtones. There is a wildness about Mala and the house. The survivor in her makes her avoid the decay and morbidity of the house with all its dark memories. What the novel achieves through border crossings of various kinds is the questioning and collapsing of the neat and comfortable binaries that patriarchy imposes on people by presenting alternative world-views.

4.7 The Silent Body and the Language of Silence

Obasan by Joy Kogawa, is an example of a text where the body is being written in an extremely subtle manner. The novel, as acknowledged by Kogawa herself is autobiographical, in that, it narrates the trials and tribulations of the Japanese-Canadians during the Second World War, when they were uprooted from their residences and dispersed in different internment camps, after having their properties and land confiscated by the government, since suspicion of them as being spies and saboteurs ran high. Coomi Vevaina notes: "History shows us that during depression or war, deep-seated prejudices are usually grafted onto new fears and anxieties to produce a rank growth of racism." (Dissertation 90)

Obasan narrates the horrifying experiences of racism and ostracism faced by the Japanese-Canadians during the war years. Kogawa, born in 1935 in British Columbia, experienced the internment camp when her family was sent to Coaldale and lived a life of field labour. She began writing in 1959. In an interview with Sue Careless, Kogawa, admitting that *Obasan* is strongly autobiographical, says: "Like Naomi, I became a person who would not speak, would not ask a question, did not expect to be heard." (1988) In the same interview, discussing the nature of silence, she says: "I have a great deal of respect for cultures of silence. My first language was silence; my second was speech. I understand the language of silence; yet I need a lot of communication." (1988)

The novel begins with these lyrical lines of the epigraph:

> There is a silence that cannot speak.
> There is a silence that will not speak.
> Beneath the grass the speaking dreams and beneath the dreams is
> a sensate sea. The speech that frees comes forth from that amniotic deep. To attend its voice, I can hear it say, is to embrace its absence. But I fail the task. The word is stone. (*Obasan*)

She ends these introductory lines by asking:

> If I could follow the stream down and down to the hidden voice, would I come at last to the freeing word? (*Obasan*)

The novel, narrated from the child Naomi's perspective, is about silence and absence. The absence and silence of her mother imposes years of silence on Naomi, whose identity is submerged but whose inner life is rich and it is that which sustains and nourishes her. Naomi's sense of loss and betrayal by her mother's sudden disappearance when she is five years old and her mother's continued absence and complete lack of communication with her daughter is almost archetypal. The sense of the loss and psychic trauma are portrayed in the most poignant terms. She is able to delve deep in the underground stream of the layers of her unconscious and relate to her mother only in her dreams. The loss of her mother and her psychological inability to sever the umbilical cord has a profound impact on Naomi's personality development and identity. This trauma is compounded by racial discrimination and the literal fragmentation that the Japanese-Canadian community has to undergo due to the dispersal policy. The desertion of the mother as the child sees it, coincides with the desertion of the community by their country, Canada. The episode where Naomi and her aunt search in the attic for something "lost" is powerful in its significance. The attic is in itself significant as a repository of the family's memories—something of an archive. It triggers powerful memories in Naomi of her mother, even as she comes upon a thin patchwork quilt her mother had made for her bed when she was four years old. These fragments of things are storehouses of painful memories:

> When I least expect it, a memory comes skittering out of the dark, spinning and netting the air, ready to snap me up and ensnare me in old and complex puzzles. Just a glimpse of a worn-out patchwork quilt and the old question comes thudding out of the night again like a giant moth. Why did my mother not return. (26)

The response to this question has always been silence—that it was a silence of protection when the facts about her mother and grandmother Kato's fate in Nagasaki are revealed Naomi realizes later. This does not take away the pain and bewilderment that Naomi feels throughout her childhood and adult life due to her mother's unexplained absence. Aunt Emily remarks on what a serious and unsmiling baby Naomi had been. The still photograph of her and her mother fill her with an old, familiar longing for home in Vancouver—the only place with pleasant, almost idyllic memories of childhood for Naomi. She remembers her mother's soft voice narrating the story of Momotaro:

> My arms are flung around my mother as she lies beside me and breathe in her powdery perfume as she continued her chant. (61)

The story which Naomi never tires of hearing is significant in that, it is about a child who is a gift to parents who are not his biological parents and who place a high value on living in honour above everything else. Memories of her mother are invariably linked with Naomi's childhood house in Vancouver and these come back to her in a sensory manner with feelings of longing in fragments:

> These are the bits of the house I remember. If I linger in the longing, I am drawn into a whirlpool. I can only skirt the edges after all. (57)

This is linked to memories of her mother:

> The woman in the picture is frail and shy and the child is equally shy, unable to lift her head. Only fragments relate me to them now, to this young woman, my mother and me, her infant daughter. Fragments of fragments. Parts of a house. Segments of stories. (57)

In the incident when young Naomi sees the white hen injure and kill her yellow chicks, she runs to her mother to rescue the chicks. The image of her strong, protective mother is imprinted in her memory:

> All the while that she acts, there is calm efficiency in her face and she does not speak. Her eyes are steady and matter of fact—the eyes of Japanese motherhood. They do not invade and betray. They are eyes that protect, shielding what is hidden most deeply in the heart of the child. She makes safe the small stirrings underfoot and in the shadows. (63)

The child Naomi does not perceive herself as different from her mother and in fact, sees herself as an appendage or an extension of her mother's body.

> I am clinging to my mother's leg, a flesh shaft that grows from the ground, a tree trunk of which I am an off-shoot—a young branch attached by right of flesh and blood. Where she is rooted, I am rooted. If she walks, I will walk. Her blood is whispering through my veins. The shaft of her leg is the shaft of my body and I am her thoughts. (69)

This is quite typical of the undifferentiated identity with the mother that a child experiences prior to the separation and sense of self achieved in the process of maturation. The sexual abuse Naomi experiences at the hands of Mr. Gower leaves her confused and guilty, especially since her mother's leaving coincides with this episode. She blames herself for it and feels that the secret had already separated her from her mother. In spite of the love showered on her and her brother Stephen by her uncle and Obasan, the feeling of security never returns to her. Naomi feels, "In the centre of my body is a rift" (69).

This separation from her mother is repeatedly enacted in her childhood and later dreams with the accompanying image of her legs being sawn in half. This recurs in several dreams throughout the novel. The confusing mixture of pleasure and fear which she experiences after Mr. Gower's sexual advances, leave her feeling guilty and powerless. The feeling of powerlessness finds expression in a dream about three beautiful oriental women lying naked on a muddy road. The women resort to seduction as a way of escaping the soldiers' bullets and in order to survive. One of the women has her legs severed above the ankles. Unable to run, Naomi identifies with Snow White in the forest, and visualizes Gower as "the forest full of eyes" (69).

When she asks for her mother, she is told that her great grandmother being very ill, needed her. This does not appeal to the child's logic and she thinks:

> My great grandmother has need of my mother. Does my mother have need of me? In what market place of the universe are the bargains made that have traded my need for my great grandmother's? (72)

The absence and silence of her mother have undoubtedly had a profound impact on Naomi's psycho-sexual development. All through the novel she constantly turns to mother earth for comfort and healing.

The other aspect that figures prominently throughout *Obasan* and the sequel novel, *Itsuka*, written ten years later is Naomi's repressed sexuality. Cecily Devereaux, in her article titled, "The Body of Evidence: Re-membering the Past in Joy Kogawa's *Obasan*" writes:

> *Obasan* is articulated in terms of the body. It utilizes a body-centred vocabulary and explores a system of maternal symbolic iconography. In Kogawa's novel, the past is figured as a body; the narrative as a process of its paradoxical exhuming and birth, and the text as its reconstitution—or resurrection—in a new form which integrates a plurality of voices in one narrative. The corporeal images that dominate the novel's language explicitly link the text—and memory—in process with the metaphor of the past as a silent—dead—body which resists burial. (236)

The act of memory is held out as being restorative not only to the individual, but the community as well as Aunt Emily tells Naomi:

> "You have to remember," Aunt Emily said, "You are your history. If you cut any of it off you're an amputee. Don't deny the past. Remember everything. If you're bitter, be bitter. Cry it out! Scream! Denial is gangrenous. (54)

To Aunt Emily, silencing the past can be gangrenous and unhealthy for the person and by extension, the community. The two aunts represent two different approaches and ways of being as Naomi understands it:

> How different my two aunts are. One lives in sound, the other in stone. Obasan's language remains deeply underground but Aunt Emily, BA, MA, is a word warrior. (33)

The house and Obasan's body are continuous, in that, both signify warmth, familiarity and protection. Both are storehouses of collective, cultural memory as well. Naomi's writing of Obasan's maternal body signifies all of these things:

> The house is indeed old, as she is also old. Every home-made piece of furniture, each pot holder and paper doily is a link in her lifeline. She has preserved in shelves, in cupboards, under beds—a box of marbles, half-filled colouring books, a red, white and blue rubber ball. . . . They rest in the corners like parts of her body, hair cells, skin tissues, tiny specks of memory. This house is now her blood and bones. (15-16)

The bonding of women through three generations prevailing in the community is portrayed in the bathing scenes earlier in the Vancouver house when little Naomi bathes with Grandma Kato and later in the public bath with Obasan and Nomura Obasan. She writes of bathing with Grandma Kato in these words:

> My body is extended beside hers and she makes waves to cover my shoulders. Once the body is fully immersed there is torpid peace. We live in this state forever. (52)

This is the idyllic period of Naomi's childhood, her grandmother's and mother's bodies signifying security and contentment. Smaro Kamboureli, in her analysis of the novel, writes:

> The reciprocity of the three bodies—mother's, grandmother's and Naomi's—shows their discourse to be at once constative and performative in that they do what they say, and they say what they do. Here, 'saying' denotes a discourse of physicality that expresses the libidinal energies connecting these bodies to each other. The corporeal map that links them is produced by the constant flow of these women's desires, a circuit of exchange established by their bodies' knowing. (180)[7]

Obasan's old body is compared to the landscape and a map to be deciphered as Naomi helps her with her bath:

> I rub the wash cloth over her legs and feet, the thin purple veins a scribbled maze, a skin map, her thick toenails ancient rock formations. I am reminded of long extinct volcanoes, the crust and rivulets of lava scars, criss-crossing down the bony hillside. Naked as prehistory, we lie together, the steam from the bath heavily misting the room. (84)

There is something indestructible and solid as the landscape about the aged Obasan's body, containing the past within as memory. Obasan and Uncle have been the only constant in Naomi's life. Naomi's identification and sex typing during her formative years would be with Obasan, who had been a mother to her almost all her life. Naomi's sexual inhibitions are perhaps, partly due to the lack of physical demonstration of feelings, which she is used to in Obasan's household. This is evident when she sees her aunt first after her uncle's death. "Oba," I say loudly and take her hands. My aunt is not for hugs and kisses" (11). She has never seen Obasan demonstrate grief either:

> Her eyes are unclear and sticky with a gum-like mucus. She told me years ago her tear ducts were clogged. In all this time I've never seen her cry. (12)

Grief is written all over and is contained within. Naomi knows this and she acknowledges the fact in these words:

> The language of her grief is silence. She has learned it well, its idioms, its nuances. Over the years, silence within her small body has grown large and powerful. (14)

This constrained person has been the major female influence in Naomi's growing up years and Naomi describes herself as having "the social graces of a common housefly" (7), knowing fully well that she was being self-denigrating. Naomi's anger at being asked if she had ever been in love stems from her dormant feelings. She wonders why she and Aunt Emily remain unmarried and again thinks in a self-derogatory way: "Must be something in the blood. A crone-prone syndrome" (8). Her repressed sexuality is again evident in her identification with several asexual fairytale heroines like Snow White, Rapunzel, Goldilocks and later, in *Itsuka*, when she is with Father Cedric, the Anglican priest, whom she is attracted to, she identifies with Alice in Wonderland and Cinderella. Even as an adult, seeing a photograph of her mother, conjures up sensations of the physical connectedness with her:

> My fat arm clings to your leg. Your skirt hides my face. Your leg is a tree trunk and I am branch, vine, butterfly. I am joined to your limbs by right of birth, child of your flesh, leaf of your bough. (266-67)

This is during the distress she feels when her mother's plight in Nagasaki is first revealed to her. Images of death with the accompanying terror continue to haunt the Naomi of *Itsuka*. She is sexually inhibited and dormant, even as a forty-year-old woman, haunted by fears of sexuality:

> I fear too, the cunning of the body's inner foes. I fear touch as much as the inability to touch. So, of course, I fear Father Cedric. (2)

Aunt Emily advises her that life has to be a hands-on experience and that she has to act and be involved. This advice applies to her at the personal and political level. Kamboureli, with reference to the impact of the gaze on Naomi writes:

> The stare visualizes Naomi's body, foregrounding her physical appearance: the body still shapes her identity, but it is the dynamics of a look that determines her sense of difference and alienation. It is through this logic of visuality that Naomi enters the realm of the body politic. (191)

Naomi's repressed sexuality is also in part, due to the rigorous Christian religious teachings she is exposed to. She associates sin with the body, "As the grid of the Christian fundamentalists' way of life descends, so too do the demons of the flesh. Every thought to do with sex is sinful" (*Itsuka* 25). She is however, fascinated by the "bad kids" and admits: "The village is still in my middle-aged views" (28). When she calls herself old, Aunt Emily exclaims, "Old! You haven't even been born yet" (99). This also refers to her sexual dormancy, in addition to her political indifference. Her dream about being dismembered is significant in this context. She dreams that she is three tiny women in an inch-high library in a miniature world and a man who loves is in the background. (One is reminded of her earlier dream of being Alice following Father Cedric, the White Rabbit). In the dream she is faced with the dilemma of either staying in the man's tiny world or going in to oblivion. She chooses the latter and loses her limbs:

> Somewhere in this no longer physical, no longer visible world is the moment of discovery. What I know is that I am without a body, but I am, I am not without consciousness. (87)

The dream concludes with her returning to the body by whispering the word "mama." The dream of being disembodied can be related to her earlier dreams of limbs being severed. This perhaps, signifies the guilt and shame she feels towards the body. When Naomi walks with Father Cedric in the woods, she feels like a Cinderella and says: "This is the closest I have ever been to the prince's ball. In this my autumn season, I am opening the book of an untimely tale" (135). She later has a dream of Cinderella sitting at the end of "the pumpkin coach bus" and describes herself as "a shadow in search of her flesh" (136).

Father Cedric appreciates her feet as being "soft and perfect as babies' feet" (138) and thinks that high heels were like foot binding and this makes Naomi think:

> My whole body has been a foot binding all my life. How have I breathed through the layers of rules and propriety, through my fears. (138)

In an interview with Janice Williamson, Kogawa, discussing the body in her works, says:

> What I want is my body, and that is the big problem that Naomi has. She is so divorced from her body, such a repressed prude, and I don't think she's ever going to come out. I have such trouble with her. And Aunt Emily doesn't have her body either. There is a lostness I despair about because I don't know how I'm ever going to have my body. (158)

Kogawa gave the interview while she was still working on *Itsuka.* She identifies with Naomi's frustrated attempts at getting in touch with her body and in the same interview says:

> You see, I think that I truly am one of these really repressed people, too. Deep down it is so severe and the scarring is so great that maybe I'm not going to come out. I don't know. Maybe that's part of the struggle. (159)

The self-awareness that Naomi shows tempts one to think that she has the potential to eventually overcome the block and she does. She begins to feel more and more comfortable with Father Cedric and comes to accept her body's needs towards the end of the novel:

> The fact of flesh is new in my life. A simple fact, as commonplace as pebbles on a beach. But I'm a pebble that was lost. Now I've been found. I'm held in a hand that's warm as song. (271)

At the end of the novel, even as she becomes politically aware, she is sexually awakened:

> To be without history is to be unlived crystal, unused flesh, is to live the life of the unborn. What I've awakened to in this new autumn day is hunger. . . . I'm hungry for this square inch of space we are inhabiting today. Our bite-sized moment of life. I'm as small and as hungry as a newborn sparrow. (271)

What distinguishes Kogawa from writers writing the body, merely in celebration of it is the fact that the body, in this case, often serves as a metaphor as well. She is not merely writing of repressed sexuality and later sexual awakening, but also using the body as a metaphor to refer to the process of memory and re/covering the history of a community. The text contains a plurality of voices which often enact the tension between silence and speech. Kamboureli sees Naomi's narrative as that of a hysteric. Referring to Naomi's silence, she sees the racialized aspect of the repressed body and writes:

> the closer she comes to full expression of what she has repressed, the more she realizes that she cannot afford to forget what has caused that repression. To do so would be tantamount to practising cultural amnesia, forgetting the history of her body and her racialization, collaborating with the appropriating and assimilating strategies of hegemony. This is why I believe, Naomi's silent discourse reflects the liminality of her subjectivity, but it also discloses her reflexive use of repression to be an important political strategy. (212-13)

In an interview with Susan Yin, Joy Kogawa says:

> To the Issei, horror and dignity is expressed through silence the twig bending with the wind. The Sensei view silence as a dangerous kind of cooperation with the enemy. (par.3)

She refers to two kinds of silence—a silence that will not speak (protective silence) and a silence that cannot speak (silence about repressed memory and the unknown past). Obasan's silence is the Issei's ancient language of grief. Aunt Emily being Nissei is energetic and a visionary. She is described as a "word warrior." She is proud of her Canadian identity. Naomi's mother is 'kibei,' born in Canada and raised in Japan and described as 'yasashi kokoro.' Naomi, a Sansei is a 'spinster' and often numb. These voices belong to Kogawa who says in an interview with Karlyn Koh:

> after writing *Obasan* and in a way being forced into public situations, the Naomi character that was within me, who basically could not talk, and which is really the way I used to be, got more and more transformed and the Aunt Emily voice came out. (30-31)

When asked about the character of Aunt Emily in the same interview, she says:

> I was simply writing out of my own life and writing in some of the way I wrote poetry. . . . When I was at the Archives, though in Ottawa, that's when I became aware of another voice that I was not conscious of being within me—Muriel Kitagawa's voice. To me, it was a voice from the outside, one that I had never encountered, and one that I could only report on. So Aunt Emily's voice was always outside of me throughout the entire writing of *Obasan.* (26)

She admits that this plurality of voices did pose problems for the narrative as she says:

> I think in *Itsuka* I was much more like Emily, but since I was writing in Naomi's voice, I had a problem because I didn't want Naomi to be transformed too suddenly. (30-31)

Like Naomi, Kogawa says she had no consciousness except in a negative sense, of Japaneseness and that she thought and wrote as a white person. Assimilation was a great pressure that they had to contend with. Naomi's attitude to Aunt Emily's ideas is one of impatience bordering on scorn. When Aunt Emily writes in "The Story of the Nissei in Canada: A Struggle for Liberty," that she knows the Nissei well, Naomi thinks smugly that none of her friends presently were Japanese Canadians. Again, dual points of view are presented with Naomi asking Aunt Emily whether one should not just turn the page and move on, to which Aunt Emily replies, "The past is the future" (45). Again, looking at Aunt Emily's package, Naomi thinks: "What is past recall is past pain. Questions from all these papers, questions referring to turbulence in the past, are an unnecessary upheaval in the delicate ecology of this numb day." (48)

Running parallel to this is the discourse contained in Aunt Emily's letters to her sister entered in her diary describing the plight of the Japanese Canadians. It is however, clear to the reader, that the narrator Naomi is a subject in the process of formation. Naomi's vision is a partial one, since she is a child and many facts are withheld from her. When the policy of relocating and dispersing the Japanese Canadians begins, Stephen, who is old enough to understand the situation poses a riddle, "We are both the enemy and not the enemy" (*Obasan* 76). This is the first time that their ethnic identity is focused on and literally targeted. There is an account of the political climate changing in Vancouver and racial hatred. When they are forced to leave the B.C. coast Naomi records: "We are dispersed, rendered voiceless, stripped of car, radio, camera and every means of communication, a trainload of eyes covered with mud and spittle." (119)

They undergo unimaginable ordeals even as they get dispersed in different ghost towns. The indignation one ought to feel is tempered by Obasan's resilience and the consolation offered to Stephen during their difficult times. She tells him that "the best samurai swords are tempered over and over again in the hottest flames and people too are made strong and excellent when they go through life's difficulties" (142). Naomi is also touched by Obasan's worldview. She internalizes the negative stereotypes about her community due to the racist slurs Stephen and she are subjected to at school. She thinks while in the hospital after she almost drowns as a small girl:

> To be yellow in the Yellow Peril game is to be weak and small. Yellow is to be chicken. I am not yellow. I will not cry however much this nurse yanks my hair. (165)

It is under Aunt Emily's tutelage, her collected data and her insistence on remembering that Naomi is compelled to come to terms with the painful past. She protests against the incumbent pain using images of surgery and physiology:

> Aunt Emily, are you a surgeon cutting at my scalp with your folders and your insistence on knowing all? The memory drains down the sides of my face, but it isn't enough, is it? It's your hands in my abdomen, pulling the growth from the lining of my walls, but bring back the anaesthetic turn on the ether clamp down the gas mask bring on the chloroform when will this operation be over Aunt Em? (214)

There is a graphic description of young Naomi's toiling body in Alberta's beet farm. Naomi adopts a detached, unemotional tone when describing it. It is much later that she can bring herself to grieve about the past and even then sees the act of remembering as futile:

> I can remember since Aunt Emily insists that I must and release the flood gates one by one I can cry for the flutes that have cracked in the dryness and cry for the people who no longer sing. I can cry for Obasan who has turned to stone. But what then? (219)

The act of remembering is the key to re/covering history and retelling it. Memory is what would save history from erasure—not official versions of it but a community's authentic experiences. Denial would lead to gangrene and further amputation. Kogawa in the interview with Karlyn Koh talks about denial:

> When you're in denial you can go on with your life—it's a great survival tactic. . . . And I look back and see that I have lived my life in denial and that's what I write about. It enables me to thrive to the extent that I did. But the fog is denial, the fog is surviving, it keeps us safe, it keeps the sun from coming through and destroying us. The sun is like the truth I mean truth is what enables things to grow. (38)

In spite of the multicultural policy of Canada, visible minorities are always asked to explain their origins and to prove their Canadianness. When asked a similar question, Naomi wails:

> Oh Canada, whether it is admitted or not, we come from you. From the same soil, the slugs and slime and bogs and twigs and roots. We come from the country that plucks its people and flings them into the roadside. (*Itsuka* 247-48)

Naomi's dream of the Grand Inquisitor signifies the terrors and trauma of the racial profiling that the Japanese Canadians were subjected to.

It is through two letters written by Grandma Kato speaking of their travails in Nagasaki that Naomi resurrects her mother's story and the years of silence get broken and Naomi thinks, "Gentle mother, we were lost together in our silences. Our wordlessness was our mutual destruction" (*Obasan* 267). One senses that Naomi, in the course of the novel, and in her maturation process, has moved from the Issei position to the Nisei position. It is significant that she dons Aunt Emily's coat for warmth as she drives to the coulee. During this time, aided by the copious data in the form of letters, reports and manuscripts collected by Aunt Emily, Naomi re/covers her personal past and that of her community as well. In doing both, she attains her selfhood and the first steps to restore the community's dignity have also been taken. This view is endorsed by Shirley Geok-lin Lim in these words, "In rescuing? Writing her maternal and racial past, the narrator/protagonist has rescued/written herself" (307).

The structures of both *Obasan* and *Itsuka* do not follow the conventional linear pattern. Kogawa begins the former when Naomi is an adult and goes back till the early forties and swings back and forth till she brings the narrative to move ahead from where it began while the fragments of the past are revealed through a variety of discourses contained in unconventional modes like diary entries, letters and official documents. *Obasan* begins with lyrical lines and ends with tersely worded lines from an excerpt from "the Memorandum sent by the Co-operative Committee on Japanese Canadians to the House and the Senate of Canada, April 1946." It maintains its tone of authenticity throughout by weaving fiction and reality. Even the fiction admittedly contains autobiographical elements. Appropriately, *Itsuka* continues as a sequel ought to, with the progress of political action for redress by Japanese-Canadians and again goes back to the Fifties, swings back and forth, unleashing more of personal and community history and then progresses to the triumph of their efforts. This political history coincides with Naomi's personal one of coming into her own as a person, with Aunt Emily and Father Cedric serving as catalysts.

The writers who have been studied in this chapter celebrate the body differently, since they are placed in different contexts, culturally and socially. Most of them do not write of 'jouissance' overtly. The body is the site of oppression for different reasons. They are not commodified in the way the white women's bodies are but their bodies are also fetishized nevertheless. Their bodies are objectified in terms of violence and economic exploitation. They are further marginalized by virtue of being the 'Other's' 'other' due to racism. Their bodies are viewed and represented stereotypically by the mainstream. Consequently, women writers of colour are faced with the special task of demystifying, not just the female body but the coloured body.

From the writers studied, it is amply clear that to them the body plays a dual role, in that, it is also a metaphor used to draw attention to their foremost agenda—that of exposing racism. Women of colour are marginalized by the mainstream as well as by their own communities. They are doubly or even triply alienated from their bodies. The sex/text metaphor does not always have a one to one correspondence in their works. The body erupts into the text much more subtly.

NOTES

1. For an exploration of postcoloniality and the coloured female body, see Kanneh's article titled, "Feminism and the Colonial Body" which has a direct bearing on this chapter.
2. For the "writing back" of women of colour, see *Returning the Gaze: Essays on Racism, Feminism and Politics*, ed. Himani Bannerji, which has the views of prominent women writers of colour drawn from different communities in Canada.
3. Philip distinguishes between memory that is mere nostalgia and kinetic memory that propels people to act. Her own works attempt to adhere to the latter.
4. Cixous' use of the metaphor of Africa, the 'dark' continent to suggest the female body is condemned as an illustration of precisely the stereotyping they resent.
5. In 1893, more than 600,000 Indians migrated to the Caribbean islands as indentured labour after the abolition of slavery in the British Empire. They left to escape conditions like casteism and poverty back home. They stayed on after their contracts expired and cultivated on the land allotted to them. They continued the extended family system, finding the elders essential for taking care of preschool children, to transmit cultural values and religious practices to the next generation. In 1967, with the growing clashes between the Afro-Caribbean people and the Indo-Caribbean people, migration to Canada began. Religion, in a fossilized way became the stabilizing force for the community. The cosmopolitan diaspora in Ontario, where the Indo-Caribbean population settled in large numbers, became the site of a unique reunion of Indians from India and the Caribbean. The

two communities do not share the same ethos. Thus the term 'the Indian diaspora' cannot be used as a blanket term.

6. The position of the Indo-Caribbean women has been discussed by the poet, essayist and activist, Ramabai Espinet, in her essay, "Representation and the Indo-Caribbean Women in Trinidad and Tobago," where she writes that the presence of Indo-Caribbean women has not been felt in the public sphere. They are absent from art, from literature, as scholars and thinkers. They are functionally equipped to operate in the world of work, but once that is done, they revert to the seclusion of the patriarchal culture, which has always kept them in the women's quarters. The article is in *Indo-Caribbean Resistance*, ed. Frank Birbalsingh (Toronto: TSAR, 1993).
7. For a recent study of the body in some diasporic Canadian texts, see Smaro Kamboureli's book, *Scandalous Bodies Diasporic Literatures in English Canada.*

Chapter Five

Respecting Differences

5.1.1 An Overview of the Emergence of Some Terms and Identities

Before the nineteenth century, a lesbian was thought of as a woman with a huge clitoris who penetrated other women. This was a male-centred view which was based on the assumption that no penis meant no sex. In the late nineteenth century, sexologists thought of a lesbian as a man trapped in a female body, an "invert" or a member of a "third sex." Michel Foucault deals elaborately with notions of sexuality in his three volumes on *History of Sexuality*. Writing on the first records of homosexuality in medical history, he observes:

> We must not forget that the psychological, psychiatric, medical category of homosexuality was constituted from the moment it was characterized—Westphal's famous article of 1870 on 'contrary sexual sensations' can stand as its date of birth—less by a type of sexual relations than by a certain quality of sexual sensibility, a certain way of inverting the masculine and feminine in oneself. (43)

There are however, no known records of how these people dubbed as 'inverts' regarded themselves or felt. By mid-twentieth century, Vera Whisman in her article titled "Identity Crisis: Who is a Lesbian, Anyway" observes:

> both sexperts and lesbians themselves had switched from the lesbian-as-invert model to lesbian-as-female homosexual and to lesbianism as a sexual preference. If the notion that lesbians had much in common with straight men lived on, the belief that they were men trapped in woman's bodies became less and less convincing. A neatly symmetrical set of categories described the sexual possibilities: female or male, homosexual or heterosexual. But the symmetry did not imply equality; the homosexual remained the "deviant" or "variant." (50)

By the 1960s, lesbians were recognized to be women attracted to women or "female homosexuals." By the 1970s lesbian feminists began to challenge such definitions and rejected the notion that lesbianism was merely a sexual preference. Adrienne Rich referred to a "lesbian continuum" and said it included "a range . . . of woman-identified experience, not simply the fact that a woman had or consciously desired genital sexual experience with another woman" (qtd. Whisman 51). Lesbianism took on political hues and lesbian theory began distinguishing 'real' lesbians from 'false' ones. Today the community resists essentialism of any sort and the foundation of identity politics, that is, the belief that 'we share an identity and therefore a politics' is on its way out. In the psychoanalytic framework, in the later part of the Oedipal stage when there is "repudiation of the mother" is the crucial point for what Freud calls "gender consolidation" (qtd. Butler *GT* 59). Summing up the Freudian position on the formation of homosexual identity, Butler writes:

> Forfeiting the mother as object of desire, the boy either internalizes the loss through identification with her, or displaces his heterosexual attachment, in which case he fortifies his attachment of his father and thereby "consolidates his masculinity." If the boy renounces both aim and object and therefore, heterosexual cathexis altogether, he internalizes the mother and sets up a feminine super-ego which dissolves and disorganizes masculinity, consolidating feminine libidinal dispositions in its place.
>
> For the young girl as well, the Oedipal complex can be either "positive" (same-sex identification) or "negative" (opposite-sex identification); the loss of the father initiated by the incest taboo may result either in an identification with the object lost (a consolidation of masculinity) or a deflection of the aim from the object, in which case heterosexuality triumphs over homosexuality, and a substitute object is found. (*GT* 59-60)

The homosexual identity is interpellated from the normative heterosexual identity formation process in Freud. Butler goes on to point out that "[a]lthough Freud does not explicitly argue in its favour, it would appear that the taboo against homosexuality in effect creates the heterosexual 'dispositions' by which the Oedipal conflict becomes possible" (64). Hence for Freud, the primary bisexuality contained within every psyche, due to the taboo against homosexuality, gives way to the heterosexual identity. It is also important to note that in Freud's thesis identification and desire are linked in that, if one identifies as a given gender, one must desire a different gender. Butler critiques this position which glosses over differences within "femininity" which "might itself offer an array of identificatory sites, as the proliferation of lesbian ferine possibilities attests" (*Bodies* . . . 239). She also notes that this treatment of identification and desire as being mutually exclusive, "leaves no room for dynamic exchanges of lesbian and gay relationships," nor any "vocabulary for describing the difficulty play, crossing and destabilization of masculine and feminine identifications within homosexuality" (239).

She writes that this is only now beginning to emerge. Foucault, by contextualizing sexuality within his notion of power, exposes the simplistic ideas of a pre-existing, untouched sexuality. He argues that "sexuality is always produced or constructed within specific historical practices, both discursive and institutional and that recourse to a sexuality before the law is an illusory and complicitous conceit of emancipatory sexual politics" (*GT* 97). This view of Foucault is of course hinged on his overall perspective on subjectivity as being subject to networks of power. Foucault's writings have been significant for the development of lesbian and gay activism and scholarship.

Summarizing the Foucauldian position on marginal identities, Annamarie Jogose writes lucidly:

> In Foucault's analysis, marginalized sexual identities are not simply victims of the operations of power. On the contrary, they are produced by those same operations. For two centuries now, the discourse on sex has been multiplied rather than rarefied; and it has carried with it taboos and prohibitions, it has also, in a more fundamental way, ensured the solidification and implantation of an entire sexual mosaic. This emphasis on the productive and enabling aspects of power profoundly

> alters the models by which traditionally it has been understood. Consequently, Foucault's revaluation of power has significantly affected much lesbian and gay analysis. (80)

Foucault assigns a productive and enabling role of power in this sense. It seems that power with its regulatory mechanisms has in fact contributed to the creation of the sexual "mosaic."[1] According to Foucault, power and resistance go together and, like power, resistance is multiple and unstable and circulates in discourse. Foucault's idea of discourse as a mode of resistance has proved to be appealing to lesbians and gay people and later for queer theory and practice.[2] "The rise of the homosexual as a 'species' exemplifies the polyvalent capacities of discourse (81). In the context of seeing discourse as a mode of resistance "insofar as homosexuality is one of his key examples, Foucault regards sexual identities as the discursive effects of available cultural categories" (82).

These ideas of Foucault have been instrumental in the formulation of Butler's notions of performativity and in her destabilizing the category of gender. As Jagose puts it:

> Instead of naturalizing the same-sex desire of homosexuality—which is the usual strategy of gay and lesbian movements—Butler contests the truth of gender itself, arguing that any commitment to gender identity works ultimately against the legitimation of homosexual subjects.
>
> No longer a natural basis for solidarity, gender is refigured by Butler as a cultural fiction, a performative effect of reiterative acts. (84)

Heterosexuality in that case merely gets naturalized by the performative repetitions of the normative gender identities. The notion of identity itself has been destabilized as also rejection of identity politics in the wake of poststructuralism and the theories of Althusser, Freud, Lacan and Saussure. This questioning of essentialism and identity has met with mixed responses from the lesbian and gay communities with some members seeing their politics getting diluted and the identity question getting co-opted by the general questioning of identity set in motion by poststructuralism.

Another theorist who problematizes the categories of sex and gender is Monique Wittig. She does not see sex and gender as different and understands sex to be gendered and as politically invested. She makes another radical claim—that a lesbian is not a woman since woman "as a term that stabilizes and consolidates a binary and oppositional relation to a man, that relation she argues, is heterosexuality" (Butler, *GT* 112). She further sees a lesbian as refusing heterosexuality and as one who transcends the binary opposition.

The lesbian to her appears as a third gender—"a category that radically problematizes both sex and gender as stable political categories of description" (112). She sees "sex" as discursively produced and feels the need to reject the hegemonizing discourse on sex since it is oppressive to women, gays and lesbians.

5.1.2 Emergence of 'Queer'

The anti-essentialist tendency and the questioning of 'identity' as a monolithic concept triggered off by poststructuralism, has paved the way for the resurrection of the term 'queer.'

Previously used as an abuse word hurled at homosexuals, it has gained respectability and intellectual rigour in its current usage. Jagose observes the emergence of this term:

> The delegitimation of liberal, liberationist, ethnic and even separatist notions of identity generated the cultural space necessary for the emergence of the term 'queer'; its non-specificity guarantees it against recent criticisms made of the exclusionist tendencies of 'lesbian' and 'gay' as identity categories. (76)

The term indicates an anti-normative positioning with regard to identity. As Butler sees it, "[t]he term "queer" emerges as an interpellation that raises the question of the status of force and opposition, of stability and variability within performativity" (*Bodies* . . . 226).

"Queer"[3] shares at least three concerns with lesbian feminism—its attention to the specificity of gender, perceiving sexuality as institutional rather than personal and critiquing heterosexuality. Ironically it is its very broad base that makes "queer" suspect to some lesbian and gay theorists in that, its "totalizing gesture is seen as having the potential to work against lesbian and gay specificity, and to devalue those analysis of homophobia and heterocentrism developed largely by lesbian and gay critics" (Jagose 112). This is a term which engages younger lesbians and gays who find common sources of oppression even with transsexuals and other groups "not straight." This is precisely why older generations of gays and lesbians see their years of analysis and politics being swept aside by this umbrella term.

5.1.3 Lesbian Sexuality and Language

Freud's theory of female sexual development based on sameness or the male model negates female desire and sexual pleasure. It traps female desire within the Oedipal situation with its concomitant guilt. Shirley Neuman critiques Freud in these words:

> The misogyny of Freud's theory of sexual difference is triple: it conceives female sexual development in terms of male development, it restricts the adult woman's sexuality to motherhood, the woman to becoming in her sexual relations with a man, like her mother-in-law; at the same time, it makes the mother, as first object of desire and of its frustration and displacement, the guilty other whom all women must mime in their sexual relationships. (393)

Irigaray, in "This Sex which Is Not One," points to the subordinate role that a woman is compelled to occupy in sexual relations where she no longer even knows what she wants. Irigaray further notes that, "[a]s Freud admits, the beginnings of the sexual life of a girl child are so 'obscure,' so 'faded with time,' that one would have to dig down very deep indeed to discover beneath the traces of this civilization, of this history, the vestiges of a more archaic civilization that might give some clue to woman's sexuality" (351). If indeed there had been such a time, Irigaray feels women's desire "would undoubtedly have a different alphabet, a different language" (351). She concludes that "woman's desire has doubtless been submerged by the logic that has dominated the West since the time of the Greeks" (351). Lacan sets a different problem by recreating the Oedipal scene in the arena of language. By propounding the phallus as the transcendental signifier, he "denies women a discourse in which to articulate their own experience" (Neuman 395). In Lacan's scheme a girl child can enter the Symbolic Order or male discourse at the point of separation from her mother and suppression of female sexuality. As Neuman sees it, "For the female as for the colonial subject, the only recourse is to foreground one's difference from the dominant discourse while speaking within that discourse" (402). There are evidently divided views on the issue of language. There is on the one hand, an extreme and utopian view which advocates the need to evolve a separate language just as the need to inhabit a different space and the other view which advocates strategies like deconstruction, intertextuality, language play, parody etc., essentially working from within. Both views have then a set of practitioners but the first view has not found complete implementation and often the utopian ideal tends to find diluted expression. Donna Bennett observes:

> [Deconstructionists] view language as a closed system, self-referential and, while, illusory, not covering up reality so much as foisting off as reality an obscuring correspondence between writing and the external world. For such writers criticism must break up language, which structures our beliefs about woman, before the nature of women's work can be perceived—much less articulated. (236)

These writers recognize such 'feminine' characteristics as circularity, spontaneity, playfulness, diffuseness, novelty and a tolerance for overlapping—as fuzzy categories (236). In the terms of Lacanian influence models, it would be termed as the language of the libido.

An apt illustration of this writing is the following part of Lola Lemire Tostevin's *Gyno Text*:

> voice
> boxed
> in
> ears
> echo
> deeper
> pounding
> typa
> tymp
> panic
> rhythm
> of a
> heart
> some
> w(here) (qtd. Hlus 288-89)

This is about pregnancy and birthing. It is expressive of a woman hearing the sounds of life within her which is a uniquely feminine experience. Although Tostevin is not a lesbian writer, she does write the body and her ideas seem close to that of lesbian writers. Tostevin is also admittedly influenced by Julia Kristeva's ideas and Kristeva writes her views on woman's language in these words:

> If it is true every national language has its own dream language and unconscious, then each of the sexes—a division so much more archaic and fundamental than the one into languages—would have its own unconscious wherein the biological and social program of the species would be ciphered in confrontation with language, exposed to its influence but independent from it. (238)

When these are the issues that confront women as writers, the lesbian writer writing the body is further marginalized from the dominant discourses and has to evolve her subject position in language which is forever in confrontation with heterosexual constructs—the first and foremost one being that of 'woman.' Elizabeth Meese expresses the difficulties faced in these words:

> The lesbian writer presents her subject as [the] one in the absence of others. Her lesbian, the lesbian in her, is made "present" in language, standing as representative for and representation of the one(s) not here. Her words contend with the polysemy and polyvocality of an unlimited field, striking (down) limits with every word she writes in a signifying system which prefers dimorphic binarism to polymorphic abundance, feigning presence when every word stands in for some one or some thing else/where. It cannot be denied that there is something of capital importance here, a capital investment in / of the letter /—a reminder, a sentence, a matter of principal importance, counting on a return. (76-77)

The lesbian writer thus has to continuously reinvent herself both as the subject of her own discourse and overturning phallogocentric language.

It is relevant at this juncture to quote a passage from Louise Cotnoir's essay "Writing Ourselves with, in and against Language" which is a parody of Saussure's theory of linguistics where she exhorts women in general to assert themselves and create a language which will truly reflect their experiences. This advice rings especially true for lesbian writers:

> Refuse to be disappeared. Order language back into the continuity of the typeset. Re-establish its proper value in human discourse. Become. Become self-assertive. Get back inside ourselves. But she implies, always be concerned and on the alert from the eternal return of annihilation and silence. Sound the silent 'e.' Make discourse sprout from the rhizome and blossom in a perpetual show of color. Make feminine discourse as universal as weather. Real. Banish illusion in language. Make it without bias/unbiased. Make the word reflect the hero, the self. 'They,' the images in the mirrors, must become we, the bodies reflected. Take the image out of the mirror and put it back in the body where it belongs. Defy 'being-for others.' Be. Re/possess essence / being / soul. (qtd. Hlus 291)

This search for a language untainted by the vestiges of patriarchy has led lesbian writers back to their bodies to articulate their difference in being and sexuality. Expressing this very view, Betsy Warland writes:

> i felt/ convinced of the connection between the one-dimensional quality of the english language and the phenomenon of our missing bodies within lesbian writing. at the same time i was reading Audre Lorde's essay "Uses of the Erotic: The Erotic as Power" when i heard Lorde name the erotic "our most profoundly creative source" and "the nurturer or nursemaid of all our deepest knowledge" i was exhilarated! (175-76)

Writers like Daphne Marlatt, Betsy Warland and Nicole Brossard are led to consider the mother-daughter relationship as the first lesbian relationship and re/cover lesbian language in the matrix of this relationship, particularly in the rhythms of the mothers' bodies. They incorporate etymology as a part of their text and assign it a crucial role in their enterprise to re/cover their mother tongue. Daphne Marlatt in a theory fiction piece titled, "Musing with Mothertongue" writes:

> The Beginning: language, a luring body we enter at birth, sustains and contains us. it does not stand in place of anything else, it does not replace the bodies around us. placental, our flat land, our sea, it is both place (where we are situated) and body (that contains us), that body of language we speak, our mothertongue it bears us as we are born in it, into cognition. (223)

These writers through the genre of theory fiction try to theorize this language as well using unconventional metaphors and images in a deliberately non-linear, seemingly non-theoretical, lyrical style. Nicole Brossard does this theorizing prolifically and in the following illustrative passage attempts to describe the strategies used:

> The movements are pendulum movement, repetition (litany) spiral movement, diffuse or suspended movement, and jerky, elliptical movement, the strategies are parody, intertextuality, use of a foreign language, anthropomorphism, and the creation of female myths. Women's experience is repressed in non-meaning, in nonsense. Strategies convey the unthinkable, transgress patriarchal meanings, and invent or produce our own meanings. (227)

5.2.1 Daphne Marlatt's Woman with(out) (Her)Story in *Ana Historic*:

Although the main thrust for écriture au feminin or writing in the feminine came from French feminist thinkers like Hélène Cixous, Luce Irigaray and Julia Kristeva, the Québecoise writers took to it in a big way, situated as they were in a crucial juncture, historically and socially. Women writers questioned the gendering of language and other established practices, including literary genres during the Quiet Revolution. Writers like Brossard were politically active during this period and this activism found expression in their works. Karen Gould lucidly documents the circumstances in which writers like Nicole Brossard, Madeleine Gagnon, Louky Bersianik and France Théoret took the centrestage in this new mode of writing since the early seventies.[4]

Their writings and ideas have had a strong influence on the Anglophone writers in Canada, particularly the new generation of contemporary writers such as Daphne Marlatt, Gail Scott, Betsy Warland etc. Daphne Marlatt has been a forerunner of this kind of writing and has taken initiatives in organizing conferences and undertaking journalistic ventures like *Tessera* (of which she is one of its founder members) to create an environment conducive to the sharing of experiences and ideas in the community of writers and readers.

In an interview with Janice Williamson, Daphne Marlatt talks about the influence the French theorists had on her particularly Nicole Brossard, who was "writing always as a woman in the process of writing" (Williamson 183). In the same interview she says she approached Freudian theory first through "the Americans, through Chodorow and, more recently, Dinnerstein" (183). She says she finds their ideas "link with Kristeva's sense of the semiotic in language." (183). She further says that feminism forced her to examine the creation of the female psyche and this led her to look at childhood and forced her "to take Freud seriously" (192).

The aspects to be focused on in this study include the interplay of body and language in Marlatt's theory as well as the novel, the problematization of the mother-daughter relationship, the centrality of the mother to language and the emergence of lesbian subjectivity. As a postmodern writer, Marlatt also examines the truth claims made by masculine discourses like history and theorizes on language and the process of writing through the narrative structure of the novel.

Writing in the feminine brought with it the writer's heightened awareness at the level of enunciation, an interest in the ways in which linguistic structures and literary focus prescribes cultural codes. This has led to a questioning of the sacrosanctness of genres and has erased the traditional boundaries between theory and practice as well. Karen Gould observes:

> In texts published by Brossard and others in the early issues of *La Barre du jour*, the notion of distinct literary genres gradually withered away, while textualité and later écriture became the theoretical passwords for a growing number of unconventional writing practices that, among other things, refused the constraints of traditional genre distinctions and privileged the mixing of discourses or interdiscussivity. (21)

Almost all the writers write theory fiction as they attempt to break down the traditional barriers between the discourse of criticism and of fiction. There is no longer the omniscient writer controlling the characters, caught in the tumult of the passionate storms of their fictitious lives. The writers' thoughts / experiences in process are lived in / through their works.

Ana Historic, a novel by Daphne Marlatt is a good illustration of this. There are stories within the story. The writer/narrator is very much in the thick of things. This leads to typically postmodern self-reflexive writing that explores the nature of the creative process itself, similar to postmodernist writing. One also finds a critique of totalizing systems and truth claims. As Linda Hutcheon puts it:

> In literature written by women in Canada and elsewhere today, we find the same kind of radical critique of totalizing systems and so-called universal Truths as is to be found in contemporary post-structural philosophy and literary theory. The difference is that this critique, brought about through the study of sexual difference, is enacted in the literature itself, particularly (but not exclusively) in the fiction of women writers. These novels—often very self-consciously—demonstrate how meaning and sexual identity are fixed through and by representation, and how one can never separate the social and the separate, the social and the sexual in dealing with the lives of women. ("Shape Shifters . . ." 220)

However, in another article Hutcheon points out that although feminist concerns may seem to overlap with those of post-structuralist philosophy and may even use its strategies, there is a vital difference:

> While feminisms may use postmodern parodic strategies of deconstruction, they never suffer from this confusion of political agenda, partly because they have a position and a "truth" that offer ways of understanding aesthetic and social practices in the production of and the challenge to gender relations, this is their metanarrative. ("Incredulity . . ." 189)

Writers like Daphne Marlatt, Betsy Warland and Nicole Brossard would go further to challenge gender relations as understood by liberal mainstream feminists with their normative ideal of heterosexuality.

Absence is a pervading feature in the novel—absence of the central figure of Ina who is merely present as a voice in her daughter Annie's memory indicates the absence of the lesbian body and sexuality which is repressed, absence also of Ana Richards—a woman in the nineteenth century whose life story Annie is trying to re/construct from her diary which she finds in the archives. The absence of history forces Annie to construct (her)story for which she is chided by her mother's voice for her fondness for making up stories. All through the novel there is a non-verbalized attempt to valorize story over history.

The novel begins and ends with the "story" of Annie, with the stories of Ana and Ina interspersed at intervals. Annie in the process of assisting her husband's historical research, chances upon an entry in the archives about Ana Richards, a school teacher who had arrived at Hastings Mill. The document's record of her existence is in stark, prosaic words, making her very existence in the past sound dull and insignificant which practically causes her to be glossed over. However, chancing upon her diary, Annie's imagination takes over and she sets about re/constructing Ana Richards' 'real' history. In the process of doing that, Annie emerges as a person and writer after coming to terms with her mother Ina's death. The novel centres around a triple heroine: Ana, Ina and Annie. Ana keeps a journal and Annie also "scribbles," as she embarrassedly admits to her husband Richard.

We as readers have close encounters with the innermost thoughts of two women living in two different centuries. In her essay titled "Self-Representation and Fictionalysis," Marlatt writes about the autobiographical fiction that *Ana Historic* is, defining what autobiography means to her, tied as it is to imagination and memory. Particularly for women, major portions of whose lives are repressed, the confluence of fiction and analysis occurs in autobiography. She writes, "[a]utobiography is not separable from poetry for me on this ground i would call fictionalysis: a self-analysis that plays fictively with the primary images of one's life, a fiction that uncovers analytically that territory where fact and fiction coincide" (124). Referring to *Ana Historic*, she writes:

> In *Ana Historic*, Annie and Ina discuss the difference between story and history, between making things up (out of nothing) and the facts, those frozen somethings of evidence. But what is evident to Annie is not always evident to Ina, because in each of them the seeing occurs in differently informed ways. Clearly, there are different kinds of seeing. For Annie the facts are "skeletal bones of a suppressed body the story is," and that suppressed body which can be resurrected by dint of making up is the unwritten story of who (else) each of the women in the book might be. It is through analysis, analysis of the social context each of them inhabits, that Annie can write her way through

> the bare bones of who they apparently are to the full sense and the full sensory body of who each of them might be, if they could imagine to their fullest the other i's, their real—(other)-i-zations. (125)

Since Annie needs only the bare skeletal outline to create a whole person, even a life—that of Annie Richards gives her imagination free play. Annie is not unduly obsessed with 'facts.' Peggy Kelly in her article "Fiction Theory as Feminist Practice in Marlatt's *Ana Historic* and Scott's *Heroine*" notes:

> Marlatt's deconstruction history, which is inseparable from the life-writing thread, is a key element of the fiction-theory practice of *Ana Historic.* At the intersection of life-writing and historiography, Marlatt examines the false oppositions of "factual" history and story-telling, public and private events, truth and fiction. (83)

There are numerous instances in the novel where the personal journal writings of Ana are juxtaposed with archival records written in officialese. This serves as a parody of "masculine" historical records where the essence of lives lived is compromised in favour of f(acts). For instance, the existence of Ana Richards in the place is recorded in the following manner in the official records:

> Miss Sweeney was shortly succeeded by Mrs. Richards who soon became Mrs. Ben Springer and her lot with the struggling little hamlet, giving place to a Miss Redfern . . . great difficulty was experienced in keeping a teacher longer than six months. (*AH* 39)

Ana's journal, as improvised by Annie has this to offer a page later:

> She could walk forever on an afternoon like this—let down her hair, feel her skin expand beyond the confines of her clothes. She wanted to kick off her boots, dance the well-being of her soul at home, for once, in her skin. (40)

This is the flesh and blood Ana. Marlatt uses conventional punctuation and capitals in Ana's writing to distinguish it from Annie's. The strategy of having multiple female voices in the text is a major point of contrast to the single, omniscient, narrator-protagonist of traditional and modernist texts. Marlatt quite overtly states her dominant ideas encompassed in the very body of her fiction in this way:

> in 1874 Mrs. Richards marries Ben Springer and the Pattersons move to Moodyville. That is all that history says.
>
> but i don't want history's voice. i want . . . something is wanting in me and it all goes blank on a word want. What does it mean to be lacking? empty wanton. . . . (48)

Annie is not the stereotypical detached researcher. The need to recreate Ana's life is connected to her own. From "want," "wanton," she launches off into etymology to expose all the ramifications of the word, laying it bare, with all the connotations that patriarchy has loaded on to words such as these. Marlatt's interests in history and etymology function together to expose and subvert patriarchal discourses.

Marlatt constantly plays on the word "history" to expose it in all its ramifications and to bring to light the hypocrisies couched in it. For this purpose she links it to "hystery" which is defined in this manner:

> hystery the excision of women (who do not act but are acted upon). hysterectomy, the excision of wombs and ovaries of repression, by mechanical compression, by ice, by the knife, because we were 'wrong' from the start, our physiology faulty, preoccupied as we are with the things of the flesh, spiritless—except for our rages—'going off the deep end' where the divers went. (88)

Annie is dealing with the trauma of her mother Ina's "bouts of rages" which are treated with shock therapy and she returns home, reduced to a ghost of her former self. Marlatt hints at a conspiracy among the institutions of patriarchy to keep woman silenced and "normal." Women in society are seen as all body, devoid of spirit and patriarchy is happy to keep them spiritless. Annie is not just dealing with the particular experience of Ina but of women in general. Time and again Marlatt succeeds in transcending the particular to achieve a wider perspective. For women it is her story rather than history that repeats itself.

In keeping with a woman's biological rhythms, time is cyclic instead of linear for feminists. As Alice Jardine puts it:

> Female subjectivity as it gives itself up to intention becomes a problem with respect to a certain conception of time: time as departure, progression, and arrival—in other words the time of history. (446)

The concept of time would be subject to radical change and ironically, contemporary science is also questioning the absoluteness of time. Julia Kristeva further adds:

> It might also be added that this linear time is that of enunciation of sentences (noun + verb, topic—comment, beginning—ending), and that this time rests on its own stumbling block of that enunciation. ("Woman's Time . . ." 446)

Marlatt deals with the distant past, the more recent past and the present. In the structure of her work itself, there are no abrupt borders to demarcate the separation of the three. On a superficial level, even, the novel begins and ends with the present. She does not seem to be showing progression from Ana to Ina to Annie. That does not seem to be her intention. Each one rebels in her own socio-historical context but the three of them are linked in the fluid medium of consciousness. The distant past, the past and the present inexorably weave into each other and freely address one another. Ana, Ina and Annie could very well be aspects of one woman's consciousness. At the very outset of the novel, Annie who is in bed, begins with, "Who's there?" and slips very easily to who's there? echoes from further back. (119). She is in the near past of her childhood. Soon she reverts to the description of timber in the archival records and is with the distant past of Ana Richards. The traversing of time is done effortlessly and without abrupt ruptures in the continuity of the narrative. The progression is in terms of heightened awareness, of consciousness of a choice for both Ana and Annie—the decision to enter into a lesbian relationship. While Annie is toying with the decision to be with Zoe, her intimate reader, as the re/creator of Ana's (her)story also places her tentatively on the threshold of a lesbian relationship with Bridie/Birdie. Both of them experience momentary panic and fear before giving in to their desires. Cixous beautifully expresses the intermingling of the private and the public thus:

> In woman, personal history blends together with the history of all women, as well as national and world history. ("The Laugh . . ." 340)

It is this continuum and fluid time that Marlatt works into the novel.

5.2.2 Language and the Body

The notions of subjectivity and language are closely linked as Catherine Belsey indicates:

> It is in language that people constitute themselves as subjects, consciousness of the self is possible only through contrast, differentiation: "I" cannot be conceived without the conception "non-I," "you" and dialogue, the fundamental condition of language, implies a reversible polarity between "I" and "you." (595)

Since language is patriarchal, it is virtually impossible for a woman to enter the Symbolic Order as Lacan's theory posits, and be true to her experiences as a woman at the same time. This poses special problems for the woman writer, particularly the lesbian writer.

The only solution would be as Hélène Cixous suggests—to subvert from within the discourses of patriarchy and appropriate language of the Symbolic Order. What Cixous lyrically suggests in her manifesto for écriture feminine is now being practised by the Québecoise and Anglophone writers like Daphne Marlatt.

Women have to re/invent language if they want to re/enter the texts as subjects. This is a necessity or else the language of patriarchy will keep their subjectivity erased. Critics like Elaine Showalter and Nina Auerbach fear women's attempt to write their body might lead to the development of a regressive biologism. Despite the controversy, écriture au feminine remains a powerful mode of writing. Referring to Marlatt's writing, Peggy Kelly observes:

> The significance of sound and rhythm to language-centred writing is most evident in *Ana Historic* because Marlatt's sound-centred writing strategies serve to develop the melody of the spoken word into poetic prose. (91)

This view is endorsed by Marlatt herself when she writes about the nature of language in "Musing with Mothertongue":

> Language is first of all for us a body of sound leaving the water of the mother's womb with its one dominant sound, we are born into this other body whose multiple sounds bathe our ears from the moment of our arrival. (223)

This precisely is the principle behind Marlatt's body-centred writing. *Ana Historic* is an attack against the repression of the female body and sexuality in Western society. As Annie writes:

> The real history of women, Zoe says, is unwritten because it runs through our bodies. We give birth to each other. (131)

Marlatt is referring to the community of women who used to work together to give life to each other in "feminine" discourse. Annie as a young girl wonders why there were no lost girls in Never, Never land. She dwells on the origin of the word 'tomboy' when her mother Ina calls her one for refusing to be 'domesticated.' She finds that the word includes a "double masculine, as if girl were completely erased" (13). She also learns from her mother all the spirited things that girls were forbidden to do. Annie examines the connotations of the word 'lady' when Ana Richards in her diary entry writes that she could not keep only to drawing rooms and the school and feels that she was perhaps not a proper lady. Annie imagines all the strictures that would have applied to ladies during Ana Richard's time and remembers the clothing ladies were supposed to wear and that nice girls even in her childhood used to brand those outside their group as "tramp, slut, bitch" (34). Ina had transmitted her fear of the body and sexuality to her daughters:

> you taught as your fear, you taught us what you knew about a world where even uncles were not to be trusted. you grew more afraid as our sexuality came budding to the fore. (34)

Annie realizes that her mother is a victim of patriarchal sexual mores and is herself trapped in its structures. An illustration she offers is the advice given by one of the "how-to-fix yourself books (caught in a fix, castrated—what is the female word of it? i mean for the psychological condition?)" (35).

She goes on to examine the gendering of words like 'soul' and 'spirit'—'Soul' being generically feminine, a servant of Spirit:

> it is the man who is Spirit, has spirit. what does Soul, what does a woman do with her unexpressed preferences, her desires? (damned up, a torrent to let loose) and this is what you were trying to live up to. the writer. (35)

Ina's repressed sexuality which is a result of her conditioning, is transmitted to her daughters. Annie comes to realize this about herself even as she is in the process of re/covering the erased story of Ana Richards' life. She intrudes into Ana's story in the same way as we readers intrude into hers:

> she is writing her desire to be, in the present tense, retrieved from silence. each morning she begins with all their names . . . each morning she begins with her name, a name that is not really hers. Each evening she enters her being, nameless, in the book she is writing against her absence. (47)

This is what Annie is also doing in her life. Marlatt feels that the Imaginary is a part of one's life story just as she portrays Ana's story to be a part of Annie's reality:

> i know that in inventing a life for Mrs. Richards, i as Annie (and Annie isn't me though she may be one of the selves i could be) invented a historical leak, a hole in the sieve of fact that led the shadow of a possibility leak through into full-blown life. History is not dead and gone, it lives on in us in the way it shapes our thoughts and especially our thought about what is possible. . . . Mrs. Richards is a historical leak for the possibility of lesbian life in Victorian British Columbia, which like some deep-paced bedrock continues to underlie the leather shops and tinted glass of our high-rise 1990s. ("Self-Representation . . . " 125)

Annie is the victim of the same patriarchal norms of beauty and its commodification of the female body as much as her mother Ina had been. There is a graphic description of Annie's adolescent body deliberately described in conventional terms as "looking a peach," watching her father work in the garden and blushing when he looks up and calls her a princess (50). This is a poignant image of a young girl on the threshold of womanhood vying with her mother for her father's attention, competing for the male gaze and getting objectified. She is aware of her rivalry with her mother:

> yes i tried to efface you, trace myself over you, wanting to be the one looked at, approved by male eyes. (50)

Soon follows an image of her father taking pictures of his wife and three daughters:

> shapes and sizes of our growing bodies you presided over, our father invisible behind the camera imaging moments of this female would. (51)

There is pain implicit in Annie's imaginary exchanges with Ina when she evokes childhood memories of attaining puberty. The lines are tinged with hurt and sarcasm aimed at the male gaze to which young women are subjected:

> I was slimming into another shape, finding a waist, gaining curves, attaining the sort of grace I was meant to have as a body marked woman's. (52)

Women's heads are filled with ideas of beauty propagated through popular media of hetero-sexist culture which encourages passivity. Youth is celebrated and the middle-aged female body is tabooed. After she meets Zoe, Annie, a middle-aged closet writer thinks:

> for here i am, thinking about being attractive, a middle-aged woman who hasn't held a job for twelve years. a middling woman muddling through as wife and mother. what have i done in all this time? (the small space a life gets boxed into). (59)

Annie, even while she is writing Ana Richards into existence, is taking stock of her conventionally "successful" life which yet seems devoid of meaning and narrow. In a following section significantly titled "Waking Up" is an account of Ana Richards gradually finding comfort in the new place and enjoying the pleasure of her body's sensations so long denied:

> Warm, wet . . . she had given in to it, the slide into the pool . . . brown water, yellow brown and flecked with leaves or green bits . . . letting go. . . . Now she is awake, the feeling seeping away, the secret pleasure of her body in its rooting place. (85)

The celebration of the body can only follow a complete consciousness of all that keeps it repressed. This process of analysis continues simultaneously in the novel through Annie's consciousness. Natural functions of the female body such as menstruation and labour pangs and blood are held out by orthodox religion as punishment for "Eve's original sin" (87).

She quotes from historical documents to show that even in the nineteenth century, "the source of hysteria was still, as in Plato's time, sought in the matrix of the female body, upon which surgical attacks were unleashed" (89) and that in Germany "Hegar (1830-1914) and

Friedrich (1825-82) were using even more radical methods, including ovarectomy and cauterization of the clitoris" (89). Writers like Marlatt see the body as the only way to inscribe female subjectivity into the text. This can be done only by listening to and understanding its rhythms and celebrating its processes. Since women have been erased or 'absenced' by virtue of their bodies they have to become centred in their discourses through the same route—the body. It is unique that Annie, who is close to menopause thinks pleasurably of menstruation in these words:

> my secret pleasure, feeling the flow, a sudden rush of blood slide out between my lips and onto the pad. . . . there is still even now the innate pleasure of seeing on a fresh white pad the first marks of red, bright red when the bleeding's at its peak. Innate because of a childish astonishment, *i made that*! the mark of myself, my inscription in blood. i'm here scribbling again. (*AH* 90)

It is significant that these thoughts come to Annie sitting across from Zoe, writing.

The transformation of her consciousness is already at work. When talking about *Ana Historic* in an interview Marlatt says:

> I think what Annie's doing in that book is that she's trying to see her own life through a new lens and she isn't really sure what a new lens is until she gets towards the end of writing Ana Richards' story. Then it becomes clearer what that lens is; when you come out, you translate yourself into another sexual being and it makes all your previous life—especially if you've lived a good portion of your life as a heterosexual woman—it makes you see it all in a new light. (Curran 115)

Descriptions of Jeannie Alexander birthing a baby are one of the most poignant and sensitive parts of the novel. The parts describing the birthing are alternated with various 'masculine' discourses ranging from biblical allusions to the historical documents of a boat race, complete with rules of the sailing competition. The writing of the body and these discourses of 'the public sphere' interrupt one another. The feminine discourse ruptures in effect the historical one and is more real. Marlatt ironically observes that women's achievements are ahistoric, erased from history whereas men's exploits and adventures invariably find their way, however trivial they may be, into the annals of history:

> the ships men ride into the pages of history. the winning names. the nameless women who are vessels of their destiny. the ship R.H., H.DO., ride into history as stars on board the mute matter of being wife and mother—a historic, muddled in the mundane, incessantly repeating, their names 'writ in water.' (121)

Earlier in an allusion to God's punishment meted out to women after the Fall:

> To the woman he said: I will greatly multiply your pain in childbearing; in pain shall you bring forth children. (118)

The following line is ironic in tone: "the vessel she is—(full) filling her destiny" (118). In contrast to these cold pronouncements is a very warm and intimate description of Jeannie's vaginal contractions and the manner in which the women around bond together assisting her in every way during the birthing. Childbirth also serves as a metaphor to signify Ana Richards and Annie coming out and coming into being as persons recognizing their desires. When talking to Zoe about how women came to be alienated from their bodies, Annie says how a woman of her mother's generation viewed her body:

> (Her body) is a burden: worn away in service to the species, bleeding each month, proliferating passively, it is not for her a pure instrument for getting a grip on the world but an opaque physical presence; it is no certain source of pleasure and it creates lacerating pains; it contains menaces; woman feels endangered by her "insides." (133)

The body was viewed with fear and resentment as a source of pain rather than pleasure. Annie speculates that perhaps that was why women's writing "which we also live inside of, is different from men's, and not a tool, not a 'pure instrument for getting a grip on the world.' 'it contains menaces,' traps, pitfalls" (133). Ina, her mother, also a "scribbler" like Annie is silenced by the electric therapy she undergoes for her psychological problems. Kathleen M. Scheel in her article "Freud and Frankenstein: The Monstered Language of *Ana Historic*" sees the novel as subverting "the paradigm of castration anxiety by showing that colonization of the land—or women—is not necessarily a desirable end" (95). She cites illustrations from the novel of historical accounts of "logging the 'virgin' country" (97) to suggest the confluence of Nature and woman as objects of male exploitation and phallic sexuality conjoined to "remove all traces of threatening difference." (97) Scheel suggests that Ina's disgust and fear of her own body needs to be read as a reflection of the cultural misogyny to which she was subjected:

> The psychiatric diagnosis of Ina as a hysteric, based on Freudian psychology, confuses symptoms with causes in a gross misreading of female experience. Freud's prediction that women are predisposed to hysteria is a further scripting of female behaviour that has particularly ominous implications for women. (100)

Scheel goes on to point out the biases in traditional psychiatry:

> Psychiatry can then be seen to "create" the monstered version of woman who, like Frankenstein's creature, has no identity of her own to speak her experience, and becomes a blank or absence to mirror man back to himself. Hysteria, the languageless resistance to objectification, results in annihilation for Ina, just as the monster's rage at his creator's refusal to recognize him as a desiring subject leads to his destruction. (101)

She sees similarities between Anna O. Joseph Breuer's patient and Annie, both of whom "have repressed sexuality and engage in imaginative fictionalizations" (102). The act of writing is central to the novel since the triple heroine Ana, Annie and Ina are writers of sorts. Marlatt assigns an important role to writing. Quoting Marlatt from an interview with Bowering, Pamela Banting points out:

> Marlatt describes the act of writing as a translation between the prelinguistic given (this given can be equally the body or the external world) and language. She states that "Everything is prelinguistic, & as soon as you get into linguism, language, humming it, uttering it, you get back into the problem of translating. . . . Plus the fact that it's even more complicated than translating, because

> language has its own presence & its own insistences & its own connections, which you have to take into account all the time." (*Body Inc.* 203)

Banting also points out that unlike Cixous, who theorizes an alternate relation between body and language on the basis of the hysterical body, Marlatt's focus is the lesbian body. (206) This is of course more evident in her poetry.

Marlatt clarifies the link she sees between language and the body in these words:

> hidden in the etymology and usage of so much of our vocabulary for verbal communication (contact, sharing) is a link with the body's physicality: matter (the import of what you say) and matter by extension mother; language and tongue; to utter and outer (give birth again); a part of speech and a part of the body; pregnant with meaning; to mouth (speak) and the mouth with which we also eat and make love; sense (meaning) and that with which we sense the world; to relate (a story) and to relate (to somebody), related (carried back) with its connection with bearing (a child); intimate and to intimate; vulva and voluble; even sentence which comes from a verb meaning to feel. ("Musing . . ." 224)

Marlatt dwells frequently on the etymology of words. The exploration of the name "Ana" as being a suffix meaning "pertaining to" is an interesting example. Ana also means new arrival. She points out earlier in the same piece that words are like atomic particles attracting each other, which gives us assonance and alliteration. Going into etymology helps her explore all the possibilities of a word and its in-built biases against women as well. This is an important feature of her entire ouevre. She also uses personal pronouns in a very deliberate way. Annie refers to Harald and Richard in the third person, thereby distancing them from the centre. The one-to-one dialogue she carries on with Ina in her imagination brings forth the intimacy that she feels with her, even in her absence. Ana Richards, whose life she re/creates, maintains a diary and Annie writes in the first person. This inevitably has the effect of centring the female subject and valorizing hitherto marginalized genres such as diaries and journals which have much more to say about a woman's life experiences.

Marlatt uses blank space with a few lines remarkably well to draw the attention of the reader to aspects of the layout of the text. As in the case of: "a book of interruptions is not a novel" (37), this is an overt statement that the novel form is being subverted and the different narratives in it are intermeshed and rupture one another. Again the beautiful signature 'Ana' with the name unusually spelt draws the reader out of curiosity into the story Annie is about to "make up." When Annie asks Joe what she should do about the ending of Ana's story, it almost has the effect of Brechtian alienation technique, where one is jolted into awareness that it is fiction and not life. Ana relives through Annie who re/merges as a new person.

5.2.3 The Lesbian Subject

The resolution in the novel seems to be the emerging lesbian subjectivities of both Ana Richards and Annie. Annie notes that "history married her to Ben Springer and wrote her off" (134). Zoe who is listening to her toying with ideas of how to end Ana's story insists "wrote her in . . . listed her as belonging" (134). Her ongoing dialogue with her dead mother Ina, interrupts her thoughts after which in a section titled "Not a Bad End," she gets to Ana's encounter with Birdie when she finally admits to her that she is scared of her own desire which is "written across my face" (139). Annie intrudes into her story again reminding the reader:

> once history's onstage, histrionic as usual (all those wars, all those historic judgements), the a-historic hasn't a speaking part. What's imagination next to the weight of the (f)actual? (139)

These lines show the doubly marginalized status of both Ana and Annie by virtue of being women and lesbian, forever silenced. In an essay titled "Lesbera," Marlatt writes:

> if women's history has been overlooked, then lesbian history has definitely been swept under the carpet, into the closet. Kept out of sight as something immoral, mutant, shameful, not by any means, a tradition we might glory in. (43)

Ana's realization of her lesbian desire is perhaps doomed to failure in Victorian British Columbia. Her diary goes silent with the sentence 'Today I have accepted' (146). Annie's conscious protests against the possible erasure of her other selves—"secret diarist, pioneer pianist, travelling companion to Birdie Stewart—invalidated, unacceptable." (146)

Annie protests that she does not want to do that to Ana. Running parallel to this is her own emerging lesbian desire and consciousness. There is self-directed irony in the words:

> (there goes Annie, assuming she's different from each of them. Safe in her parentheses, her own cover story. (150)

This self-reflexivity is what makes the novel a postmodern text. Also, the Anna Richard story is left open-ended. In an interview, Marlatt discusses the climax of the novel:

> The climactic point in the novel is when Annie says her name, the name she gives herself, Annie Torrent, which internalizes all the negative wildness of her mother, her heritage and makes it positive. She confronts her own desire, and she says to Zoe, you are what I want and she names it. And once she names it, that's the end of that particular story which is the coming to that point, and then a new story begins which the last page just suggests. She moves from being the author who is on the sidelines, writing about someone else, to the author who takes responsibility for the enactment of her own life and she moves into enacting her desire which is the enactment of her life. (Curran 115-16)

The lesbian eroticism in the novel is very subtle and suggestive as compared to Marlatt's poetry. She is however, very vocal about this eroticism elsewhere. She coins the word '*lesbera*,' "to mark eros with lesbian identity: a new word, *lesbera* the *lesberetic* (yes, heretic) expression of erotic power as a transforming energy we revel in each time we move our lovers, our readers and ourselves to that ecstatic surging beyond limits" (*Lesbera* 49).

She conceptualizes the lesbian erotic as power which lesbians come into as they gain their identity. Referring to the creation of such an identity in Annie, Marlatt in her interview with Janice Williamson says:

> Once I had located Annie as a very sexual woman, the writing kept moving towards her actually making love with Zoe, and yet that could only come at the very end of the book, because she had to

> go through all these shifts of identity and coming to consciousness of what the latent desire really was. Yet I didn't want that final scene to be the end of the story, because it's never the end, it's always the beginning of new stories, so how could I honour that? The only way I could honour that was by moving back into the writing and the reading, using the metaphor of the continual turning of the page as the working of desire. (188)

If it were not for this fluid ending, the lesbian identity again runs the risk of being boxed into the particular text, silenced once again. It is easier to understand Marlatt's continuous engagement with language, particularly as a lesbian writer in the context of Bonnie Zimmerman's views on it:

> Speaking, especially naming one's self 'lesbian' is an act of empowerment. . . . [P]owerlessness on the other hand is associated with silence and the 'speechlessness' that the powerful impose on those dispossessed of language. In a sense, then, contemporary lesbian feminists postulate lesbian oppression as a mutilation of consciousness curable by language. (qtd. Marlatt *Labyrinth* . . . 37)

5.2.4 Mother-Daughter Link

Most women writers writing the body view the mother-daughter link as a principal one since they are either drawing on the Lacanian schema or subverting it. In both cases they are working from it as Marlatt confessedly is. *Ana Historic* foregrounds this relationship interestingly through the mother's physical absence and linguistic presence as a voice continuously in dialogue with her daughter within her psyche. This link is even more significant for the lesbian subject and Marlatt writes in an essay titled, "For the private reader: interplay in the public realm": "Mother as first love and first source of love; mother as first model of how to be someone marked female." (221)

One can see the problematic that the mother-daughter relationship poses in *Ana Historic* in the context of this view. There are possibly autobiographical elements embedded in this which seem to be evident from what Marlatt says of herself in an interview with Janice Williamson:

> I had a very close bond with my mother, I realize now looking back to when I was little, and I can actually see in my relationship to her such an appreciation of her femininity that it almost supports Freud's notion (although I dislike this notion because he couldn't recognize a female libido as female; it always had to be modelled on the male libido) of the little girl as the 'little man' courting the mother. I can recognize that behaviour when I look back. But then we went through such a difficult time together during my adolescence when she denied me and I denied her, and we never really got back to any kind of *rapprochement* before she died; so writing about her is my way of doing that, of getting to a place where I can feel some of that affection and empathy and understanding. It's a really different bond from the little girl's bond, because my understanding comes from empathizing with her experience as a mother, having had my own experience as a mother. And recognizing in myself the difficulties I had as an immigrant, and seeing how those were magnified for her. I can only realize what we had in common by also expressing where I felt she betrayed me as a mother, because she was in such deep psychological trouble herself that she couldn't go on mothering. (184)

These ambivalences of the relationship are clear in *Ana Historic*. Marlatt later in the same interview cites the moment in the novel when Ina says to Annie "your mother's gone" and says that it is a primal experience to have the mother deny that she is the mother figure—figure the child always counted on and "because she is saying it, language makes it real and her absence is suddenly there as a frightening possibility" (185). In terms of memory which is again crucial for a writer and its relation to language, Marlatt says:

> There is in memory a very deep subliminal connection with the mother because what we first of all remember is this huge body which is our first landscape and which we first of all remember bodily. We can't consciously remember it, but it's there in our unconscious, it's there in all the repressed babble, the language that just ripples and flows—and it isn't concerned with making sense. It's concerned with the feel of that body, of the contours of early memory. The wholeness of memory, these early memories that suddenly flash upon you, probably has something to do with the earliest sense of a whole body image, and later, much later, a whole landscape. Anyhow, it's only later that we separate ourselves and everything into subject and object. (185)

It is easy to see the link Marlatt establishes between the mother's body, early sensory perception and language. Marlatt's search for her mother's past leads her to close family, the English landscape and finally The Great Mother in *How Hug a Stone*. In "*Lesbera*" she writes, extending the idea of mother from the literal to literary:

> For our own survival we need to know not only our biological mothers but our/historical foremothers and our literary mothers, those whose work help us begin to recognize the largeness of who we are or who we can be. (45-46)

Marlatt in a poem titled "kore" uses the Demeter-Persephone myth to show lesbian love. The myth is used in a subversive way to write about lesbian sexuality. Pamela Banting in an article titled "The Phantom Limb Syndrome: Writing the Postcolonial Body in Daphne Marlatt's 'Touch to My Tongue,' analyzes the poem in these words:

> the lesbian relation both accumulates elements of the mother-daughter relation and deconstructs them at the same time. Even as the mythological parallel is drawn, it is reduced, played down, and problematized within the context of the poem. For example, within the poem it is undetermined which lover plays the role of Demeter and which Persephone. The title, "kore," might suggest that not the poet but her lover is Kore. Yet the lover's eyelashes, "amber over blue," recall "(amba, amorous Demeter, you with the fire in your hand, i am coming to you)," which implies that the lover is Demeter instead. (18)

In *Ana Historic* Annie moves from the position of a child distressed by her mother's absence (she is grieving over her mother's death) as also her threatening to become absent in her childhood to her mothering (nurturing) her mother who is reduced to a ghost of her former self and memories of her:

> I-na, I-no-longer, i can't turn you into a story. there is this absence here, where the words stop. (and there i remember) (11)

She is distraught at having to re/construct and piece together this figure of her mother from memories:

> the worst is that it's up to me to pull you through. this crumbling apart of words. 'true, real.' you who is you or me. she. a part struck off from me. apart. separated. (11)

In the finality of the absence of her mother, the reality of her mother's existence in the past has to be established by her daughter. The anguish of the severing of the mother-daughter connection is evident. Her mother, having migrated from England, tries to instil English values and 'proper' language in her daughters. These are again echoes from Marlatt's own life for she says, "I had to come to terms with the oldest layer of my language, the language I inherited from my mother, which was generated within certain national class and period mores. (Williamson 193). Even in her later interview Marlatt acknowledges: "That bond, that mother-daughter bond is very much an oral bond, we internalize that voice so much" (Curran 117). Annie collaborates with her mother's language, her own versions of it and her friend Zoe's responses. In each voice there are other voices echoing and talking to each other. Along with the mother's voice and language, daughters also internalize value systems which are encoded in language. Annie internalizes her mother's fear and disgust of her own body and she notes this bitterly:

> the mothers, the inheritance of the mothers. you taught me a lot. you taught me the uneasy hole in myself and how to cover it up—cover girl, the great cover-story women. (60)

Annie internalizes her mother's patriarchal attitudes to fashion and makeup as also her sexual body parts. She refers to the fact that these patriarchal attitudes are built into language and women as much as men conspire to sustain these negativities about female sexuality inherent in language:

> but the words for our bodies betrayed us in the very language we learned at school: 'cunt,' 'slit,' 'boob' ('you boob, you dumb broad') . handed down from friend to friend, sister to sister, mother to daughter. hand-me-downs, too small for what i really felt. (62)

The rage and protest she feels towards her mother subside towards the end when her mother returns from the hospital barely able to look after herself, a mere shadow of her former self:

> they erase whole parts of you, shocked them out, overloaded the circuits so you couldn't bear to remember. (149)

In a journal entry dated April 21, 83, Marlatt writes referring to Annie:

> unlike her mother she uses her immigrant experience as a way of belonging by seeing it through a feminist lens & fusing love-of-place with love of a woman (in the body because the body doesn't speak in systems of power, its "speaking," an upheaval, breaks out through the codes that repress it). (*Labyrinth* 15)

In addition to using an unconventional narrative form full of ruptures, Marlatt also uses a plurality of voices to decentre the unified subject. This also allows her to bring to centrestage not just Annie's voice but also that of Ana Richards, Ina and Zoe. In an essay titled "The In-Between Is Reciprocal" she writes about her mother's voice:

> I was never more aware of this than when I was writing *Ana Historic*, a fictional autobiography in which whole phrases came back to me that were my mother's, habitual phrases that sounded the very texture of who she is in me and through her the residue of my grandmother—and beyond her, who knows? (116)

Marlatt also uses intertextuality for Freudian theory runs as a subtext which she continuously questions as much as the biblical allusions and historical documents of nineteenth century surgical practices. The story of Ana Richards running as a parallel text, serves to illustrate Victorian mores of sexuality, further interspersed with "masculine" discourse of logging in the "virgin" country. Intertextuality allows her to simultaneously expose numerous patriarchal discourses, particularly history. These have conspired to silence women's life stories and even completely erase them out of existence.

Lola Lemire Tostevin has criticized Daphne Marlatt for being essentialist and prescriptive, particularly with reference to the ending of *Ana Historic*. She also criticizes her for her nostalgic desire for origins meaning her interest in etymology. Pamela Banting in a logical defence of Marlatt writes:

> if French feminist Hélène Cixous can be permitted the use of certain key words without being entrapped in the various systems they carry with them, then surely Canadian feminist Daphne Marlatt may be permitted a similar licence. Instead the impression Tostevin leaves us with is that to differ from Cixous is merely to dream comfortably on the couch of nostalgia rather than that of analysis. (*Body Inc.* 147)

Banting in her spirited defence further points out: "Etymology is for Marlatt a source of delight, inspiration, historical information, memory, and collaboration" (161).

Banting astutely observes: "This controversy within feminist critique over essentialism and biologism in the work of important writers, indicates a series of untheorized gaps pertaining to the relations between corporeal and linguistic substances" (151). Marlatt, in her unassuming manner, has the final word in the controversy in a journal entry dated Aug. 89. Referring to Tostevin and Frank Davey's criticism, she says:

> if differences among women are crucial, as they are, why should i expect L to understand my work any better than F? it's that "our," it's that "we" again & the false assumptions of unity implicit in a shared poetic, a friendship, a shared politic—feminism which isn't one, i keep learning over & over. (*Labyrinth* 129)

5.3.1 Betsy Warland's Subversive Project

For the purposes of this study have been selected two of Betsy Warland's books: *Serpent (W)rite* and *Double Negative*. The selection of these two books is based on Warland's main concerns. *Serpent (W)rite* is a book written by her after being grounded fully in her lesbian subject position and *Double Negative,* since she is passionate about collaborative writing is significantly with her lesbian partner Daphne Marlatt. In *Serpent (W)rite,* a book tracing her evolution into a lesbian writer, she coming out fully she articulates and undertakes a brilliant critique of a wide range of patriarchal discourses. This critique from a lesbian subject position, grapples with issues of sexuality, language and identity. Hence the book is broad in its perspective and concerns in that, it not only represents the lesbian erotic but also broader social issues like genetic engineering, war and the prospect of nuclear holocaust and the annihilation of mankind. Warland in re/presenting these ideas often takes an ecofeminist position as well. Her writing is informed by a wide range of disciplines from theology to biological sciences, modern physics, mythology, anthropology, sociology, psychology and linguistics. A range of texts from these disciplines intersect in her work. she undertakes the work of a linguistics archeologist. As suggested by Mary Daly, she undertakes the work of a linguistic archeologist in unearthing the various ways in which language has been gendered. She also demonstrates how systems of patriarchal power work in unison to erase feminist knowledge systems to sustain themselves. As Luce Irigaray suggests in *An Ethics of Sexual Difference,* establishing any position of difference requires a critique of totalizing and homogenizing systems:

> A revolution in thought and ethics is needed if the work of sexual difference is to take place. We need to reinterpret everything concerning the relations between the subject and discourse, the subject and the cosmic, the microcosmic and the macrocosmic. Everything, beginning with the way in which the subject has always been written in the masculine form, as *man*, even when it claimed to be universal or neutral. Despite the fact that *man*—at least in French—rather than being neutral, is sexed. (7)

This enterprise is executed with brilliance and thoroughness by Warland in her works. She does this by employing various linguistic devices grounded in her philosophy so that the compartmentalization of form and content is negated.

5.3.2 Warland's Lesbian Subject

In an essay titled "moving parts" Warland writes of the evolution of her own lesbianism and the hurdles that lesbians in general are compelled to overcome, marginalized as they are by heterosexist society. She writes:

> In the process of becoming a self-named lesbian, any woman must find her way through a myriad of fears. As she does, she becomes less afraid. As she does, she becomes the focus of fear within the heterosexual world. (248)

She feels that the challenges of living unprotected in a male-dominated society are far greater for lesbians as compared to heterosexual women and the prospects of responsibility for oneself quite terrifying:

> For lesbians, who are twice defined by our feminine gendered bodies this struggle is doubly crucial. As our bodies propel us away, inciting a desire which is greater than fear—we take a leap into the unknown, which is unnamed. With our desire we rename everything: slowly; passionately. And with the gathering of our words we own ourselves: become self-responsible. This takes years. This takes a lifetime. (248)

These views find their way into her writing. There is also a special relationship to language that lesbian writers like Warland seek to establish to assert their difference both in theory and praxis. The notion of separatism or being on the margins of society is critical for the lesbian identity which is forever under the threat of erasure. Therefore, the lesbian subject position is not only based on sexual preference but is a political position as well. As Adrienne Rich defining lesbianism puts it:

> I mean the term *lesbian continuum* to include a range—through each woman's life and throughout history—of woman-identified experience; not simply the fact that a woman has had or consciously desired genital experience with another woman. If we expand it to embrace many more forms of primary intensity between and among women, including the sharing of a rich inner life, the bonding against male tyranny, the giving and receiving of patriarchal and political support . . . we begin to grasp breadths of female history and psychology which have lain out of reach as a consequence of limited, mostly clinical definitions of "lesbianism." (qtd. Zimmerman 121)

In order to "unlearn" and "uncondition" oneself as a lesbian, it would be absolutely essential to delve into the area of language and invent new uses of language and genres to articulate different ways of being. Bonnie Zimmerman[5] lucidly writes:

> If we have been silenced for centuries and speak an oppressor's tongue, then liberation for the lesbian must begin with language. Some writers may have reconciled their internal censor with their speech by writing in code, but many critics maintain that modern lesbian writers, because they are uniquely alienated from patriarchy experiment with its literary style and form. (127)

Warland is an experimental writer of this sort whose choice has been a deliberate one. This choice compounds the challenges faced by her as she puts it in "the breasts refuse":

> Sometimes I say, 'Why make it so difficult for yourself, Betsy? You're already up against it as a woman writer, who is not only a feminist, but a lesbian as well—why be a language-focused, writer too? Let's face it: this isn't a very smart approach if you'd like to reach a larger audience—which every writer longs to do. I have no choice—this is my script my inherited limits (times, borderlines, between fields. These are my de/marcations: the sites of my vision. (292)

In an interview with Janice Williamson, she further clarifies her need to be an experimental writer. When questioned as to whether lesbian language-centred writing does not take on the rhetoric of a vanguard, she says:

> Experimental writing writes in resistance to the more familiar and valorized forms and ideas. Experimental writers must extricate themselves from the prevailing literary expectations. I'm still puzzled as to why this is so offensive particularly to the heterosexual feminist writers who have been the most critical of our work. Their most frequent remarks are that our writing is exclusive, difficult to understand, and prescriptive. There's almost this sense of betrayal—that difference is misinterpreted as intentional rejection. Does this spring from a deeply internalized stereotype that we're all alike and consequently that we should have the 'right' to understand each other? There's also a feeling that our work has been privileged, but in fact most of these women writers are in a much more privileged position than any of us who come to experimental work from a slant because

> we're almost invariably from a different race, a different culture, a different language, or a different sexual orientation. (312)

Lesbian writers like Warland would be anxious to maintain their strategic position in the margin as well as their difference from other marginalized groups. In her conclusion titled "Where our loyalties lie" to the *Telling It Conference,* she writes:

> It is within the outlawed communities of active feminists, lesbians, incest survivors, differently-abled, single mothers, goddess worshippers, etc., that we can begin to find the resources we need for throwing off our oppression. It is here, on the margin, that we can also experience a growing awareness of the necessity to refuse our former complicity with other forms of patriarchal oppressions which differ from our own. (195)

Her writing is characterized by this conscious, well-thought out lesbian subject position and is marked by respect for plurality of voices, including those of other marginalized groups like the aboriginals of Australia in *Double Negative*. The two texts will be studied with a focus on the articulation of lesbian sexuality with specific attention to the text and the philosophy of language that emerges through the linguistic devices used.

5.3.3 Serpent (W)rite[6] and the Critique of "Master" Narratives

There is a visible subversion at work in the very title with the (W) in parentheses signalling, woman with a capital 'W' and the word 'write' being split into 'w' and 'rite.' There is a hint that the mysteries and mysticism associated with the semi-divine figure of the serpent are going to be explored and perhaps unravelled. It is evident later that the serpent with its forked tongue becomes a metaphor for lesbian writing. The epigraph to the book contains lines by Adrienne Rich:

> In speaking of lies, we come inevitably to the subject of truth. There is nothing simple or easy about this idea. There is no 'the truth,' 'a truth'—truth is not one thing, or even a system. It is an increasing complexity.

The book sets out to establish just that by deconstructing various white, androcentric, phallogocentric, "master" narratives. When asked about the significance of the epigraph, Warland said:

> There's a growing awareness of the need to understand, articulate, respect difference, and to avoid universalisms which have repressed women all along. Rich's statement has a real resonance in my work because I find that my writing has more integrity and fascination for me when I'm involved in an ongoing investigation of form, language and content. What seems difficult for us all to circumvent is the desire to say I have the right point of view. While it's a very interesting time to be writing and living, it's not easy. (Williamson 303)

Warland in fact questions the truth claims by these so-called "universals" through alternate discourses, equally rigorous. She elaborates on some of the writings that influenced her perspective in "moving parts." Referring to *Serpent (W)rite* she writes:

> This book represents my most intensive work in decoding and analyzing language as the bedrock of The Great White Fathers' value system. Dale Spender's *Man Made Language* (1980) was a crucial source of confirmation about the necessity of this language—deconstruction project, as was Nicole Brossard's deconstruction of woman in *These Our Mothers* (published translation in 1983). Eve and Adam, the original moulds of gender indoctrination, are also deconstructed as is the experience of being lost (our post-Garden condition). As the writer, I submerge myself in the experience of being lost: through relentless deconstruction of clichés and decodifying language; through the interruption by other voices excerpted from a wide variety of material I was reading during the writing; and through the resolution to not go back over and read any of the writing until the text came to its resting point. Consequently, the writing wanders in circles (as one does when one is physically lost), sometimes with recognition of earlier passings but more often with no conscious recognition of the textual landmarks—and so another perspective is laid down in the groove. There are no page numbers, and only in the latter editorial stage did I set the text into eight "turns" which function as indicators of the text's inherent movement (which also evokes women's cyclical orgasmic movement). (252)

With these explanatory notes from the writer herself, the analysis of the text becomes somewhat manageable. In deciphering experimental writing like Warland's, the reader has a participatory role in the creation of the text's multiple meanings by decoding the text. Warland writes in the same article comparing *Serpent (W)rite* with her earlier books *Gathering Instinct* (1981) and *open is broken* (1984):

> Although the lesbian body continues to be site-specific in *Serpent W(rite)*, it is no longer foregrounded. Out of 128 pages, there are only eight erotic lesbian passages. In essence, the lesbian body now becomes the ground from which the writing in *Serpent (W)rite* is generated. Having established the terms of the speaking voice in open is broken as lesbian, I am centred and prepared to speak of the world as I know it beyond the lesbian littoral. (253)

Warland at the outset positions herself writing out of lesbian sexuality and from the lesbian body. In the very first line addressed to her lover she says:

> We lose ourselves in each other
> smell . . .

The vowels are listed horizontally and vertically with a play on the word 'last':

> last lest list lost lust
> lest
> list
> lost
> lust

The sentence following this is "your smell in/lists me" (turn one). From this follows the act of bringing her lover to orgasm with the vowels forming the sound of her cry. The page ends with the sentence referring to her own work as: "this lost manuscript" (turn one). The lesbian text of desire is marginalized, even erased. The use of the vowels of the master('s) tongue to signify orgasmic sounds is truly subversive. The next page has the lines: "willing to be lost/a will to be lost accept our condition give up the Garden" (turn one). She extends the notion of loss from personal to the loss of Eden. The line, "(our resolve) to make this place home" signifies the creation of her own literary space as a lesbian.

There is a highlighting of the sense of smell and its role in memory with language and the sense of smell playing similar roles—that of the ability to convey messages. The lesbian erotic erupts into the text with the words:

we write on our bodies with
the tide of Yin
hot wordsmells pour on cunt belly
breasts
claiming presence to/ in each
other (emit, transmit, submit)
our fluids marking where we have been
odors our fluency, bhleu—to swell, well up, overflowing
    sheets upon sheets

    smell signals scent/ence
    sheet signals paper (turn one)

The lesbian sexual pleasure yields to writing. There is a pun on the word "sheets" signifying bed sheets as well as sheets of paper. This pleasure or 'jouissance' marks the beginnings of language and the lesbian text. In "the breasts refuse" Warland writes on the connection between the body and says:

> In my early thirties, i reached a crisis with language. In relocating my writing within my lesbian body, i found that language, by omission and negative connotation, had denied the intimate world of my eroticism and love. Brossard, Rich, Lorde, Cixous and Irigaray broke sexual taboo, and i discovered my words; marked the page; have never been the same. (279)

Warland's use of deconstruction to expose the "master" narrative of patriarchy begins with the subversion of the story of the Fall from Genesis. She begins by re/surrecting the figure of the serpent "cursed to the dust / upon your belly you shall go / and dust you shall eat. Goddess Nidaba, the first deity of writing has been depicted as a serpent. There is a re/presentation of the figure of:

Eve standing beneath the Tree
with a need in her breast
something missing in paradise . . .
a longing for words (turn one)
Adam's naming not an ending
more words wanted out
words which spoke of experience interpreted perception
words of discourse (turn one)

Adam, the first patriarch has named Eve with propriety. She needs language to represent her experience, powerful language that centres her as the subject of discourse. The serpent as a figure linked to "wisdom and counsel" subverts the conventional figure of serpent in Christian mythology. Warland lists the names of goddesses from different myths depicted by the serpent to illustrate the androcentrism of the Christian myth. The image of Eve by the tree is similar to that of the poet herself at the age of thirteen in a small town in the American Midwest in turn four:

> at the age of thirteen i
> was confirmed, hot summer
> hours beneath the walls,
> a foreigner tree memorizing
> for public catechism, one
> morning a voice said,
> you can ask for one
> thing. i asked without hesitation: 'wisdom.'

The poet has grown up in a milieu of orthodox Christianity and the image of her beneath the tree asking for wisdom is similar to the earlier image of Eve beneath the Tree of Knowledge longing to know. Warland further gives wisdom a feminine gender and capitalizes the letter 'W.' She resurrects the figures of both Eve and Pandora, both of whom are considered as foolish, overly curious women by Western myth:

> Eve, Pandora damned for *openings,* upo, evil
> their *lid, klei, clitoris*
>
> the body condemning the body condemned the body lost
> i afraid of losing myself. (turn one)

This refers to the negativity loaded on to these two figures and is connected with their sexuality and their thirst for knowledge. She is also referring to the Western woman's alienation from her body as a result of religious strictures. She repeats the image of Eve at the tree following the intermeshing lines by the goddess such as

> I am the woman of the great   expanse of water, says   sabina
> I am the woman of the expanse of the divine sea, says. . .

with lines addressed by a woman to her lesbian lover as from a love poem beginning with:

> i am the woman who receives you, says
> i am your shore your harbour, your territory
>
> moan gathering above
> tremor shout down hot floods my cunt. (turn one)

The poem seems to suggest that it is from the body, particularly the lesbian bodies in their sexuality that language comes into being. She includes lines by Audre Lorde that "the erotic offers a well of replenishing and provocative force to the woman who does not fear its revelation."

Creativity arises out of the lesbian erotic for Warland. "Cracking the code broken is open"—the lesbian code is the subtext. This is followed by the image of Eve at the tree, "longing for her history, wisdom." Her story is juxtaposed with Genesis to demarcate the feminine from the patriarchal text:

> Eve at the tree the bheudh—
> make aware, bode (boda, messenger),
> ombudsman, Bo Tree, Bodhisattava, Buddha . . . (turn one)

Her combined use of deconstruction of words, etymology and finding 'relative' words of Indo-European origin enables her to scrutinize myths from other cultures and understand the erasure of matriarchal principle from Western religions. She suggests that there has been a usurping of the original goddess by the male God figure of Yahweh. The parallels she draws from Buddhism show how the tree is conceived differently in that it promises self-realization. She deconstructs the Greek mythic goddess, Demeter's name to 'Dē-mater' 'De' is the delta, or triangle, 'D/e—ve' to the Sanskrit 'dwr' or 'door' to the door of birth—"yoni yantre" or "yantra of the vulva."

This is followed by the all-too-familiar command of patriarchy "nip it in the bud" (repeated in the text). The bud of course signifies the female vulva. She then proceeds to examine the word "vulva" with its attendant symbolism in Indian tradition:

> Personifying the yoni, the
> Goddess Kali bore the title of Cunti or Kunda,
> root of the ubiquitous Indo-European word "cunt"
> and all its
> relatives: cunnus, cunte,
> cunning, cunctipotent, ken, kin,
> country.
> (cunt-tree) (turn one)

In this manner Warland sets about feminizing the English language making connections with root words from other languages. In an essay, "f.) is sure" she writes of the need for dialects:

> We need all the dialects, to fill in the gap, make up a deficiency, fill in a vacant space. Because we are absent in the English language as women who are self-defined and name. so, we're free to invent, reclaim, re-dis-cover language on a word-to-word basis: like children—the power, the sensuousness and the magic of words. This is where language becomes very spiritual for me; when it is not a given but a gift. (35)

In this context it is useful to see Irigaray's views on linguistics:

> The *linguistic sciences* have concerned themselves with models for utterances, with synchronic structures of speech, with language models 'known intuitively to any normally constituted subject.' They have not faced, and at times even refused to face, the question of sexuation of discourse. They

> accept, perforce, that certain items of vocabulary may be added to the established lexicon, that new stylistic figures may potentially become acceptable, but they refuse to consider that syntax and the syntactic-semantic operation might be sexually determined, might not be neuter, universal, unchanging. (*Ethics* . . . 24)

This gendering of discourse is what writers like Irigaray and Warland are interested in exposing. In turn eight, after locating the feminine origins of the Torah, Warland quotes Saussure's statement that "in language there are only differences." The concept of difference has been critical to the Derridean notion of deconstruction which has been appropriated by radical feminist writers like Warland.

In turn two and turn four, Warland lashes out at modern reproductive technology which seeks further control over women's bodies. She seeks the origin of the use of the letter 'X' to signify the female chromosome and finds a connection with the X form of sign used in 1000 BC by Phoenicians and other Semites of Syria and Palestine. Over time, X came to be used to signify an illiterate person, an unknown person, an unknown quantity etc. Towards the end of turn four, alternately the letters "XOXO" she endows the letters with the power of the female body, both being mouths—one upper and the other lower. Using modern genetics she establishes that in the course of fetal development, "the *fetus* is said to be chromosomatically female in the first few weeks" and that we have all been fe(male) not every androgynous till sexual differentiation occurs. This is offered as indisputable fact from modern genetics which goes contrary to the story of Genesis with Eve having been created out of Adam's rib. She addresses the issue of artificial insemination and parodies the exchange of marriage vows in this context. She attacks man's need to control women's bodies through reproductive technology which would further fragment her body and alienate it. In these short, cryptic lines she ironically observes that the preoccupations of men and women have been exchanged:

> Eve be /got the Womb
> Adam be / got the Word
> now man discovers reproductive technology
> now woman dis/covers the word
> this could be wholeness
> this could be war (turn four)

Their roles are reversed as it were in that, man wants to gain control of the womb now and woman, language. She refers to the three symbols of patriarchal power:

> man's throwback to Adam—test(icle) tube babies
> trei—, three, testament, contest, trine (trinity)
> Yahweh procreating with Adam
> it's a man's wor(l)d (turn four)

In turn four she refers to the ethical question of motherhood posed by surrogate motherhood quoting a report from *The Globe and Mail* dated April 4, 1987 which stated that a surrogate mother Mary Beth Whitehead was stripped of her parental rights by a court verdict. (She spells it as VerDICK to show the male bias encoded in it). This was due to the contract she had signed relinquishing her parental rights once the baby was born. Her change of heart was struck down. The fetus as well as the woman's womb is commodified by the verdict. Similarly in turn four, Warland deconstructs, the word 'hysterectomy' to 'his-tear-economy' and dubs it as "America's favourite operation." In a reversal of Freudian theory of 'penis-envy' she posits "womb envy" and cites evidence from anthropology to show that there is no evidence of "known female ceremonials in which women pretend to be men, as the men who conduct puberty rites pretend to be women or as in couade." Neither is there any evidence of "Freud's even having analyzed a little girl." She cites the various branches of knowledge used by man to appropriate the womb:

reproductive technology
(boy)cott biology
terrortory theology
(man)ipulator mythology (turn four)

She proceeds to warfare, both traditional and biological warfare—both current preoccupations of man. Even in the face of new evidence to the contrary

yet he remains ADAMant
using Garden Grammar he
writes an opposite story (turn four)

He names the clitoris / a homologue of the male penis, present as a rudimentary organ. In this manner man creates more discourses to maintain his position of power and Warland terms it "X-propriation." In turn three, Warland subjects the objectified condition of woman to closer scrutiny. She discovers that "the Word appears in league with the highest Lord of creation, either as the tool which he employs or actually as the primary source from which he, like all other Beings and order of Being, is derived." This is true of creation accounts of all cultures, where the word is a source of authority. She writes:

Adam's mind over matter,
mother, matrix (turn three)

Matter, mother and matrix are again connected and man wields power over them through language which is conceptual. She points to the crux of man's subjectivity being grounded in the position of women as object:

objects of desire
woman as object
word as object (turn three)

She also points out that language as a system of representation has always depended on this subject position of man. Referring to her early incest experience, Warland writes in "f) is sure":

> I learned very profoundly that language is not to be trusted. it is all too often a vehicle for deception. . . . My silence was all I had to protect me from losing myself and my reality. (33)

Referring to her development as a writer she writes in the same article:

> Later as I became more grounded in my life as a lesbian, and my vision as a lesbian, I came smack up against the reality that there were no words for my experience—my erotic, sexual and spiritual experiences as a lesbian. In my second book, *open is broken* (which came out in 1984), I started to sink myself into language; I began to take it apart and make up words and reclaim it. that's when I came into a deep realization that language is a value system. (34)

In turn three she examines Irigaray's statement, 'But what if the "object" started to speak?' in the light of her earlier reference to Lacan's theory, without naming him she says:

> man master / baiting himself
> into The Transcendental Signifier
> of no / body

She later refers to his Mirror Stage too. She starts speculating on what writing would emerge if the object started to speak or became the subject of discourse. Referring to Monique Wittig's text, Namascar Shaktini writes, "Through a major reorganization of meaning within Monique Wittig's text, the lesbian body has displaced the phallus as the central point of reference" (291). This is the central point from which writing emerges according to Warland as well:

> the text is full of holes
> mouth cunt ears urethra
> nostrils anus eyes
> infinite constellation of pores
>
> i am a figure of speech
> we are figures of speech in
> each other's arms
> (to fit together, read, riddle, rite)

Later she writes:

> we meet in fluid
> rushes from sources unknown
> over our bodies and claiming
> we provoke its pouring require
> territorial marking a wildness
>
> remember the way wet
> in want encountered, these holy
> waters current us down (turn three)

This section is filled with images of fluidity. The fluid images of lesbian eroticism are connected to the Great Goddess whose urine rained over the face of the earth:

> Sophia, spirit of Female Wisdom,
> 'once represented God's female
> soul, source of his power'

present when He created the
heavens and earth—
'Then I was there beside him
[all] together;
I was his daily joy' (turn three)

This image of the Goddess is close to the concept of Shakti as Shiva's consort, presiding over the universe. Sophia is usurped by a masculine figure. She refers to "Sophia tide of yin rising on the face of the earth" and quotes from Chang that 'the Tao discovered the female ejaculation phenomenon at least 2,000 years ago and called it the tide of yin.'

Warland writes that 'we are now just learning of our waters.' Knowledge about woman's sexuality itself has been repressed till recently. She concludes turn three with the damning statement: "phallus? Fell us." In characterizing the experimental feminine Joan Retallack writes:

> we note current identifications of "the feminine"—that it is open, diffuse, multiple, complex, decentred, filled with silence, fragmented, incorporating difference and the other (Hélène Cixous, Luce Irigaray, et al) undefinable, subversive, transgressive, questioning, dissolving identity while promoting ethical integrity (Julia Kristeva, Judith Butler, et al); materially and contextually pragmatic, employing nonhierarchical and nonrationalist associative logics—"weblike" connective patterns (Carol Gilligan); self and other interrupted, open/interrogative (Sally McConnell-Ginet, Mary Field Belenmy, et al); marginal, metonymic, juxtapositional, destabilizing, heterogeneous, discontinuous. (367)

Betsy Warland's works exhibit most of these listed features of the experimental feminine. Warland parodies the "split Adam theory" by which Eve was created and terms it "Evectomy of Adam's dark side." She terms the anxiety of Adam at the removal of a rib as "primal castration." She conflates the two "master" narratives—Freudian theory and Story of the Fall from Genesis for subversion. She does not spare even common usages such as "i've half a mind to" from her scrutiny and finds that it probably emanates from the relegation of the right side of the brain (associated with feminine, non-verbal activities), the dark side to a lesser role.

By using the archaeology of language to trace the Greek origins of 'chaos,' Warland inverts the meaning of chaos pointing to the fact that Eros was born out of chaos. She equates that with female sexuality by interjecting a quote from Brossard: 'Female desire resists closure.' (turn five). She draws on different cultural myths to demonstrate the primacy of woman's blood as being the source of earth's life and presents different images of fluids from the amniotic to the "holy waters" pouring from the Goddess Sophia's womb. Man has suppressed knowledge of female sexuality to such an extent that female ejaculation, which was termed as the tide of yin by Tao centuries ago, until 1980 was not accepted by the medical community. She uses these fluid images to describe female sexuality as well as to foreground history of the language of the feminine:

kykeon soma sa ambrosia
fills mouth

pours over
face neck breasts belly cunt legs
amniotic fluid ofour in-fount-cy
when our waters break in-, not +
                    fari, to speak
we begin the course of our fluency
river, re-, to scratch, tear write,
                    writan, to tear, scratch
reverwrite
          branching wherever earth will
                    receive us
A-dam had no sea legs
but he smelled something fishy (turn five)

Language which is dammed, breaks out even when woman's sexuality breaks free from the shackles and the fluency of language is compared to the fluids of woman's body. Warland deconstructs words in the middle of sentences to disrupt the comfort of readers who are habituated to conventional meanings given by patriarchy. In her interview with Janice Williamson, she expresses her views on the relationship between the body and language:

> The era in which I developed as a feminist has been intrigued with the significance of the body: the body (and gender) has been a major focus of psychology, sociology, linguistics, politics and literature. As a lesbian writer, it has been important for me to articulate the particular sensuality, eroticism, and language of my body. Because this is a language that has not been articulated, it can seem very unfamiliar—even to ourselves! And it doesn't stop there—it impacts whatever I write about. (306)

In these lines she clarifies her perspective on the relationship between the body and language and this perspective does inform her work. In turn six she offers some prescriptions for this body-centred writing and begins the section with the line, "HOW NOT TO GET LOST The main rule for not getting lost is to know at all times where you are."

She is of course implying that one needs to be grounded in a stable subject position. One needs to begin in the body "where word begins." Woman becomes her own figure of speech. At this juncture she quotes Irigaray's words: 'Instead of being a recipient of meaning she becomes a producer and as such begins to deconstruct her muted state.'

This is what Warland suggests women writers ought to do. She warns of the obstacles that stand in the way of such an enterprise and quotes Drucker's statement, we are the line of discourse 'continually being structured/circles within circles sss-piraling/ around A-dam 'manglish.' (turn six). She combines man and english to coin the word 'manglish.' She is suggesting that woman is discourse constructed by male language. The gendered English language and its sciences discriminate against woman.

In turn seven and eight she evokes the spectre of nuclear holocaust and links war to male sexuality. She terms the prospect of nuclear catastrophe as "The Phallusy of the phalloids." She creates images of the aftermath of a nuclear holocaust with the world plunged in sub-zero temperatures and an image of a new Noah's Ark with no animals and women perhaps in functional numbers. War seems to heighten sexuality according to people who have been in combat. Warland thus outlines man's alienated condition in all aspects of life.

Unlike animals who live superstitiously, "Christianity can't abide superstition because it has overcome animism . . . and that move represses your inherent religiosity in relation to the world" (turn eight). Christianity, according to Warland, alienates man from nature and puts him in opposition to the rest of the species. This is not true of ancient religion. Man is alienated in his heterosexual relationship as well. Warland suggests that he has a parasitic relationship to woman:

He shares the body as *guest,*
hospes, stranger
is not host is afraid of host of
being held (host) age
A-dam creating an ecto Genesis
ectogeneous, able to live and develop
outside a host (turn eight)

Man is alienated from her but thrives on her life force. She writes:

He writes with penis, pes-, pencil
Eve (w)rites with nipples, nadja-, nib
She (w)rites two
not opposite but different
speaks both sides of Her brain

A-dam speaks left—feels left (turn eight)

Since she uses both sides of her brain, she is bound to think more holistically whereas man uses his left (rational) part and "feels left"—abandoned. There is a pun here again signifying his alienation. Adam is alienated in spite of all the power he wields for he longs for a 'Mother.'

Warland refers to the Lacanian Mirror Stage and the development of the self in alienation. Language acquisition takes place in this alienated condition:

language is loss
is how we bridge our separation
after Paradise
after the womb (turn eight)

She subverts this Lacanian image by turning to the lesbian subject and puns on the notion of 'the split subject.'

we are the split subject
split, slit, slot
hollow between the breasts
no longer divided against our/selves

are the subject of two mouths
which now *face, form*
words of our own
prefix and suffix in dialogue
no longer waiting to be heard
no longer eating our hearts out

my word!
eating pussy
        cat got my tongue
we make love in the company of
      four
two Eves four mouths. (turn eight)

Warland suggests that it is in this position that plurality emerges as also by using dialects. She writes in "the breasts refuse," "in naming ourselves we finally accept our babbles' necessity" (290). She writes about the destruction of this plurality and dialects by patriarchy:

the danger of dialects

divisive
disruptive
difficult to control

historically having been
either gradually absorbed into one
            dominant language
or
splintering off into
independent 'foreign' languages (286)

Plurality and differences have always been viewed as threatening by the establishment. She recommends a return to the body which is the lost place, the home one ought to write from. Referring particularly to the lesbian body, she says:

head between my legs
you are daughter emerging returning
sucking your source (mouth to mouth resuscitation)
whirling spinning us around to
        m(O)ther body we shared
synaptic syntax of our sensuality
you urge uterus utterance
de-, away, off+rivus, stream
tide of yin
pouring over your 'whole face'
here in fluency
we are The Flood which sustains us
(the form is the cuntext) (turn eight)

There is a play on 'form is content' to a new statement on lesbian writing. She seems to be somewhat utopian in recommending this ideal. This view is corroborated by her writing in "moving parts":

> Lesbian writers, along with other marginalized writers, are the voices of the future (which is the present) simply because our voices have been so absent in the past. We are the source of the knowledge that has been repressed, and it is that very repression that has put the world at such risk. (257)

In the conclusion of turn eight she suggests that it is not an easy task for lesbian writers since they have to re/cover lost meanings from 'other' 'foreign' languages and dialects which are the sap of contemporary languages, often destroyed by the colonizer and the poet is compelled to examine each given word:

> with my hands I catch word after word that holds us
> captive set us free wordsmells wombwords word-
> prints we track endlessly. (turn eight)

5.3.4 *Double Negative*—Collaborative Writing

Double Negative is an illustration of collaborative writing which is rare among white, Western writers. The writing is located literally and metaphorically in the desert space conventionally considered to be negative space. Again the aspects to be focused on in this text are the construction of the lesbian identity through sexuality and language.

Positioned as lesbian women writing on the margins of dominant culture, they are enabled to look at the colonization of the aboriginals of Australia by conjuring up images of colonization through the aboriginal names of places that the poets retain in the original. When asked about collaborative writing at an interview with both the writers, Daphne Marlatt says:

> with Betsy, collaborating is much more *collaborative*. For one thing, we were not so much competing with each other as trying to open out the experience of being women together on this train. We both had this project of writing our lesbian bodies into the phallic symbolic of the train. This allowed not only for more sharing but for a lot more eroticism and joy in the writing. (Williamson "in companionship. . ." 197)

The text is divided broadly into two sections—the first section denoted by time and place in the style of journal entries, written by both the poets whose authorship is deliberately kept undistinguishable. The second section is titled "Crossing Loop" with Marlatt and Warland alternately explaining their writing, again followed by a sub-section titled "Real 2" where they continue writing larger pieces, again with authorship left unstated. In the same interview Betsy Warland explains the process of collaborative writing adopted by them:

> Well, we were on the train for three days, and the two rules that guided us were that we were to alternate entries and read one another's previous entries. The second rule was to refer to the names of the places we were passing through; you had to at least mention one in each poetry entry which makes up the first part of the book. We seemed to make two entries each day, so there were four al-

> together each day for the three days. The middle of the book is the interview section, where we talk about wanting to break the frame of the lyric poem, go off track, so we could be free to explore all our sub-textual thoughts that we had set aside because they weren't located within the narrative context of the poem. In the third prose poetry section we take excerpts and phrases from one another's poetry and spark a whole derailing of thought. The interview and prose poetry sections were done in Canada. It was a lot of fun to break the frame ourselves, and to do that twice: to find out what happened when we wrote beyond our own endings. (Williamson "in companionship . . ." 196)

Within the text there is a conflation of the lesbian body's eroticism and the landscape/contours of the Australian desert. They are literally and metaphorically travelling in a reverse direction, "travelling backwards through Australia/rim of glass on our lips." (*DN* 12) As Brenda Carr explains:

> 'Re-versed' on one level, reflects Marlatt and Warland's literal experience of writing while sitting in train seats facing backwards. Movement in reverse is double as they engage in 're-vision' of literary ground, in Adrienne Rich's sense of 'entering an old text from a new critical direction.' Such re-versing facilitates transformation of the historical subject of poetry from monolithic, male, and heterosexual to multiple, female and lesbian. (114)

They are keen on re/presenting the female travel experience even in the evocation of images of the female body to feminize the landscape as is evident in these lines:

> traine, to
> feminize (part of a(d)dress)
> and not merely in tow
>
> you, you who know
> we go inside
>
> out
> into the womb of the continent
> ochre, red earth, salt plain. (13)

Even the colours are sensual, warm, and earthy body colours. They are aware of themselves as outsiders and of the impossibility of going back to the absolute origins of cultures or language. At the same time they are respectful of the aboriginal culture:

> we don't know where they came
> from
> we can't go back
> not to the roots we know
> Indo-European words, deadwood
> sentences tracking
> across the untracked, the
> intractably here (15)

Language creates itself through the uncharted territory like the train. She implies the wild, uncharted territory of lesbian sexuality as well. Even as they mouth new words of the oldest living language, they are aware of the new language they need to articulate lesbian love in:

we are fed we sleep are held nameless
and content
umbilical track leading us to
names a map
Yunta, Paratoo, Ucolta, Yongala
words we head for down this
birthing canal
"the oldest living language" shaping
our tongues lips
to speak it out (though we do not
know the meanings)

magnetic fields of sounds
mouths move in an Other motion (16)

Their mouths move forming the words in a child like manner. From the interview section it is evident that Marlatt and Warland saw the track's symbolism differently.

According to Marlatt, "What we really didn't deal with is how when you're on a train you are on the one track. It's not cyclical." (37)

Warland writes, "It wasn't that way for me because I saw the tracks as the umbilical cord, the track as representing our continuous dependency on the earth which we're never really cut free from. Also, the train is constantly starting and stopping, departing and arriving, coming and waiting at crossing loops and in that sense it's cyclical [as rhythm is cycling back repeating itself, the rhythm of our movement everything] (37).

The V shape in the landscape makes the poet meditate on the erotic symbolism of the Venus mound or V of the female body:

's incessant stream
the landscape pours through

us filled with it, held and
rocked backward, content or not
kinetic at all points in touch
with coming incessantly
into
THIS, this
image cattle climb the
soft mound of hill lost
dip or cleft a
V to view
"this little entry"
"mine take forever"

take forever
crossed then by
V
V
(a cloud, rose-breasted
this the imaginary
we enter (18)

Again later:

off the map
opening up the Subject
hands a manual alphabet
i sign your V

PROHIBITED AREA

CONS: "French cunt"

the imaginary
two women in a birth (21)

Earlier she refers to the two of them as "two negatives make a positive." The prohibited area refers to strictures against female sexuality, particularly lesbian sex. They are asked whether they are alone in the dining car. In an article titled "Where our loyalties lie" Warland writes about the unprotected lives lesbians lead:

> Lesbian women relinquish the protection of men. And in a world that is so systematically and arbitrarily distrustful of and violent to women, this is serious business. It means that as lesbians, we are responsible for ourselves in every way: economically, socially, spiritually. (198)

Explaining the significance of the V in the text Carr writes that the V shifts the gaze from the phallus as a term of reference in the Lacanian theory of subject formation to the Venus mound.

The text refers quite overtly to 'The Gaze' and all that it signifies in terms of patriarchal values:

there are birds, insects, mammals,
reptiles, scrub trees,
bushes, grasses
thriving outside The Gaze
(can we see what we do not value) (24)

Since Western patriarchal culture does not value nature and other species, it adopts merely an exploitative stance against it. The poet gives us an ecofeminist viewpoint. There is need to identify and empathize with all those marginalized or erased by 'The Gaze.' There is a need felt to reinvent language to articulate lesbian eroticism in the following lines:

Rock bottom seabed we lie in
You pulled me under last night

Sucking me out through my womb
Inside out
Re-versed writing across bed into
Sky
Touching holding everything
Words my only boundary
The desert on other side of my
Mind (23)

In their re-versed writing sex erupts into the text and the lesbian erotic finds its way into writing. The images of fluids of nature are again conflated with those of the body with innuendos contained in the words "breaking waters" in these lines:

then its down to breaking waters
Indian Ocean at down
your Mound of V pulling me
O contraction Star of V-us
first letter of another alphabet
let language we stare at

We will open the bed and chant
our stars down
into the sway of unuttered texts
as the matter of language reinvents
itself all over again. (28)

In articulating lesbian sexuality and 'jouissance,' language needs to reinvent itself repeatedly. Marlatt writes about this in the interview section of the book:

> We talked about coming but made it female coming and the cyclical nature of female orgasm is really different from the on-track crescendo of male orgasm. (37)

One sees evidence of this intermeshing of body and text in the following excerpt from "Reading and Writing Between the Lines" by Daphne Marlatt and Betsy Warland. Writing about collaborative writing is "reciprocal in this, that the holes we make in such a definite body leak meaning we splash each other with, not so much working as playing in all this super-fluity, wetting ourselves with delight even, whetting our tongues, a mutual stimulation we aid and abet (entice) in each other" (81).

In the interview section of the text Betsy Warland refers to Nicole Brossard and Jane Rule's use of the desert in their works:

> Thinking about their work i began to have a sense that there is some kind of a North American lesbian tradition of exploring the feminine in relation to the desert which is usually seen as an arena for male activities. I find it quite exciting that there's this female movement into the desert saying "this is mine too and i relate to it in a different way." (38)

In the piece titled, "traveling backwards through Australia" is contained the idea that the reversed position gives a new perspective. There is a reference to Betsy Warland being born breached "unable to see what lies ahead" (42) meaning her life as a lesbian. The last section of the text contains a parody of popular, macho, "reel" heroes. In the prose poem titled "light thoughts" are references to the exploitation of the desert and mining of sacred aboriginal sites by the white colonizer (46). In the poem titled "two women in a birth" is the notion of the doubling of the lesbian subject. Carr suggests:

> Here, as the end of 'coming into Port Pirie' also suggests the monolithic subject is opened up to allow for the birth of a twinned subject: two women in a train giving birth to each other as desired and desiring subject in and for each other's writing. (119)

In fact juxtaposed with the image of women chanting slogans at a nuclear testing site in the desert, multiple voices emerge. This view is endorsed by their writing in "Reading and Writing Between the Lines":

> in our doubleness, no, our plurality as we read (for) and write (to) you, all the you's in each other reading and writing too—a polylogue, such bends and twists—you see how this writing rivers out to various mouths immediately? (80)

There is the tendency among these writers to ally themselves with ecofeminist and pacifist causes. This goes to show that their concerns as lesbian writers extend to issues of marginal identities and sexuality. This is illustrated in the poem titled, "imagin-a-tion in the heart of." The human heart is compared to the "heartland laid waste" due to exploitation of the land for its resources. She writes, "the heart is not allowed to throb for pleasure in what surrounds it (imagine a nation at home in the deathless body). There is a reference to the fragility of the ecosystem and economies which thrive on surplus profit. They use run-on lines with no punctuations or capitals to break the conventional, linear syntax, and use open-ended sentences which allow for freer use of language. Their language play and deconstruction of words to yield new meanings and sounds, innuendo, puns and incomplete sentences. These leave room for the reader's participation and collaboration in constructing the text. An illustration of the unusual syntax formations and possibilities is the following line:

> she is also she is desert come in waves the waves she rides she rises up and overflows the words a round around the word surround (50)

Sexuality, desert landscape and birth of language are signified simultaneously. This device allows for multiple layers of meanings to surface. In the poem titled, "he says we got to stay on track," the poet wants to escape from the Symbolic Order with its strictures of patriarchy. She argues for separatism in these lines:

> she wants to migrate she wants to mutate she wants to have no natural predators be nothing look at nothing thrive in her own absence be out of focus out of range of The Gaze hide out from the Law . . . here she can rest here she can play encounter her anima (l) self pre-sign pre-time touching you i touch kangaroo words forming then shifting desert dunes her desire to untrain herself undermine every prop(er) finition. (51)

She wants to escape from the hold of phallogocentrism, learn afresh and undermine known, conventional norms. Carr puts the poets' enterprise in the text lucidly:

> Such a textual connection between two colonized territories—desert and female body becomes the means for a literal and symbolic gesture, an ecofeminist gesture of double decolonization. (120)

In the poem titled "no train of thought" the desert becomes a metaphor for the self:

> "the self in a desert becomes more and more like the desert"(s) and word wavering sense boundaries "stretched out for ever." (53)

"Wavers" has dual meaning in that it signifies hesitation and used in a new way as a verb, it can mean create waves or act. "This, which everything acts upon, acts." The passive object gains subjectivity. The poet asks a rhetorical question: "Do parallel lines meet?" (54) and answers it herself:

> in light years perhaps yet
> it's *what* we see this illusion
> the eye momentarily believing in
> unity (believing is desire) seeing is. . .
> we believe ourselves into ecstasy. (54)

There is a utopian faith in the possibility of the merging of two separate entities. In the final poem titled "we had not wanted it to end" she writes of the lesbian identity as being on the fringes of society:

> reading us in what is out of place out/standing out of that/which (normally) is we are arctic we are summer/tasting a water not so salt as marked by it forever/lingual tongue in alkaline caves succeeds accedes to the pre(prairie free) symbolic flowers here a desert's/standing seen the ocean in us throbs to meet/
>
> we bilingual reading rock reading sand word reading (56)

The poets are outsiders to the mainstream by virtue of being women and lesbian.

They try to inscribe themselves into being through the desert landscape which is conventionally negative space like them.

5.4.1 Body in Motion

Nicole Brossard is the only writer from Quebec selected for this study, since the Québecoise writings are in French and translations have to be used. She is one of the earliest pioneers of the movement of "writing in the feminine" and has influenced most of the Anglophone women writers in Canada writing the body. The novel selected is *French Kiss or Pang's Progress* since it is one of her earliest works where her key ideas of lesbian sexuality, the "writing self" and the hologram germinate. Here is one of the earliest voices of the modernity movement in the province of Quebec in the late 1960s and this connected with the feminist movement and the rising feminist consciousness as well. As Karen Gould in her extensive study of the Québecoise writers puts it:

> Brossard formulated as well as conveyed the new mood of experimental writing in Quebec—what has been described by many contemporary critics and writers alike as an emerging "crisis" of confidence in the representational powers of language and a mounting mistrust regarding the organic wholeness, the ostensibly unified sign system, and the presumed signification or predetermined meaning of the literary text. (54)

In addition to this, Brossard's preoccupation with and theorizing about the process of writing itself provided the impetus for a lot of theorizing about writing in the feminine in Quebec. Referring to this body of writing, Louis Dupré writes:

> Writing is central to the whole investigation. . . . A meaningful intertextuality of dedications, quotations and references is emerging by means of which women writers name, greet, stimulate, re-read and interpret one another ("Experimentation . . ." 357)

In the writing of the Québecoise writers there is a free mixing of genres based on an outright rejection of traditional literary genres. These writers are engrossed in practising what Irigaray suggests:

> If we don't invent a language for our body, there will be too few gestures to portray our history. We will weary of the same few gestures, and our desires will remain latent, and in limbo. Lulled to sleep, unsatisfied. And delivered to the words of men. (qtd. Dupré in "Doubly Complicit . . ." 29)

The preoccupation with language and literary forms is intimately connected with the feminist enterprise in general but is particularly evident in the case of lesbian writers like Brossard. In an interview with Janice Williamson she speaks of the development of her feminist consciousness:

> Before I became a feminist, I suppose I was an angel, a poet, a revolutionary, which I still am (laugh), but I was definitely not identifying with women. In fact, I became a feminist when I became a mother. Almost at the same time I fell in love with another woman. Suddenly I was living the most common experience in a woman's life, motherhood, and at the same time, I was living the most marginal experience in a woman's life lesbianism. Motherhood made life absolutely concrete for me, and lesbianism made my life absolute fiction in a patriarchal heterosexual world. Motherhood shaped my solidarity with women and gave me a feminist consciousness just as lesbianism gave me new ideas about almost everything and opened new spaces for me to explore. (60)

When asked by Beverly Daurio in an interview about people who have influenced her writing, Brossard says:

> I make a distinction between people who have influenced you and people who are accompanying you in the writing. In the beginning when you are writing, you are much more impressed by other texts. For me the main influences were Mallarmé and Maurice Blanchot. And then, in terms of women's writing, when I was much older, Adrienne Rich in her feminist essays; Mary Daly; Ti-Grace Atkinson and Kate Millett were important to me at the time that I read them; Clarice Lispector, Brazilian writer who is stimulating and exciting. (19)

Just as much as the writers who have influenced her, Brossard has been concerned early on with issues of language as a system of representation which needs to be questioned and re-worked. Louise Forsyth notes Brossard's interest in language in these words:

> Since 1965 her focus has been on the power of language to liberate the individual and restructure social institutions. She has worked primarily on the word as signifier—an active agent carrying and seeking meaning—in her lucid exploration of woman's imaginary realm, her body, and her condition in society. In all her texts, Brossard considers writing to be a praxis, a means to intervene effectively on the forum of society while giving form to woman's vision of the universe. Since language is symbol, the body and its desire are transformed by writing so that they enter the symbolic dimension where they become political by being communicated and shared. Brossard writes for herself; she writes for other women who are also writing and reading. She writes so that the image and symbols arising out of women's experience can circulate dynamically and be exchanged in the many dimensions of human space—geographic, psychological, socio-cultural—which must open and unfold if women are to be able to situate themselves in their authentic place ("Traditionalism . . ."158)

In her explorations of language and literary genres she has been mainly propelled by her lesbian identity. This defines her theory and creative writing, although she herself does not distinguish one from the other. Brossard expresses her thoughts on her lesbian identity in these words:

> Lesbians inspire me in the sense that we are a challenge for the imaginary, and in a certain sense for ourselves, insofar as we bring ourselves literally into the world that we can make our being known to the world and that we can then manifest our presence in the order of the read and the symbolical. . . . Writing, for a Lesbian, is learning to take down the patriarchal posters from her room. It is learning to live for a certain time with bare walls. It is learning not to fear the phantoms which take on the colour of the bare wall. In more literary terms, it is renewing comparisons, establishing new analogies, risking certain tautologies, certain paradoxes. ("Tender Skin . . ."181)

The best example of the way in which her lesbian identity shapes her writing, is *French Kiss* which focuses on three mains aspects, namely, writing the lesbian body, her adopting 'the writing self' and the mingling of the body and city metaphors.

5.4.2 Lesbian Body in *French Kiss*

Although her later works inscribe the lesbian body into the text more overtly than her earlier works, the process began as early as this novel. The body erotic is brought into the text by the writer/narrator to celebrate 'jouissance' and also to signify the new space inhabited by this body. Alice Parker in her analysis of Brossard's works writes:

> The Brossardian text takes desire and pleasure, or in other worlds writing, as its point of departure. Conflating *emotion and thought* ("the thought of emotion/the emotion of thought"), as well as *language and desire* (words are an irreducible source of pleasure). Brossard eroticizes the body—the text's body and the body's text. She focuses on the lesbian—as desiring subject of the imaginary—as semantic field. The figure of the lesbian is at once an object of desire, and a "double" through which the passion (for/in writing) can be channeled. Two key images suggest the interplay in-

> volved in this process: the cortex (corps/texte or body/text) and the spiral. These figures encode not only lesbian experience and identity, by which are meant the stories we construct in order to found an ontological presence in the world, but also the movement of lesbian memory. (310)

The novel is about the events in the lives of five characters, three women and two men in Montreal. Marielle/'Elle' drives through the streets of the city in her convertible, *la Mauve* (Violet). Each of the five characters are on their own search. The novel is also about the production of the text itself and the writing of a novel within the novel through Lucy Savage, one of the characters who is evidently a writer. The characters are shown as moving throughout the city almost all day and night. The city itself is a major presence, as a living body with its arteries and movements of pedestrians and traffic lights. Louise Forsyth in her study of the novel writes:

> Brossard has succeeded in *French Kiss* in superimposing three spatial fields and in exploiting the polysemic qualities of her words and images in such a way that they work simultaneously in each of the three fields. The space of the city, with its arteries and incessant movement, is homologous with the space of the body, particularly the female body, with its arteries and incessant movement, which in turn corresponds to the lines traced by words in the space evoked by the text. As Marielle circulates in her jalopy she is seen by the narrator as moving concurrently along three conceptually distinct trajectories. ("Destructuring . . ." 338)

In "Seven Times" (seventh chapter), the narrator observes:

> By day and by night a cirque ringed in red where centripetal and centrifugal forces make round Camomille and Lucy not just a motion of emotion but a vortex of desires: an ocean, 'a womb where death and life transmute one into the other.' (*FK* 28)

The images are fluid and female. Their sexuality evokes images of "an ocean," "a womb" which generates and sustains life. Again in "Thirteen Times" (thirteenth chapter) she writes:

> Camomille and Lucy making love like excited mermaids, sirens to some, double-takes, topless (voice) and bottomless (pit), membranes dilated beltline high, mouths open and kif-kif (inhale/exhale). Cloud. (40)

The passion, excitement of the love-making lesbian bodies in motion, a flurry of activity is expressed in those lines. There is a breathless quality to them with "Kif-kif (inhale-exhale)"—the mingling of the two bodies with separate identities submerged into one, not identifiable—"topless," "bottomless (pit)"—are evoked by these lines. In the interview with Janice Williamson, Brossard talks about the ways in which lesbianism has affected her writing and her perception of her body:

> Lesbianism has affected my writing in the sense that is raised new questions, clarified others. It definitely changed my *rapport d' adresse.* It multiplied my senses, energized my body in a new way. It offered me new metaphors; for example, the spiral and the hologram. In other words, lesbianism gave me new feelings and new ideas about life, power, memory, identity. It gave another rhythm to my voice and therefore to my sentences. It stimulated me to look for the missing link between what we call fiction and reality. (60-61)

The notion of the hologram, although associated with Brossard's picture theory makes its appearance in any early novel like *French Kiss*. She uses this notion to give a three-dimensional picture of the 'jouissance' experienced by the lesbian lovers. She writes:

> Behind the fiction is a mirror, silvered glass, Comomille and Lucy in holograph projection, tridimensional faces on the curtain, a screen that reveals their pleasure, doesn't hide it in some shadowed fold, unthinkable circumstance. (29)

Alice Parker throws some light on Brossard's use of the hologram in her article:

> Stealing terms from technology, science and mathematics, Brossard regrounds her vision by designing texts (literally inventing new signs) for a symbolic order within which words will respond to revised codes. Figures like the hologram and the laser drawn from new optics, references to differential equations and a fourth dimension, focus unsuspected energy on dormant centres of our minds. (307)

Interestingly Brossard says in the Williamson interview that she did not remember that the hologram was already there in *French Kiss* when she wrote *Picture Theory* and that she had been bearing this word for almost ten years in her mind. She clarifies the significance of the hologram in these words:

> Well, I think that my questioning about woman, women, the real, the symbolic, the imaginary, and the notion of fiction versus reality, all came together in such a way that only the metaphor of the hologram could account for them. The hologram deals with a 'real' object, which through 'virtual' image produces a 'fictive' image. It is as if using 'real' characters through imagination—which is the virtual part of the real—I wanted to envision a symbolic woman, fictive but yet changing the perception of womanhood. (72)

The women in *French Kiss* are fearless, autonomous entities inhabiting urban space. According to Karen Gould they are women true to the spirit of modernity and feminist consciousness. Even apart from these explicit episodes of lesbian sex, the text is replete with images of orality like the mouth and the tongue with its central episode of the kiss. The tongue has multiple associations of meanings in the text. It signifies the writer/narrator's grappling with language to produce the text as well as it being an important organ in lesbian sex. After "Twenty Times" (the twentieth chapter), there is a further fracturing of the linearity of the text with the highlighting of the kiss with the section titled "Just Once." From thereon the sections are fragmented with a prolonged dwelling on and focusing on the kiss and the tongue. The first account of the kiss appears in these words:

> Prolong the desires with the telling, the narration of a long uninterrupted kiss. How hard it is to articulate or devise compromise. The kiss, a ball of fire. Life's serum restored with undulant and penetrating movement, a reliving of the taste and smell of birth for a tongue consumed in dance beneath Camomille's palatal dome, Camomille whom I love with all my power of intervention. A wish: to abolish walls between mouths. Mm-mmm the taste of it. (57)

The writing of the kiss assumes as much importance as the kiss itself since writing yields re-living the memory of the pleasure of the kiss. The narrator actively intervenes and enters the narration by re-telling the kiss and dwelling on it:

> Begin again: on Camomille's lips a kiss, rather chaste Nibbled lips. Pain/relaxation. Pleasure, lips licked, left wet. I slip through the slot the text provides and enter Lucy's homosexual fantasies, seductive Lucy in total control of herself. The slot, parted lips, saliva. Like victims in a racy murder mystery, the membranes yield oh so gently to my tongue probing deeper DEEPER INTO THEM? OOF. (59)

There seems to be a cinematic close up on Camomille's lips that the narrator is getting at this time so that every small movement can be recorded. Louise Forsyth in her perceptive analysis of Brossard's novel writes on the metaphoric significance of the kiss:

> When used with passion and intensity, words can push back horizons, shed light on areas which have previously remained in the dark, open territories the existence of which has been unknown, oppose oppression and transform the spatial constructs on which it relies. Brossard uses a rich constellation of images associated with lips, the tongue, the kiss, to convey such a passionate use of language. She extends these images in her third prose work, *French Kiss*—tongues being understood here as meaning both the organ of the body and the body of language—where, in the central section entitled 'Une Seule Fois' the tongues of women meet in passionate jouissance. ("Destructuring . . ." 336)

In an article titled "The Idea of Your Lips," Brossard writes of the creative role of lesbian eroticism in lesbian writing:

> lesbian desire has no rest. It is a subtle floating desire which binds lesbians to lesbians but also lesbians to other women, it is a key element inspiring projects and activating creativity. (127)

There is also the political dimension to the lesbian stance taken by virtue of the lesbian's position vis-à-vis patriarchy and Brossard clarifies her commitment to writing as a political act in her preface to *The Aerial Letter*:

> I believe there's only one explanation for all of these texts: my desire and my will to understand patriarchal reality and how it works, not for its own sake, but for its tragic consequences in the lives of women, in the life of the spirit. Ten years of anger, revolt, certitude and conviction are in *The Aerial Letter*, ten years of fighting against that screen which stands in the way of women's energy, identity and creativity. (35)

She assigns an important role to 'the aerial' woman, Marielle in *French Kiss* being one. The aerial woman is one with "clear vision" which dislocates patriarchal images and fiction. The term aerial, Parker notes "moves the text beyond linearity. The poet privileges "echo, return, repetition" because of "the vitality of cycles" (322). As to the vitality of words in encoding lesbian desire Brossard writes, "Words are a way of devouring the desire which devours us with comparisons taking us to where we become the desire of science and the science of consciousness" ("Certain Words" 48). However, Brossard states categorically, that "lesbian politics is unthinkable outside lesbian eroticism" ("Idea . . ." 128). She captures the image of the free thinking, aerial woman in the character of Marielle, driving around the streets of Montreal:

> Elle in a nutshell, animated by all possible pulsations, varying the spaces, invention at play. Emcee for herself and for lines of force—prospects in mouths duplicated—a tracing.
>
> Now to put her tongue in the other's mouth. Her desire in the city and geography. (63)

She inhabits the urban space of Montreal's roads in her convertible, conventionally considered male space.

5.4.3 The Writing Self

The next aspect from which the novel is to be studied is that of the act of writing itself. The narrator in *French Kiss* is a writer who writes in a deliberately self-reflexive way intruding into the narrative frequently to rupture the linearity, disconcerting the reader into awareness of the fiction that is in the process of creation. One of the characters is a writer in the process of writing and her chapters emerge as enlarged, framed sections in the middle of the original narrative. This self-reflexivity calls to mind Doris Lessing's *The Golden Notebook,* which likewise, deals with the process of writing and also has the seeds of novels within the main framework of the text. In the interview with Williamson when asked about the process of writing Brossard says:

> on a larger scale writing is full of risks because you don't know where it will take you. After all, we write with that *fragile coherent system full of contradictions* which we call the self. . . . If my writing is elliptical and full of rupture, it is not because I want to be nasty to the reader. It is my way of creating new spaces for new meaning which would not appear if I wrote in a linear way. (68-69)

In *French Kiss* at the very outset, the narrating 'I' reminds the reader of the fiction being created:

> Ride astride grammar. I spread myself, eager, inconsequential and desire. (11)

She soon follows the above lines introducing the character of Camomille:

> And Camomille intervenes, forcing the I, making circumstances that require her presence in this text. Not a parasitic chess-game I but an I that's exploring, autonomous and anarchistic—and spans all the dimensions of Camomille's worlds, and my own, ambiguous one. (11)

The subject here is clearly the writer whose own position is not stable. There is a constant conniving with the reader in the creation of the text. Almost all the characters are introduced in the first section titled "Once" where there are references to Camomille being fiction's "shewolf" and to her "fictional lips." There are frequent comments on the work of creating fiction and use of language. An illustration is:

> To do-scribe is to reanimate an occasion on occasion. Narrator/detonator . . . a narrator set to pounce on any theme or romp. . .
>
> Ride astride syntax. Which boads an ode or goads me to something anyway. (15)

Karen Gould throws light on Brossard's evolution as a writer in these lines:

> From formalism to radical feminism, Brossard's extreme literary self-consciousness and fundamental questioning of virtually every aspect of the writing process have never really ceased, even though the act of writing itself has also become a way of exploring feminist consciousness, as well as a way of articulating her own desire for other women and for other ways of organizing reality. (56)

In an in interview in 1977 Brossard spoke about her relationship to writing and desire in these words:

> I am a being of desire, therefore a being of words, a being who looks for her body and looks for the body of the other: for me, this is the whole story [also the 'history'] of writing. (qtd. Gould 70)

Louis Dupré finds certain features of the style of writing common to the Québecoise writers:

> A desire . . . to de-articulate the dominant discourse, to split open syntax, to let the over-flowing feminine into the signifier, to reinvent vocabulary, to reinvest it with new signifieds. And so, in Quebec, the coincidence of the literary avant-garde with the works by women: a dialectic relationship which has allowed both the new writing and women's texts to spill over, to sustain an innovative dynamism. ("Doubly Complicit . . ." 30)

The characters in *French Kiss* embark upon a collective search and that culminates in the writing of a book, the author of which seems to be Lucy Savage. The three chapters of this book are incorporated and framed in the final pages of *French Kiss*. The chapters as well as *French Kiss* remain open and unfinished. The places and characters of this novel within the novel are those of *French Kiss* itself. The novel within is written five years after their collective experience of Montreal. The narrator speaks for all the characters and expresses their collective objectives. Marielle and Lexa have a baby and all five of them are present during the birthing—this is again symbolic of their collective, creative activity. Forsyth in her analysis suggests that "[t]ogether they found a source of energy so powerful that they went through the looking glass of appearances created by their social conditioning and almost seemed to make space burst apart." ("Destructuring . . ." 338)

On the subject writing in the feminine France Théoret suggests: "it is a shifting subject which often tends to mark the fragility of the present time/tense" (364).

In *French Kiss* the present is an unstable time as also the writing self. There is also a shifting of the eye of the narrator from a close up on the characters to the cityscape with a distancing effect, again in a cinematic manner in collaboration with the reader:

> Take another puff reader chum. The microscopic eye. Aerial view of the Island of Montreal. Marielle's purple Plymouth moves slowly now with other autobodies on all sides, blue, black, white, purple; colour patches in the rising mist. (21)

There is self-reflexivity even in the progress of the text, drawing the reader into the act of creation:

> Diffusion of the text complete with interference real and fictional: parasites. Creepy-crawly creatures—or bacteria (characters). Must feed on the text without destroying it. Bit by bit remove all its play (what's loose in it) and voids. With a pen-point fill it to the brim with pleasure. (27)

Lucy Savage in a presumed discussion on patriarchy and writing female experience says to Camomile or it could be a general remark:

> trouble is your heroes real or fictional are always men and if they're women they always end up thinking like males, producing as much etc. etc. variations on a double standard threaded in a spiral. Camomille, you stupefy me, woman. You get me stored but good. 'Symbolic pollution' is something to talk about, I've heard. The kind of thing you just don't leave up in the air. (29)

Brossard seems interested in the corporeality of the lesbian body, the text and the city. The text is a living entity as it were in which the narrator takes up the narration of Lexa she comments: "Here the text groans like a rusty stomach" (36). She blurs the distinction between fiction and reality in a postmodernist manner:

> Imitation: fiction/reality. Whether to beat a retreat or stay and look it over carefully and at length. This is fiction but then I don't know what isn't anymore. Phantazise a writing. Marielle drives along a Sherbrooke Street projected into space, an unsubstantial street, a fragile mental ground where first one word then another sprouts, forming images of introduction to a surrogate existence elicited by a fiction, or a reality; gives a yen for harmony, re-equilibrium in the laws of—what? Nature, word is a potential sense. (45)

Brossard seems to suggest that the concrete and 'real' structures like the city itself are in the imaginary of the writer as the narrator writes: "If writing dies, so will the city and its harlots. Will wrap about itself like a grieving young widow's luxuriant neurosis" (71). Similarly there is a lot of self-reflexivity about language within—the text. In the Williamson interview she discusses the 'slipperiness' of language:

> I like to be surprised by language. Sometimes the surprise pops out haphazardly. Sometimes it is the result of a difficult crafting; sometimes it is the result of a 'coherent contradiction.' Slipperiness has also to do with the aura of words, their connotations. In fact, the life of a language takes place with connotations, it is there that the meaning displays and renews itself. I also believe that there is a memory in language which leads to reconstituting patterns of ancient meaning. (71)

The tongue is used in a literal sense. It is also used symbolically to mean language. This serves the narrator's self-reflexivity. Similarly the mouth also performs this dual functron:

> Tongue 'a nimble mass of muscle' activates a traffic back and forth, particles of food. Meet up, thrash about, buffet the muscles of the cheeks. Break into speech like English cannonballs nibbling gnawing at the Plains of Abraham. Syllables dilate. Delphie's articulation's bad. Lucy Savage grabs the opportunity, slicks out her tongue, lets Delphie know the tongue she'll use is sharp and curious and out to touch on every surface imaginary or real. (18)

We are told that Lucy Savage the writer will put the tongue to multiple uses. She is sharp-tongued in her speech, her love-making and use of language as a writer. Camomille's effort to speak or mouth words is described sensuously:

> Effort to speak. Camomille salivates. Gets wet. Mucin. The saliva clings to the inner surfaces. Buccal membrane, the phrase alone wafts her to a site of sweet delight where the longest spaces—of undetermined length—at once seem lubrified as for erotic use, an unexplored syntactic. Slope on

> which we might however touch and there inconsequentially rub up some urges and convictions. Sparks. Erectile, eremitic narrator we. (18)

Brossard seems to be thinking of the "unexplored erotic" in language, reversing the conventional process of language being used to describe the outer world: as in the section titled "seventeen times":

> Layer, texture and overlapping as in the pauses Camomille and Lucy take while strolling down the street. A layer of words in very superficial word—word sequences like ice-flow—an active and animated overneath. For the seventeenth time the text's attracting clumps of words, clusters, magnetic the way a field draws the flitting yellow butterflies of summer and also the architects who think up plans to make them disappear. (50)

The formation of words in the text is compared to flitting yellow butterflies drawn to a field. Alice Parker describing the linguistic devices used by Brossard writes:

> Whether she is writing theory, fiction, or poetry, or a blend of the three in "fiction-theory," Brossard inscribes a sensual excitement in the text by wordplay, sound play, syntactical inversion and reversal, and other manipulations that call attention to the surface (skins, screen) of the text. The text and the body write each other; signifiers function in differential equations that locate the continuously transformed curves (velocity) of the lesbian body whose pan-eroticism refigures meaning in/of the text. The reader hears the rhythms and sounds of the language resonating in her ears as the syllables pulse through her blood and nerve circuits . . . stressing out grammar and syntax, she spins her texts and the reader's perceptions out of (conventional) control in order to displace traditional rules and patterns, to set uncanny processes in motion and make radically altered generic and sexual/textual schema possible. (312)

5.4.4 **The Body and the City**

Nicole Brossard draws an extended analogy between the female body and the city of Montreal. By so doing, she feminizes the cityscape conventionally considered threatening by women. Examining the working of this analogy Karen Gould writes:

> Brossard projects the female body in *French Kiss* onto virtually every section of the city's surface, which becomes a veritable topography of bodily excitement and sexual energy. Streets, lights, traffic and pedestrian movement serve as important narrative generators and as-analogies for the female body's arteries, breasts, pulsations, and constantly changing rhythms. Brossard's political strategy here is to carry women's bodies (both fictional and real) into the urban sphere and, in so doing, to radically alter our own conceptions of urbanity and modernity as well—the space of the city, says Brossard, "habitee autrement" ("lived otherwise"). The unusual approach in *French Kiss* to the city-body correlative involves superimposing various narrative movements by mapping the interval terrain of female organs and arteries as well as the body's exterior surfaces onto continuously changing scenes of urban geography. (72)

Brossard talks about this aspect of the novel in her interview with Janice Williamson:

> in *French Kiss*, there is a metaphoric network among the city, the body, the streets, the veins. The city has a nervous and erotic system just as the tongue and language are movement in the kissing or

speaking mouth. The pleasure given by city life is associated with the pleasure given by the complexity of language. . . . Cities are a reservoir of differences, contrasts, contradictions. They can be monstrous as well as sumptuous. Because of their eccentricities they keep you alert in thinking. They remind you of solitude and togetherness, of fun and suffering. They offer their past, and their future/no-future at the same time. . . . In fact very often cities will reverberate your feelings: if you are scared, the city will seem more dangerous; if you fell good, the city will be gorgeous; if you feel bad the city will be hell. You say that cities are a space of male aggression against women, but isn't home also a place of male aggression? (63-64)

These views are evident in her treatment of the city-body metaphor. Marielle begins her drive from the eastern tip of Montreal and goes to the west. It is a meandering and not a linear, well-defined route like the structure of the novel itself. The novel unfolds even as she covers the distance between east and west of Montreal. The narrator referring to the city, writes:

> *Different* surfaces to be captured and recognized, the singular and strategic textures of a body and a place. (22)

The city-body metaphor deepens as the narration continues and is sustained to the end. As Gould writes:

> By constructing numerous analogies that break down the distance between women and the urban city, between the female body in motion and the male-dominated metropole, Brossard turns an impressive symbol of male power (Montreal) into a physical site of female self-discovery and an exciting point of entry for écriture au feminine. (72)

The city at night is not intimidating to the characters. It has a throbbing and a life of its own:

> The night goes by at an urban pace. The city has a shifty uncertain air with its artificial light. By analogy at this hour it's a city conceived in space, over land reborn bountiful, or floating over the seas. An arborescent structure of wishes, converging at the top, its fruits, as imagined, the abode of a brain composed of polyvalent and proliferating cells. . . . Night. The city sprouts in Georges and Lexa like a mushroom. (24)

It is as if the city suddenly grows on itself Georges and Lexa, bringing them into existence. Georges' full name is Georgraphy, suggesting spatializing of character. By evoking female body parts and menstrual blood Brossard feminizes the urban space in a conscious way. Referring to the city she writes:

> The circulatory system's transgressing its appointed laws. The traffic too. Veinous, intravenous. Syringes and sirens, dual purpose for body and city both. Circulatory mechanism: blood slips easily along, moves as normally as a multiplier in an arithmetic table. . . . Blood flows menstrual between thighs and spots the crotch of pants. Coagulates on curly hair. (27)

The movement of the city's life has to be foregrounded against the space—the space of the text and the narrator wonders:

> But how to get two such scattered things together, my text and that Plymouth driven by Elle? With elevating elusions, rhymes and mimes? Babullshit. Elephantine acrobatics, aerial permutations. (39)

The reconciliation of inner and outer spaces become the narrator's problem. She refers to it more lucidly again in these words:

> But most important is the narration of the inner odyssey in terms of Montreal's geography, its contours and harsh angles, side streets and lanes sharing the circulatory problems with the major arteries, from the heart of the city to the epicentre of oneself, the target and motive source. (43)

Louise Forsyth examines Brossard's use of inner and outer space as fields of energy in her article. She writes:

> This interweaving of spatial fields underlines the universality of space in Brossard's work, and also puts into clear perspective the relations among the body, the inner space of consciousness, sensation and emotion, the outer space of the material world and conceptual space, all of which are structured by forms of language. ("Destructing . . ." 338)

Bodies in motion merge with the motion in the city and this in itself creates energy as Camomille is seen experiencing in the midst of the city's traffic:

> The traffic's heavy. Everything vehiculates. Everything circulates and animates space and time too when it's dead. Camomille's in fine form with forms visual and/or tactile to produce. Her imagination's at the gallop, riding astride grammar. Full gallop hell-bent for elation. Each moment widening her field of exploration, her experimental ground. (46)

Camomille's creative energies are at a peak against the backdrop of the hub of the city throbbing with a life of its own. Marielle's horizontal movement through the city is significant too:

> Marielle will move through this book as she will along Sherbrooke Street. Horizontally, on an open map of the city-spread out on the desk with the corners curled up like the thoughts of a crafty fox plotting a theft of tender young hens. (55)

Forsyth in her analysis writes of the vertical axis as being that which opens onto inner space—"a pole of stillness and silence, intense contained energy, whiteness or transparency, and the voids which exist both in the most distant galaxies as well as between the smallest molecules of the human body" ("Destructuring . . ." 343)

Forsyth sees the character of Camomille as the one through whom Brossard explores the complexity of vertical axis. Forsyth explains the significance of the horizontal axis:

> The horizontal axis extends in the double dimension of the form cardinal points and is the realm of surface, of distance, of the ambiguous boundary of horizon, of colors—very frequently red or rust—of context. It is on this axis that one explores the city and that one shares passion with others. Marielle in *French Kiss* orients herself by this axis as she drives her car in both a north-south and an east-west direction through the streets of Montreal. This is the realm of texture, of sensual pleasure of the skin's endless sensations. It is on this horizontal axis that ink flows on the plane of the paper, whose white margins nevertheless receive the traces emerging along the vertical axis. . . .
>
> The eye of the narrative presence in Brossard's texts simultaneously watches and participates fully in the dynamic tension and complexity created between the two poles. ("Destructuring . . ." 343)

There is no closure to the text just as the city continue to be and the characters continue to inhabit its space and that of the text. The lesbian writers considered in this chapter explore 'jouissance' fully and attempt to either twist conventional language for this purpose or seem to be in the process of evolving a language of their own. Their experimental writing affords challenges to literary critics, inviting them to delve deep into the numerous layers of meanings and messages contained in their texts.

NOTES

1. Foucault's ideas in *History of Sexuality* are central to Butler's conception of the fluidity of the category of gender.
2. Foucault's notion of power enables Queer theorists to contextualize gender within culture and to free it from biological determinism. It facilitates their critique of the "norms" imposed by patriarchal societies.
3. The term "Queer theory" is also attributed to the theorist Eve Sedgwick Kosofsky.
4. Karen Gould's study of prominent Québecoise provides a useful background to the study of 'écriture au feminine.'
5. Bonnie Zimmerman's book, *The Safe Sea of Women: Lesbian Fiction 1969-89* provides a sound basis for lesbian studies by proving an historical overview and tracing trends in the lesbian movement.
6. Warland consciously has not assigned page numbers to the book and in the original draft had not divided the book into 'turns' that she later did.. The eight turns, according to her, evoke women's cyclical orgasmic movement.

Chapter Six

Conclusion

The preceding chapters show that unlike Indian women writers, perceptions of the self are invariably tied to the body in the works of the Canadian women writers studied. The female body and sexuality are marginalized spaces from which writers write. For more contemporary writers like Margaret Atwood and Susan Swan, the body serves as a take off point to examine the alienated female subject in consumer society and to subvert phallocentric discourses of patriarchy like history but this is done in a covert way. Theories of "writing the body" with their emphasis on celebration and 'jouissance' cannot be applied in facile ways to these writers, since they write from within the Symbolic Order, using conventional language and forms. However, they make serious inroads into the questioning of the "master('s) narratives" of patriarchy as given. Their works have subversive potential and yield to contemporary feminist readings.

As an Indian woman my response to "writing the body" remains ambivalent. If the western woman suffers from commodification and fetishization of the body, oppression of the female body, particularly of the working class, lower caste woman continues at a basic and physical level in Indian society. It is ironic that it should be so in a country that has produced a classic text like the *Kamasutra* and has always prided itself on goddess worship. However, one has to remember that the *Kamasutra* is a patriarchal text with the focus being on male pleasure. Goddess worship, likewise, far from empowering women, can trap her into social moulds. Beginnings have been made in India at the grass root level by rendering help to abused women and in the academia, in the form of sociological studies of violence against women. Here, again much of what goes on in middle and upper class homes goes unreported and therefore the data can be misleading. Studies on women's sexuality continue to be few and far between. In this sense, the Indian woman's body continues to be within marginalized space with a lot of taboo still surrounding it. There are hardly any known studies for instance, of the middle-aged and aged female body and sexuality in our country.

Creative women writers in English seem to be more concerned with middle class social issues and less with the female body in our growing consumer society. The effects of the male gaze and issues of sexuality and identity have not received the attention they deserve.

Writers like Audrey Thomas, Lola Lemire Tostevin and Penn Kemp write the body in all its nuances and in more open and uninhibited ways. Their works are very deeply informed by psychoanalysis and myth. They attempt to bridge the gap between women's inner and outer spaces, thereby transgressing alienation from the body to a great extent. They try to re/claim the female body to empower themselves as women and as writers. Penn Kemp constantly uses goddess myths across cultures in order to re/store women's bodies and energies. Maternal space gets valorized in the works of all these writers. They also advance feminist ventures into questioning the language of patriarchy by making excursions into etymology and indulging in word play. To add to it they adopt a postmodern polyvocality in their narratives to decentre any homogeneous, unified, original self, in order to foreground the female subject as being in-process. This approach enables them to be self-reflexive in their writing and explore the creative process of writing itself. This is often done from a postmodern angle, using strategies of deconstruction and blurring genre boundaries but their overall feminist perspective remains intact.

Women writers of colour question the very notion of a homogeneous female body and the body in their works, becomes a site for other power conflicts. They highlight the process of stereotyping of the coloured female body in society and expose inherent biases of white, mainstream feminism. They reject monolithic, umbrella categories like the "third world" and "women of colour" and work from a multiracial position, stressing differences within their diverse ethnic identities and experiences of the diaspora.

Lesbian writers of colour like Shani Mootoo and Dionne Brand are keen to maintain their unique positions, on the margins of dominant culture by virtue of their sexual preferences. This position evolves into a political stance from which to critique heterosexist, patriarchal culture. In the process, they resist normative oppressive heterosexual gender identity foisted on them as much as white lesbian writers do. They would, however, for strategic reasons not splinter off from their communities and maintain separatism like their white counterparts as they face the larger and more severe reality of racial oppression. Their involvement with issues of language is of a different kind where they seek to strip language bare of its sexist biases as well as the racist ones. Afro-Caribbean and some South Asian writers do not hesitate to adapt the English language by using the demotic or Indian words to reflect their pride in their respective ethnic realities. The alienation experienced by them is due to the male gaze and doubled due to the white male gaze. The female body in their works often serves to foreground their triple bind of race, sex and class and therefore, is a contested site in and of itself. This presents special problems to an esoteric mode of writing like "writing in the feminine" and is an area which needs to be researched separately. Their techniques of subversion and using the female body as a metaphor hinges on their larger concerns.

There is a lacuna in theorizing of the coloured body, which needs to be filled. Interpellating from mainstream, white theories do not always work well. Some beginnings have been made by theorists like Audre Lorde and Gloria Anzaldua, but more needs to be done, particularly in the context of the plurality of ethnic identities also by heterosexual women of colour. Theories of "writing the body" by French feminists and the Québecoise theorists emanate from the Freud-Lacan model which is a Eurocentric one and which needs to be critiqued from the outside. There is nothing 'universal' about the psycho-sexual stages of development suggested by the model.

Lesbian writers go still further to maintain their difference in gender identity. They are radical in their attempts to evolve language and peel layers of patriarchal connotations of words to get to the core as it were. Their works generally seem to find resolution in the emergence of a lesbian subject. The mother-daughter link seems to be a crucial one for all the three lesbian writers studied. They invariably engage with language as one of the representational systems of patriarchy and their texts collide with discourses of patriarchy like history which they seek to re/write to re/inscribe women's bodies and lives, particularly the lesbian body, which remains outside discourse. They create discourses for the lesbian to be a speaking subject. Their works point to a need to study literature from the perspective of semiotics and to perceive it as a system of signs, where the reader-critic constantly decodes layers of meanings contained. Their works in fact, constantly challenge the reader to do so. This is an interesting area of research which needs to be developed with reference to the complexity inherent in lesbian texts. Their works generate new genres since they constantly blur traditional genre boundaries. Literary experimentation is inextricably intertwined with political statement. Their involvement with language and its deconstruction being very intense, linguistic and stylistic studies of their works need to be undertaken. Beginnings have been made by writers like Elizabeth Meese but Queer theorists also need to address issues of race and class.

Almost all the writers studied foreground the havoc wrought by the mind-body dichotomy perpetrated by western, patriarchal culture. This compartmentalization has also led western capitalist societies to ruthlessly exploit nature as well since Nature has always been categorized as feminine and conflated with the female body. The female body has always been associated with sexuality and therefore denigrated by Western religions. There has been a narrow understanding of the erotic as Audre Lorde demonstrates in her powerful essay, "Uses of the Erotic: The Erotic as Power." There has been a failure in understanding the creative potential contained in the power of the erotic. This suspicion of the erotic has been internalized by women as she says, "As women, we have come to distrust that power which rises from our deepest and non-rational knowledge. We have been warned against it all our lives by the male world, which values this depth of feeling enough to keep women around in order to exercise it in the service of men, but which fears this same depth too much to examine the possibilities of it within themselves. So women are maintained at a distant/inferior position to be psychically milked, much the same way ants maintain colonies of aphids to provide a life-giving substance for their masters" (208).

Lorde laments the fact that the spiritual and the erotic have been separated just as the spiritual and political have been and this is due to a superficial understanding of the power of the erotic. She does not believe in these false dichotomies. Clarifying the meaning of the word erotic she writes: "The very word *erotic* comes from Greek word *eros*, the personification of love in all its aspects—born of Chaos, and Venus, the Goddess of Beauty personifying creative power and harmony. When I speak of the erotic, then I speak of it as an assertion of the life force of women; of that creative energy empowered, the knowledge and use of which we are now reclaiming in our language, our history, our dancing, our work, our lives" (210).

This denial of the erotic's creative energy in our lives seems to be the bane of contemporary civilization, in which men and women are content to unquestioningly accept "received truths." This denial has led to an impoverished quality of life on the planet and has even led to the degradation of the environment. Lorde points out how this understanding has enriched her life and writes, "In touch with the erotic, I become less willing to accept powerlessness, or those other supplied states of being which are not native to me, such as resignation, despair, self-effacement, depression, self-denial" (212).

Naomi Goldenberg, in her article, "Archetypal Theory and the Separation of Mind and Body: Reason Enough to Turn to Freud?" calls for a fresh look at Freudian theory, which is rooted in physicality and is the first major departure in the modern era from transcendent theories. She finds that apart from the sexism that his theory is accused of, it does root the human being's life in the body. She explains in the following words: "It is worth stressing the degree to which thought is seen arising from body in Freudian theory. Psychoanalysis views all of our thinking as motivated by instincts. "The whole of our mental life," said Freud, "and everything that finds expression in our thoughts are derivations and representatives of the multifarious instincts that are innate in our physical constitution." "An instinct," he insisted, "cannot otherwise be represented than by an idea." Therefore, in Freudian thought, all of our notions, all of our images, all of our fantasies, and all of our ideals have their sources in our bodies. Our mental and physical lives are of one piece—just as a plant is continuous with both its foliage and its roots" (251).

Whether feminists would agree to the resurrection of Freud along these lines or not, it goes without saying that the theory turns the focus on the physicality of cognition itself. Suffice it to say that men and women's lives on the planet would see more harmony and tranquillity if they were to reject archaic and false dichotomies and incorporate the erotic in their lives and enhance their creative and positive energies.

Bibliography

Primary Sources

Atwood, Margaret. *Edible Woman.* 1980; London: Virago, 1998.

_____. *Lady Oracle.* 1976; New York: Avon, 1982.

_____. *Surfacing.* 1972; Toronto: Paperjacks, 1992.

Brand, Dionne. *No Language is Neutral.* Toronto: The Coach House Press, 1990.

Brossard, Nicole. *French Kiss or Pang's Progress.* Trans. Patricia Claxton. 1974 (French original 1974), Toronto: The Coach House Press, 1986.

Culleton, Beatrice Mosionier. *In Search of April Raintree.* 1983; ed. Suzack Cheryl. Winnipeg: Portage and Main Press, 1999.

Kemp, Penn. *Animus.* Mayne Island, B.C: Caitlin Press, 1983.

_____. *Binding Twine.* Charlottetown, P.E.I: Ragweed Press, 1984.

_____. *Four Women.* Guelph, Ontario: Red Kite Press, 1999.

_____. *Some Talk Magic.* London, Ont: Ergo Productions, 1986.

_____. *Throo.* Ontario: Moonstone Press, 1988.

_____. *Travelling Light.* Ontario: Moonstone Press, 1986

Kogawa, Joy. *Itsuka.* 1992; Toronto: Penguin, 1993.

_____. *Obasan.* 1981; Toronto: Penguin, 1994.

Laurence, Margaret. *The Fire-Dwellers.* 1969; Toronto: McClelland and Stewart, 1984.

______. *A Jest of God.* 1966; Toronto: McClelland and Stewart, 1982.

______. *The Stone Angel.* 1964; Toronto: McClelland and Stewart, 1983.

Marlatt, Daphne. *Ana Historic.* Toronto: The Coach House Press, 1988.

_____ and Betsy Warland. *Double Negative.* Charlottetown: Gynergy, 1988.

Mooto, Shani. *Cereus Blooms at Night.* 1996; New York: Avon, 1999.

Philip, Marlene N. *She Tries Her Tongue, Her Silence Softly Breaks.* 1989; Charlottetown, P.E.I: Ragweed Press, 1999.

Swan, Susan. *The Biggest Modern Woman of the World.* Toronto: Lester and Orpen Dennys, 1983.

Thomas, Audrey. *Mrs. Blood.* 1970; Vancouver: Talonbooks, 1992.

______. *Blown Figures.* Vancouver: Talonbooks, 1974.

______. *Songs My Mother Taught Me.* 1973; Vancouver: Talonbooks, 1988.

Tostevin, Lola Lemire. *Frog Moon.* Ontario: Cormorant, 1994.

Warland, Betsy. *Serpent (W)rite.* Toronto: The Coach House Press, 1987.

Wiseman, Adele. *Crackpot.* Toronto: McClelland and Stewart, 1974.

Interviews

Ayre, John. "Interview: Engendering Myth." (An interview with Susan Swan) *Books in Canada.* Vol. XXIII, No. 3 (April 1994), 12-15.

Careless, Sue. "Author on Journey of Self-Discovery." Kogawa interviewed during Festival of Faith and Arts. Writing Conference at Calvin College, Grand Rapids, Michigan in April.www.anglican

journal.com/124/06/afor.html. Last updated July 17, 1998 at 14:33 @1997-2003-Anglican Journal. March 9, 2003.

Carey, Barbara. "Interview: Secrecy and Silence" (interview with M. Nourbese Philip). *Books in Canada*. Transcultural Issue, vol. XX, No. 6 (Sept. 1991) 17-21.

Curran, Beverley with Hirabayashi Mikoto. "Conversations with Readers: An Interview with Daphne Marlatt." *Studies in Canadian Literature*. Vol. 24, No. 1 (1999) 109-23.

Daurio, Beverly. "The Language of Resistance" (An interview with Dionne Brand). *Books in Canada*. Vol. XIX, No. 7 (Oct. 1990), 13-16.

______. "Order and Imagination: An Interview with Nicole Brossard." *Books in Canada*. Vol. XX, No. 2 (1991) 19-21.

Dhaliwal, Sarinder. "Shifting Perceptions, Changing Practices." (An interview with Shani Mootoo). No. 2 (18-25).

Hayes, Kenneth. www.fusemagazine.org/voll22.html. March 9, 2003.

Koh, Karlyn. "Joy Kogawa talks to Karlyn Koh: The Heart of the Matter Questions." *The Other Woman: Women of Colour in Contemporary Canadian Literature*, ed. Makeda Silvera. Toronto: Black Women and Women of Color Press, 1995, 19-41.

Sherman, Barbara J. "Interview with Shani Mootoo." B.C. Institute on Family Violence. www.bcif.org/resources/newsletter/1993/fall/ mootoo/1.html. March 9, 2003.

Tihanyi, Eva. "Unredeemed Grace" (An interview with Dionne Brand). *Books in Canada*. Vol. 26, No. 2 (March 1997) 8-9.

Wachtel, Eleanor. "Putting up Fences in the Garden: Audrey Thomas talks to Eleanor Wachtel." *Tessera*. 5 (September 1988) 7-61.

Williamson, Janice. "Before I became a feminist, I suppose I was an angel, a poet, a revolutionary" (An interview with Nicole Brossard). *Sounding Differences: Conversations with Seventeen Canadian Women Writers*. Toronto: University of Toronto Press, 1993, 59-72.

______. "In companionship with another voice" (An interview with Daphne Marlatt and Betsy Warland). *Sounding Differences*. 195-99.

______. "Inventing ourselves on the page" (An interview with Lola Lemire Tostevin). *Sounding Differences*. 271-80.

______. "A language that holds us." (An interview with Betsy Warland). *Sounding Differences*. 303-15.

______. "When we change language" (An interview with Joy Kogawa). *Sounding Differences*. 148-59.

______. "In writing I keep breathing, I keep living" (An interview with Daphne Marlatt). *Sounding Differences*. 182-93.

______. "Writing a memory of losing that place" (An interview with M. Nourbese Philip). *Sounding Differences*. 226-44.

Yin, Susan. An interview with Joy Kogawa.www.vancouver foundationbc.ca/about Vancouver foundation/downloads/bf-ar-oo. March 9, 2003.

Secondary Sources

Abel, Elizabeth. "Black Writing, White Reading: Race and the Politics of Feminist Interpretation." *Critical Inquiry*. 19-3 (1993): 470-98.

_____, ed. *Writing and Sexual Difference*. Brighton: Harvester, 1982.

Acoose, Janice. "The Problem of Searching for April Raintree." *In Search of April Raintree*. Critical Edition, ed. Suzack Cheryl. Winnipeg: Portage and Main Press, 1999, 227-36.

Allen, Jeffner. "Motherhood: The Annihilation of Women." *Feminist Frameworks: Alternative Theoretical Accounts of the Relations between Women and Men*, ed. Alison M. Jaggar and Paula S. Rothenberg, RPT.1993, New York: McGraw Hill, 1978, 380-85.

Amos, Valerie and Pratibha Parmar. "Challenging Imperialist Feminism." *Feminist Review*. 17 (1984):3-19.

Allen Lillian. "A Writing of Resistance: Black Women's Writing in Canada." *In the Feminine*: *Women and Words Conference Proceedings*, ed. Ann Dybikowski, Barbara Pulling and Betsy Warland. Edmonton: Longspoon Press, 1985, 63-67.

Antonelli, Judith. "Feminist Spirituality: The Politics of the Psyche." *The Politics of Women's Spirituality*, ed. Charlene Spretnak. New York: Anchor, 1982, 399-403.

Anzaldua, Gloria. "Speaking in Tongues: A Letter to Third World Women Writers." *This Bridge Called My Back: Writings by Radical Women of Colour*, ed. Cherrie Moraga and Gloria Anzaldua. New York: Kitchen Table Women of Color Press, 1981. 165-73.

Ashcroft, Bill, Gareth Griffiths and Helen Tiffin. *The Empire Writes Back: Theory and Practice in Post-Colonial Literatures*. London: Routledge, 1989.

Atwood, Margaret. *Survival. A Thematic Guide to Canadian Literature*. Toronto: Anansi Press, 1972.

______. *The Journals of Susanna Moodie*. Ontario: Oxford University Press, 1970.

Bannerji, Himani. "Popular Images of South Asian Women." *Returning the Gaze: Essays on Racism, Feminism and Politics*. Toronto: Sister Vision, 1993. 144-52.

_____. "The Sound Barrier: Translating Ourselves in Language and Experience." *Language in Her Eye: Writing and Gender*, ed. Libby Scheier, Sarah Sheard & Eleanor Wachtel. Toronto: The Coach House Press, 1990, 26-40.

_____, Makeda Silvera, et al. "We Appear Silent to People Who Are Deaf to What We Say." *The Issue is ISM: Women of Colour Speak Out. Fireweed's Issue*. No. 16. Toronto: Sister Vision Press, 1983, 9-29.

Banting, Pamela. *Body Inc: A Theory of Translation Poetics*. Winnipeg: Turnstone Press, 1995.

______. "The Phantom Limb Syndrome: Writing the Postcolonial Body in Daphne Marlatt's *Touch to My Tongue*." *Ariel*. Vol. 24, No. 3 (July 1993): 7-30.

Bauer, Dale. "Gender in Bakhtin's Carnival." *Feminisms: An Anthology of Literary Theory and Criticism*, ed. Robyn R. Warhol and Dianne Pria Herndl. New Brunswick, N.J: Rutgers University Press, 1991. 671-83.

Beauvoir, Simone de. *The Second Sex*. Trans & ed. H.M. Parshley. 1969; London: Everyman, 1993.

Beckman-Long, Brenda. "Authorizing her Text: Margaret Laurence's Shift to Third-Person Narration." *Studies in Canadian Literature*. Vol. 24, No. 1, 1999. 64-78.

Belsey, Catherine. "Constructing the Subject." *Feminisms: An Anthology of Literary Theory and Criticism*, ed. Robyn R. Warhol and Dianne Pria Herndl. New Brunswick, N.J: Rutgers University Press, 1991. 593-609.

Bennett, Donna. "Naming the Way Home." *A Mazing Space*: *Writing Canadian Women Writing*, ed. Shirley Neuman and Smaro Kamboureli. Edmonton: Longspoon/Newest, 1986, 228-45.

Bhabha, Homi K. "Cultural Diversity and Cultural Differences." *The Post-Colonial Studies Reader*, ed. Bill Ashcroft, Gareth Griffiths and Helen Tiffin. London: Routledge, 1995, 206-9.

_____. *The Location of Culture*. London: Routledge, 1994.

_____, ed. *Nation and Narration*. New York: Routledge, 1990.

Bők, Christian. "Sibyls: Echoes of French Feminism in *The Diviners* and *Lady Oracle*." *Canadian Literature*. No. 135 (Winter 1992): 80-93.

Bolen, Jean Shinoda. *Goddesses in Everywoman.* 1984; New York: Harper & Row, 1985.

_____. *Gods in Everyman.* New York: Harper & Row, 1989

Brand Dionne. "A Working Paper on Black Women in Toronto: Gender, Race, and Class." *Returning the Gaze. Essays on Racism, Feminism and Politics.* Toronto: Sister Vision, 1993. 220-42.

Brossard, Nicole. "Certain Words." *Collaboration in the Feminine: Writings on Women and Culture from Tessera*, ed. Barbara Godard. Toronto: Second Story Press, 1994, 47-49.

______. "Movements and Strategies for the Writing of Fiction." *Gynocritics: Feminist Approaches to Writing by Canadian and Québecoise Women*, ed. Barbara Godard. Toronto: ECW Press, 1987, 227-30.

______. "The Idea of Your Lips." *Tessera: Changing the Subject.* Vol. 9 (Fall 1990): 126-29.

______. Tender Skin My Mind." Trans. Dympra Borowska. *In the Feminine: Women and Words Conference Proceedings*, ed. Ann Dybikowski, Barbara Pulling and Betsy Warland. Edmonton: Longspoon Press, 1985. 180-83.

_____ and Daphne Marlatt. "Only a Body to Measure Reality by: Writing the In Between." *Journal of Commonwealth Literature.* 1996. 31:2. 5-17.

Brydon, Diana and Helen Tiffin. *Decolonizing Fictions.* Sydney: Dangaroo, 1993.

Butler, Judith. *Gender Trouble: Feminism and the Subversion of Identity.* New York: Routledge, 1990.

_____. *Bodies That Matter: On the Discursive Limits of "Sex."* New York: Routledge, 1993.

Campbell, Joseph. *The Hero with a Thousand Faces.* 1949; Glasgow: Paladin Grafton, 1988.

Carr, Brenda. "To Heal the Word Wounded: Agency and the Materiality of Language and Form in M. Nourbese Philip's *She Tries Her Tongue, Her Silence Softly Breaks.*" *Studies in Canadian Literature.* Vol. 19:1 (1994): 72-93.

_____. "Collaboration in the Feminine: Daphne Marlatt/Betsy Warland's Re-versed Writing in Double Negative." *Tessera: Changing the Subject.* Vol. 9 (Fall 1990): 111-22.

Chodorow, Nancy. *The Reproduction of Mothering: Psychoanalysis and the Sociology of Gender.* Berkeley: UCLA Press, 1978.

Christ, Carol P. "Why Women Need the Goddess: Phenomenological, Psychological and Political Reflections. *The Politics of Women's Spirituality.* 11-86.

_____ and Charlene Spretnak. "Images of Spiritual Power in Women's Fiction." *The Politics of Women's Spirituality*, ed. Charlene Spretnak. New York: Anchor, 1982. 327-43.

_____ and Plaskow Judith, ed. *Weaving the Visions: New Patterns in Feminist Spirituality.* San Francisco: Harpersan Francisco, 1989.

Cixous, Hélène. "The Laugh of the Medusa." Trans. Keith Cohen and Paula Cohen. *Feminisms: An Anthology of Literary Theory and Criticism*, ed. Robyn R. Warhol and Dianne Pria Herndl. New Brunswick, N.J: Rutgers University Press, 1991, 335-49.

_____. "Sorties." Trans. Ann Liddle. *New French Feminisms: An Anthology*, ed. Elaine Marks and Isabelle de Courtivron. New York: Shocken, 1981. 90-98.

Collins, Patricia Hill. *Black Feminist Thought: Knowledge, Consciousness and the Politics of Empowerment.* Boston: Unwin Hyman, 1990.

Combahee River Collective. "A Black Feminist Statement." *This Bridge Called My Back: Writings by Radical Women of Color*, ed. Cherrie Moraga and Gloria Anzaldua. New York: Kitchen Table Women of Color Press, 1981. 210-18.

Cook, Meira. "The Partisan Body: Performance and the Female Body in Dionne Brand's *No Language is Neutral.*" *Open Letter: A Canadian Journal of Writing and Theory.* Ninth Series, No. 2 (Spring 1995): 88-91.

Cotnoir, Louise. "The Marked Gender." *In the Feminine: Women and Words Conference Proceedings*, ed. Ann Dybikowski, Barbara Pulling and Betsy Warland. Edmonton: Longspoon Press, 1985. 99-104.

Daly, Mary. *Gyn/Ecology: The Metaethics of Radical Feminism*. Boston: Beacon Press, 1978.

Davey, Frank. "Marrying the Hangman: The Biggest Modern Woman of the World." *Post-National Arguments: The Politics of Anglophone Canada Since 1967*. Toronto: University of Toronto Press, 1993. 182-94.

Debrida, Bella. "Drawing from Mythology in Women's Quest for Selfhood." *The Politics of Women's Spirituality*, ed. Charlene Spretnak. New York: Anchor, 1982, 138-51.

Devereaux, Cecily. "The Body of Evidence: Re-membering the Past in Joy Kogawa's *Obasan*." *Intersexions: Issues of Race and Gender in Canadian Women's Writing*, ed. Coomi S. Vevaina and Barbara Godard. New Delhi: Creative, 1996, 231-43.

Donaldson, Laura E. *Decolonizing Feminisms: Race, Gender and Empire-Building*. Chapel Hill: University of North Carolina, 1992.

Drinker, Sophie. "The Origins of Music: Women's Goddess Worship." *The Politics of Women's Spirituality*, ed. Charlene Spretnak. New York: Anchor, 1982, 39-48.

Dupré, Louise. "The Doubly Complicit Memory." Trans. Kathy Mezei and Daphne Marlatt. *Collaborations in the Feminine. Writings on Women and Culture from Tessera*, ed. Barbara Godard. Toronto: Second Story Press, 1994, 26-33.

______. "From experimentation to experience: Quebecois modernity in the feminine." Trans. A.J. Holden Verburg. *A Mazing Space: Writing Canadian Women Writing*, ed. Shirley Neuman and Smaro Kamboureli. Edmonton: Longspoon/Newest. 355-60.

Eliade, Mircea. *Images and Symbols*. Trans. Philip Mairet. London: Harvill Press, 1961.

Emberly, Julia. "The Logics of Discovery: Border/Body Dispute." *Canadian Review of Comparative Literature*. Vol. 22:3-4 (Sept-Dec. 1995), 603-21.

Engel, Marian. *The Bear*. 1976 rpt; Toronto: McClelland and Stewart, 1982.

Fanon, Frantz. *Black Skin, White Masks*. Trans. Charles Lam Markmann. 1952; St. Albans, Herts: Paladin, 1970.

Fee, Margery. "Deploying Identity in the Face of Racism." *In Search of April Raintree*. Critical Edition, ed. Suzack Cheryl. Winnipeg: Portage and Main Press, 1999, 211-26.

Felman, Shoshana. "Women and Madness: The Critical Phallacy." *Feminisms: An Anthology of Literary Theory and Criticism*, ed. Robyn R. Warhol and Dianne Pria Herndl. New Brunswick, N.J: Rutgers University Press, 1991. 6-19.

Forsyth, Louise. "Beyond the Myths and Fictions of Traditionalism and Nationalism: The Political in the Work of Nicole Brossard." *Traditionalism, Nationalism and Feminism: Women Writers of Quebec*, ed. Paula Gilbert Lewis. Conn: Greenwood Press, 1985. 157-72.

______. "Destructing formal Space/accelerating motion in the work of Nicole Brossard." *A Mazing Space: Writing Canadian Women Writing*, ed. Shirley Neuman and Smaro Kamboureli. Edmonton: Longspoon/Newest. 334-44.

Foucault, Michel. *The History of Sexuality: An Introduction*. Trans. Robert Hurley. Vol. 1, New York: Vintage, 1990.

Fouque, Antoinette, qtd. "The MLF is you, is me." *New French Feminisms: An Anthology*, ed. Elaine Marks and Isabelle de Courtivron. New York: Shocken, 1981. 117-18.

Franks, Jill. "Jesting Within: Voices of Irony and Parody as Expressions of Feminisms. The Writing of Margaret Laurence: *Challenging Territory*, ed. Christian Riegel. Edmonton: University of Alberta Press, 1997. 99-117.

Frawley, David. "Tantric Yoga and the Wisdom Goddesses." Condensed Indira S. Aiyan. Bombay: *Tattvaloka* (Oct.-Nov. 1995): 63-93.

Freud, S. *The Standard Edition of the Complete Psychological Works of Sigmund Freud* (SE), London: The Hogarth Press. (nd.)

_____. *The Three Essays on the Theory of Sexuality*. SE 7 (1905)

_____. *Totem and Taboo*. SE 13 (1912-13)

_____. *On Narcissism: An Introduction*. SE 14 (1914)

_____. *Beyond the Pleasure Principle*. SE 18 (1916)

_____. *The Interpretation of Dreams: An Outline of Psychoanalysis*. (1938)

Friedan, Betty. *The Feminine Mystique*. 1963; Middlesex: Penguin, 1983.

Frye, Northrop. "Conclusion." *Literary History of Canada*, ed. Carl F. Klinck. Vol. II. Toronto: University of Toronto Press, 1965. 342.

Gitlings, Christopher. "A Collision of Discourse: Postmodernism and Postcolonialism in *The Biggest Modern Woman of the World*." *The Journal of Canadian Literature*, Vol. 29:1, 1994, 81-91.

Goldenberg, Naomi R. "Archetypal Theory and the Separation of Mind and Body: Reason Enough to Turn to Freud." *Weaving the Visions. New Patterns in Feminist Spirituality*, ed. Judith Plaskow and Carol P. Christ. San Francisco: Harper San Francisco, 1989, 244-55.

Godard, Barbara. *Audrey Thomas and Her Works*. Toronto: ECW, 1989.

______. Body I: Daphne Marlatt's Feminist Poetics." *American Review of Canadian Studies*. 1985. vol.15:4. 481-96.

______. "The Politics of Representation: Some Native Canadian Women Writers." *Canadian Literature*. Nos. 124-125 (Spring-Summer 1990), 183-225.

______. "Voicing Difference: The Literary Production of Native Women." *A Mazing Space: Writing Canadian/Women Writing*, ed. Shirley Neuman and Smaro Kamboureli. Edmonton: Longspoon/ Newest. 1986.

Goldman, Marlene. "Citing the Body: The Discursive Mapping of the Woman and the Subversive Mapping of the Carnivalesque in Susan Swan's *The Biggest Modern Woman of the World*." *Paths of Desire: Images of Exploration and Mapping in Canadian Women's Writing*. Toronto: University of Toronto Press, 1999.

Gould. Karen. *Writing in the Feminine: Feminism and Experimental Writing in Quebec*. Carbondale and Edwardsville, Illinois: Southern Illinois University Press, 1990.

Grant, Agnes. "Abuse and Violence: April Raintree's Human Rights (if she had any). *In Search of April Raintree*. Critical Edition, ed. Suzack Cheryl. Winnipeg: Portage and Main Press, 1999, 237-46.

Graves, Robert. *The Greek Myths. Complete Edition*. 1955; London: Penguin, 1992.

Griffin, Susan. *Woman and Nature: The Roaring Inside Her*. New York: Harper and Row, 1978.

Grosz, Elizabeth. *Jacques Lacan: A Feminist Introduction*. London: Routledge, 1990.

______. *Sexual Subversions: Three French Feminists*. Sydney: Unwin and Hyman. London and Boston, 1989.

Grosz, Elizabeth. *Volatile Bodies: Towards a Corporeal Feminism*. Bloomington: Indiana University Press, 1994.

Gunew, Sneja, ed. *A Reader in Feminist Knowledge*. London: Routledge, 1991.

_____ and Yeatman, ed. *Feminism and the Politics of Difference.* St. Leonards, NSW (Aust.): Allen & Unwin. 1993. (Canadian Distributor: Fernwood Press, Halifax)

Harris, Claire. "Poets in Limbo." *A Mazing Space: Writing Canadian Women Writing*, ed. Shirley Neuman and Smaro Kamboureli. Edmonton: Longspoon/Newest. 1986.115-25.

_____. "Working w/out a net." *Crisis and Creativity in the New Literatures in English Canada*, ed. Geoffrey Davis. Amsterdam-Atlanta, 1990, 71-75.

Hawthorne, Nathaniel. *The Scarlet Letter.* 1850; New York: Bantam Classic Edition, 1986.

Heffernan, Teresa. "Tracing the Travesty: Constructing the Female Subject in Susan Swan's *The Biggest Modern Woman of the World.*" *Canadian Literature.* No. 133 (Summer 1992): 24-37.

Hlus, Carolyn. "Writing Womanly: theory and practice." *A Mazing Space: Writing Canadian Women Writing*, ed. Shirley Neuman and Smaro Kamboureli. Edmonton: Longspoon/Newest 1986, 287-97.

Howells, Carol Ann. *Private and Fictional Words: Canadian Women Novelists of the 1970s and 1980s.* London: Methuen, 1987.

Hoy, Helen. "Nothing but the Truth: Discursive Transparency in Beatrice Culleton." *In Search of April Raintree.* Critical Edition, ed. Suzack Cheryl. Winnipeg: Portage and Main Press, 1999, 273-93.

hooks, bell. *Feminist Theory: From Margin to Centre.* Cambridge: South End Press, 2000.

_______. *Talking Back: Thinking Feminist, Thinking Black.* Boston: South End Press, 1989.

Howells, Coral Ann. "A Shared Queerness: Liminal Identities in Shani Mootoo's *Cereus Blooms at Night.*" *Articulating Gender*, ed. Anjali Bhelande and Mala Pandurang. Delhi: Pencraft International. 2000. 163-70.

Hunter, Lynette. "After Modernism: Alternative Voices in the Writings of Dionne Brand, Claire Harris and Marlene Philip." *University of Toronto Quarterly—A Canadian Journal of the Humanities.* 62:2 (Winter 1992-93), 256-81.

Hutcheon, Linda. "Shape-Shifters: Canadian Women Novelists and the Challenge to Tradition." *A Mazing Space: Writing Canadian Women Writing*, ed. Shirley Neuman and Smaro Kamboureli. Edmonton: Longspoon/Newest. 1986. 219-27.

______. *The Politics of Postmodernism.* New York: Routledge, 1989.

______, ed. *Double-Talking: Essays on Verbal and Visual Ironies in Contemporary Canadian Art and Literature.* Toronto: ECW Press, 1992.

______. "Incredulity toward Metanarrative: Negotiating Postmodernism and Feminisms." *Collaboration in the Feminine: Writings on Women and Culture from Tessera*, ed. Barbara Godard. Toronto: Second Story Press, 1994. 186-92.

Irigaray, Luce. *An Ethics of Sexual Difference.* Trans. Carolyn Burke and Gibian C. Gill. Ithaca: Cornell University Press, 1984.

______. *Speculum of the Other Woman.* Ithaca: Cornell University Press, 1985.

______. *This Sex Which Is Not One.* Ithaca: Cornell University Press, 1985.

Jacobus, Mary. *Reading Woman: Essays in Feminist Criticism.* London: Methuen, 1986.

Jagger, Alison and Paula Rosenberg. *Feminist Framework: Alternative Theoretical Accounts of the Relations between Women and Men.* 3rd edition, McGraw-Hill, 1993.

Jagose, Annamarie. *Queer Theory: An Introduction.* New York: New York University Press, 1996.

Jakashi, Aso. "Strategies of Writing: Of the Feminine, Bodies and Postmodern Aesthetic." *Dissertation Abstracts.* Int. Ann Arbor. 1996. Dec. 57:6, 2466A-67A.

Jardine, Alice. *Feminisms: An Anthology of Literary Theory and Criticism*, ed. Robyn R. Warhol and Dianne Pria Herndl. New Brunswick, N.J: Rutgers University Press, 1991, 446.

Jay, Karla and Joanne Glasgow, ed. *Lesbian Texts and Contexts: Radical Revisions*. New York: New York University Press, 1990.

Johnson-Odin, Cheryl. "Common Themes, Different Contexts: Third World Women and Feminism." *Third World Women and the Politics of Feminism*, ed. Chandra Talpade Mohanty, Ann Russo and Lourdes Torres. Bloomington and Indianapolis: Indiana University Press, 1991, 314-27.

Jones, Ann Rosalind. "Writing the Body: Toward an Understanding of l'écriture féminine." *Feminisms: An Anthology of Literary Theory and Criticism*, ed. Robyn R. Warhol and Dianne Pria Herndl. New Brunswick, N.J: Rutgers University Press, 1991, 357-70.

Kamboureli, Smaro. "The Body in Joy Kogawa's *Obasan*: Race, Gender, Sexuality." *Scandalous Bodies: Diasporic Literatures in English Canada*. Don Mills, Ont: Oxford University Press, 2000. 175-221.

_____. "Dialogue with the Other: The Use of Myth in Canadian Women's Poetry. *In the Feminine: Women and Words Conference Proceedings*, ed. Ann Dybikowski, Barbara Pulling and Betsy Warland. Edmonton: Longspoon Press, 1985.105-9.

_____ and Lola Lemire Tostevin. "Women of Letters: Envois between Victoria and Toronto." *Tessera*. Vol. 5 (September 1988): 13-26.

_____. "*The Biggest Modern Woman of the World*: Canada as the Absent Spouse." *Studies in Canadian Literature*. Vol.16:2, 1991. 95-110.

Kanneh, Kadiatu. "Love, Mourning and Metaphor." *New Feminist Framework: Critical Essays on Theories and Texts*, ed. Isobel Armstrong. Routledge: London, 1992. 135-53.

_____. "Feminism and the Colonial Body." *The Post-Colonial Studies Reader*, ed. Bill Ashcroft, Gareth Griffiths and Helen Tiffin. London: Routledge, 1995. 346-48.

Keller, Lynn and Cristianne Miller, ed. *Feminist Measures: Soundings in Poetry and Theory*. Ann Arbor: University of Michigan Press, 1994.

Kelly Peggy. "Fiction Theory as Feminist Practice in Marlatt's *Ana Historic* and Scott's *Heroine*." *Open Letter*. Ninth Series, No. 4 (Fall 1995): 69-98.

Kemp, Penn. "A musing I would like to have shared with Gwendolyn MacEwen." *Tessera: Dialogue Conversation*. Vol. 5 (Sept. 1988): 49-57.

_____. "Changing Subjects, Changing Places." *Tessera: Changing the Subject*. Vol. 9 (Fall 1990): 97-101.

Kristeva, Julia. "Women's Time." *The Kristevan Reader*, ed. Toril Moi. Oxford: Blackwell, 1986.

_____. *Desire in Language: A Semiotic Approach to Literature and Art*, ed. Leon S. Roudiez. Trans. Thomas Gora, Alice Jardine and Leon S. Roudiez. New York: Columbia University Press, 1980.

_____. "Women's Time." *Feminisms: An Anthology of Literary Theory and Criticism*, ed. Robyn R. Warhol and Dianne Pria Herndl. New Brunswick, N.J: Rutgers University Press, 1991. 443-61.

Kudchedkar, Shirin. "The Play of Line and Image in the Poetry of Penn(y) Kemp." *Canadian Literature: Perspectives*, ed. Jameela Begum. Madras: Macmillan India, 1994, 103-11.

Lacan, J. *Écrits. A Selection*. London: Tavistock, 1977.

Laurence, Margaret. *The Diviners*. 1974; Toronto: McClelland and Stewart, 1984.

_____. *Heart of a Stranger*. Toronto: McClelland & Stewart, 1980.

_____. *Dance on the Earth*. Toronto: McClelland and Stewart, 1989.

Lauretis, Teresa de. *Technologies of Gender: Essays on Theory, Film and Fiction*. Bloomington: Indiana University Press, 1987.

Lim, Shirley Geok-lin. "Japanese American Women's Life Stories: Maternality in Monica Sone's *Nissei Daughter* and Joy Kogawa's *Obasan*." *Feminist Studies*. 16.2 (1990): 288-312.

Lorde, Audre. "An Open Letter to Mary Daly." *This Bridge Called My Back: Writings by Radical Women of Colour*, ed. Cherrie Moraga and Gloria Anzaldua. New York: Kitchen Table Women of Color Press, 1981. 94-97.

_____. "The Master's Tools Will Never Dismantle the Master's House: Comments at the Personal and the Political" Panel *This Bridge Called My Back*. 98-101. (Second Sex Conference, Oct. 29, 1979)

_____. "Uses of the Erotic." *Weaving the Visions: New Patterns in Feminist Spirituality*, ed. Judith Plaskow and Carol P. Christ. San Francisco: Harper San Francisco, 1989. 208-13.

Maitland, Sara. "Margaret Laurence's *The Stone Angel*." *Canadian Woman Studies/les cahiers de la fenime*. No. 3, Special issue, Margaret Laurence: A Celebration. Guest editor, Clara Thomas. 8, No. 3 (Fall 1987), 43-45.

Marks, Elaine and Isabelle Courtivron, ed. *New French Feminisms*: Amherst, Mass: University of Massachusetts Press, 1980.

Marlatt, Daphne. Her words appear on the jacket of Throo.

______. "Musing with Mothertongue." *Gynocritics: Feminist Approaches to Writing by Canadian and Québecoise Women*, ed. Barbara Godard. Toronto: ECW Press, 1987. 223-26.

______. "Self-Representation and Fictionalysis." *Readings from the Labyrinth*: The Writer As Critic Series VI, ed. Smaro Kamboureli. Edmonton: Newest Press, 1998. 122-27.

______. "Lesbera." *Readings from the Labyrinth*. 42-49.

______. "For the private reader: interplay in the public realm." *Readings from the Labyrinth*. 217-24.

______. "The In-Between is Reciprocal." *Readings from the Labyrinth*. 108-18.

______. *How Hug a Stone*. Winnipeg: Turnstone Press. 1983.

______ and Betsy Warland. "Reading and Writing Between the Lines." *Tessera*: Dialogue Conversation. Vol. 5 (September 1988): 80-90.

Martin, Mathew. "Dramas of Desire in Margaret Laurence's *A Jest of God*, *The Fire-Dwellers*, and *The Diviners*." *Studies in Canadian Literature*. Vol. 19.1, 1994. 58-71.

McCance, Dawn. "Julia Kristeva and the Ethics of Exile." *Tessera*. Vol. 8. (Spring 1990): 23-39.

McNay, L. *Foucault and Feminism: Power, Gender and the Self.* Oxford: Polity Press with Blackwell Publishers, 1992.

Meese, Elizabeth A. *(Sem)erotics: Theorizing Lesbian Writing*. New York: New York University Press, 1992.

Minh-ha, Trinh T. *Woman, Native, Other: Writing Postcoloniality and Feminism*. Bloomington: Indiana University Press, 1989.

Mitchell, Judith. *Psychoanalysis and Feminism*. London: Allen Lane, 1974.

Mohanty, Chandra Talpade. "Under Western Eyes: Feminist Scholarship and Colonial Discourses." *Contemporary Postcolonial Theory: A Reader*, ed. Padmini Mongia. London: Routledge, 1996. 172-97.

_____ et al, ed. *Third World Women and the Politics of Feminism*. Bloomington: Indiana University Press, 1991.

Moi, Toril, ed. *French Feminist Thought*. Oxford: Blackwell, 1989.

______. *Sexual/Textual Politics, Feminist Literary Theory*. London: Methuen, 1985.

Munt, Sally, ed. *New Lesbian Criticism. Literary and Cultural Readings*. New York: Columbia University Press, 1992.

Murray, Heather. "Women in the Wilderness." *A Mazing Space*: *Writing Canadian Women Writing*, ed. Shirley Neuman and Smaro Kamboureli. Edmonton: Longspoon/Newest. 1986. 74-83.

Mycak, Sonia. *In Search of the Split Subject: Psychoanalysis, Phenomenology and the Novels of Margaret Atwood.* Toronto: ECW Press, 1996.

Neuman, Shirley. "Importing Difference." *A Mazing Space: Writing Canadian Women Writing*, ed. Shirley Neuman and Smaro Kamboureli. Edmonton: Longspoon/Newest. 392-405.

Panofsky, Ruth. "From Complicity to Subversion: The Female Subject in Adele Wiseman's Novels. *Canadian Literature.* No. 137 (Summer 1993): 41-48.

Parker, Alice. "Nicole Brossard: A Differential Equation of Lesbian Love." *(Sem)erotics: Theorizing Lesbian Writing.* New York: New York University Press, 1992, 304-29.

Pennee, Donna Palmateer. "Technologies of Identity: The Language of the Incontinent Body in Margaret Laurence's *The Stone Angel.*" *Studies in Canadian Literature.* Vol. 25, No. 2 (2000): 1-23.

Philip, Marlene N. "Father Tongue." *A Genealogy of Resistance and Other Essays.* Toronto: The Mercury Press, 1997. 128-32.

_____. "Dis Place—The Space Between." *A Genealogy of Resistance.* 74-112.

_____. "Gut Issues in Babylon: Racism and Anti-Racism in the Arts." *Frontiers.* 211-31.

_____. "The Absence of Writing or How I Almost Became a Spy." *She Tries Her Tongue, Her Silence Softly Breaks.* 10-25.

Philip, Nourbese M. "Making the House Our Own: Colonized Language and the Civil War of Words." *Fuse.* 8.6 (1985): 43-45.

_____. "Echoes in a Stranger Land." *Frontiers: Essays and Writings on Racism and Culture.* 1984-1992. Stratford, Ont: The Mercury Press, 1992. 9-25.

_____. "Why Multiculturalism Can't End Racism." *Frontiers.* 181-86.

_____. "Who's Listening?" *Frontiers.* 26-46.

_____. "Journal Entries against Reaction: Damned if We Do and Damned If We Don't." *Frontiers.* S59-71.

_____. "Making the House Our Own: Colonized Language and the Civil War of Words." *Fuse*, 8.6 (1985), 43-45.

Retallack, Joan. "Re: Thinking: Literary· Feminism: (three essays onto shaky grounds)." *Feminist Measures: Soundings in Poetry and Theory*, ed. Lynn Keller and Cristianne Miller. Ann Arbor: University of Michigan Press, 1994.

Rhys, Jean. *Wide Sargasso Sea.* London: Penguin, 1966.

Rich, Adrienne. *Of Woman Born.* New York: Bantam, 1977.

Rigby, Kate. "The Goddess Returns: Ecofeminist Reconfigurations of Gender, Nature and the Sacred." *Feminist Poetics of the Sacred.* (www.oup-usa.org/sc/0195144686/0195144686-01.pdf.accessed on March 9, 2003)

Robin, Morgan, ed. *Sisterhood is Powerful: An Anthology of Writings from the Women's Liberation Movement.* New York: Random House, 1970.

Rubin, Lillian B. "The Sexual Dilemma." *Feminist Frameworks: Alternative Theoretical Accounts of the Relations between Women and Men*, ed. Alison M. Jaggar and Paula S. Rothenberg. New York: McGraw Hill, 1978. 461-68.

Said, Edward. *Culture and Imperialism.* New York: Knopf, 1993.

_____. *Orientalism.* London: Routledge & Kegan Paul, 1978.

Sarbadhikary, Krishna. *Dis-Membering/Re-Membering: Fictions of Audrey Thomas.* New Delhi: Books Plus, 1999.

Saul Joanne. "Home Free." *Canadian Literature.* www.cdn.lit.ubc.ca/ reviews/saul.html.accessed on March 9, 2003

Scheel, Kathleen M. "Freud and Frankenstein: The Monstered Language of Ana Historic." *Essays on Canadian Writing*. No. 58 (Spring 1996): 93-114.

Scheier, Libby. "Body Language." *Books in Canada*. (March 1985): 17-19.

_____, Sarah Sheard and Eleanor Wachtel. *Language in Her Eye: Writing and Gender*. Toronto: Coach House Press, 1990.

Schuyler, George S. *Black No More*. 1931; Boston: Northeastern University Press, 1989.

Scott, Gail. *Spaces Like Stairs*. Toronto: Women's Press, 1989.

Sedgwick, Eve Kosofsky. *Between Men: English Literature and Male Homosocial Desire*. New York: Columbia University Press, 1985.

Shaktini, Namascar. "A Revolutionary Signifier: The Lesbian Body" *(Sem)erotics: Theorizing Lesbian Writing*. New York: New York University Press, 1992, 291-303.

Showalter, Elaine. *A Literature of Their Own: British Women Novelists from Brontë to Lessing*. London: Virago, 1978.

_____. "Feminist Criticism in the Wilderness." *Critical Inquiry*, Special Issue Writing and Difference, ed. Elizabeth Abel. 8, No. 2 (Winter 1981), 179-205.

_____. *The New Feminist Criticism: Essays on Women, Literature and Theory*. London: Virago, 1988.

Silvera, Makeda. "How Far Have We Come?" *Fireworks: The Best of Fireweed*, ed. Makeda Silvera. Toronto: The Women's Press, 1986. 191-95.

_____, ed. *The Other Woman: Women of Colour in Contemporary Canadian Literature*. Toronto: Black Women and Women of Colour Press, 1995.

Smart, Patricia. *Writing in the Father's House*. Toronto: University of Toronto Press, 1990.

Spivak, Gayatri Chakravorty. *In Other Worlds: Essays in Cultural Politics*. New York: Methuen, 1987.

Starhawk. "Ethics and Justice in Goddess Religion." *The Politics of Women's Spirituality*, ed. Charlene Spretnak. New York: Anchor, 1982. 415-22.

Stein, Arlene, ed. *Sisters, Sexperts, Queers: Beyond the Lesbian Nation*. New York: Penguin, 1993.

Stovel, Nora Foster. "Sisters Under Their Skins." *The Writing of Margaret Laurence: Challenging Territory*, ed. Christian Riegel. Edmonton: University of Alberta Press, 1997, 119-39.

Suleri, Sara. "Woman Skin Deep; Feminism and the Postcolonial Condition." *Contemporary Postcolonial Theory*, ed. Padmini Mongia.

Swan, Susan. "Desire and the Mythology of Femininity." *Language in Her Eye: Writing and Gender*, ed. Libby Scheier, Sarah Sheard & Eleanor Wachtel. Toronto: The Coach House Press, 1990. 260-62.

Théoret, France. "Writing in the feminine: Voicing consensus, practising difference." *A Mazing Space: Writing Canadian Women Writing*, ed. Shirley Neuman and Smaro Kamboureli. Edmonton: Longspoon/ Newest. 1986. 361-73.

Thompson, Dawn. "Technologies of Ethnicity." *Writing Ethnicity: Cross-Cultural Consciousness in Canadian and Québécois Literature*, ed. Winfred Siemerling. Toronto: ECW Press, 1996, 59-69.

Tong, Rosemarie. *Feminist Thought: A Comprehensive Introduction*. 1989. London: Routledge, 1992.

Torrance, Robert M. *The Spiritual Quest: Transcendence in Myth, Religion and Science*. Berkeley and Los Angeles: University of California Press, 1994.

Tostevin, Lola Lemire. *'sophie*. Toronto: The Coach House Press, 1988.

_______. "re." *Collaboration in the Feminine: Writings on Women and Culture from Tessera*, ed. Barbara Godard. Toronto: Second Story Press, 1994, 40-43.

_______. "Contamination: A Relation of Differences." *Tessera*. Vol. 6 (Spring 1989): 13-14.

_______. *Gyno Text*. Toronto: Underwich Editions, 1983.

_______. "The Muses Have Learned to Write: The Journal diary crosses borders and boundaries in Canadian Women's Writing." *Crisis and Creativity in the New Literatures in English Canada*, ed. Geoffrey Davis. Amsterdon-Atlanta, 1990. 215-26.

_______. "Daphne Marlatt Writing in the Space That is Her Mother's Face." *Line* 13 (Spring 1989): 29-32.

Turner, Kay. "Contemporary Feminist Rituals." *The Politics of Women's Spirituality*, ed. Charlene Spretnak. New York: Anchor, 1982. 219-33.

Verduyn, Christl. "Language, Body and Identity in Margaret Laurence's *The Fire-Dwellers*." *Margaret Laurence: An Appreciation*, ed. Christl Verduyn. Peterborough: Journal of Canadian Studies Broadway Press, 1988. 128-40.

Vevaina, Coomi. "Black Woman, 'Righter' and the Anguish of English." *Women in Canadian Society: International Journal of Canadian Studies. Les Femmes Et La Société Canadienne Revue Internationale D'Edudes Canadiennes*, 11 (Spring 1995), 261-76.

______. "Naming, Un-naming, Re-naming: Epistemological Challenges in the Afrocentric Feminist Writings of Dionne Brand, Claire Harris and Marlene Nourbese Philip." *Literary Theory: (Re)Reading Culture and Aesthetics*, ed. Jameela Begum and B. Hariharan. Delhi: Pencraft Interanational, 1997. 208-22.

______. *Re/Membering Selves: Alienation and Survival in the Novels of Margaret Atwood and Margaret Laurence*. New Delhi: Creative, 1996.

______. "Searching for Space: A Conversation with M. Nourbese Philip." *Open Letter*. 9.9 (18 May 1996): 14-26.

Walker, Alice. *The Color Purple*. London: Women's Press, 1982.

Warland, Betsy. "Surrendering the English Language: The Lesbian Writer as Liberator," *In the Feminine: Women and Words Conference Proceedings*, ed. Ann Dybikowski, Barbara Pulling and Betsy Warland. Edmonton: Longspoon Press, 1985, 175-79:

_____. "moving parts." *Proper Definitions: Collected Theorograms*. Vancouver: Press Gang Publishers, 1990.

_____. "the breasts refuse." *Language in Her Eye: Writing and Gender*, ed. Libby Scheier, Sarah Sheard & Eleanor Wachtel. Toronto: The Coach House Press, 1990, 279-92.

_____. "When our loyalties lie." *Telling It: Women and Language across Cultures*, ed. Sky Lee, Lee Maracle, Daphne Marlatt and Betsy Warland. Vancouver: Press Gang Publishers. 191-02.

_____. ".f) is sure." *Telling* It. 31-41.

Waugh, Patricia. *Feminist Fictions: Revisiting the Postmodern*. New York: Routledge, 1989.

______. *Feminine Revisiting the Postmodern Fictions*. London: Routledge, 1989.

Weedon, Chris. *Feminist Practice and Poststructuralist Theory*. Oxford: Basil Blackwell, 1987.

Whisman, Vera. "Identity Crisis: Who is a Lesbian Anyway?" *Sisters, Sexperts, Queers: Beyond the Lesbian Nation*, ed. Arlene Stein. New York: Penguin, 1993. 47-60.

Wilson, Ethel. *Swamp Angel*. 1954; Toronto: McClelland and Stewart, 1986.

Wilson, Sharon Rose. *Margaret Atwood's Fairy Tale Sexual Politics*. Jackson: University Press of Mississippi, 1993.

Wittig, Monique. "One Is Not Born a Woman." *Feminist Frameworks. Alternative Theoretical Accounts of the Relations between Women and Men*, ed. Alison M. Jaggar and Paula S. Rothenberg, New York: McGraw Hill, 1978, 178-82.

Young, Robert. *White Mythologies: Writing History in the West*. New York: Routledge, 1990.

Zacodnik, Teresa. "I am Blackening in My Way: Identity and Place in Dionne Brand's *No Language is Neutral.*" *Technologies of Gender*. 194-211.

Zimmerman, B. "Feminist Fiction and the Postmodern Challenge." *Postmodern Fiction: A Bio-Bibliographical Guide*, ed. Larry MaCaffrey. New York: Greenwood Press, 1980. 175-88.

_____. "What Has Never Been: An Overview of Lesbian Feminist Criticism." *Feminisms: An Anthology of Literary Theory and Criticism*, ed. Robyn R. Warhol and Dianne Pria Herndl. New Brunswick, N.J: Rutgers University Press, 1991. 117-37.

______. "Lesbians Like This and That: Some Notes on Lesbian Criticism for the Nineties." *New Lesbian Criticism*. 1-16.

______. *The Safe Sea of Women: Lesbian Fiction. 1969-1989*. Boston: Beacon Press, 1990.

Zinn, Maxine Baca and Dill Bonnie Thornton. "Theorizing Difference: From Multiracial Feminism." *Feminist Studies*. Vol. 22, No. 2 (Spring 1996): 321-31.

_____, ed. *Women of Color in U.S. Society*. Philadelphia: Temple University Press, 1994.

Zwicker, Heather. "The Limits of Sisterhood." *In Search of April Raintree.* Critical Edition, ed. Suzack Cheryl. Winnipeg: Portage and Main Press, 1999, 323-37.

Abbreviations

Abbreviation	Title of Book	Author
AH	*Ana Historic*	Daphne Marlatt
AR	*In Search of April Raintree*	Beatrice Culleton Mosionier
BMWW	*The Biggest Modern Woman of the World*	Susan Swan
CBN	*Cereus Blooms at Night*	Shani Mootoo
DN	*Double Negative*	Daphne Marlatt and Betsy Warland
EW	*Edible Woman*	Margaret Atwood
FD	*The Fire-Dwellers*	Margaret Laurence
FK	*French Kiss or Pang's Progress*	Nicole Brossard
GT	*Gender Trouble*	Judith Butler
JD	*A Jest of God*	Margaret Laurence
LO	*Lady Oracle*	Margaret Atwood
NLN	*No Language is Neutral*	Dionne Brand
SA	*The Stone Angel*	Margaret Laurence
SMTM	*Songs My Mother Taught Me*	Audrey Thomas
SS	*Sexual Subversions*	Elizabeth Grosz
STHT	*She Tries Her Tongue, Her Silence Softly Breaks*	M. Nourbese Philip